VIETNAM... AGAIN

By

Marc Cullison

VHPA INDIANAPOLIS
JULY 5, 2017

Acknowledgements

This book is dedicated to the memory of Donald Hooper, a short-time friend of long-lasting influence.

If it were not for the sage, wifely counsel I received prior to embarking on this adventure, this book would never have been written. Thank you, Bobbie, for all of the wonderful things you do for me.

And my thanks to the folks at Imzadi Publishing for their patience and efforts in bringing this book to life. A special thanks to Anita Dugan-Moore for her help with trailers and audio previews.

CONTENTS

MEET THE MEMBERS OF THE VC PLATOON

CHAPTER 1

GETTING THE CALL

Vietnam veterans can be a funny lot. You will recognize one if he is wearing some article of clothing, patches, or pins broadcasting his participation in the war. Many of them used to wear nothing to give any indication that they had anything to do with it. Now, you see the patches, and Huey logos everywhere.

I avoided marking myself as a Vietnam vet for many years. I never received a hearty welcome home, a handshake, or even a kind look when I returned from Vietnam. It was something we veterans felt was better left alone, unacknowledged. Let the dust settle lest it choke us with it enmity. Some vets had it tough, some did not. Many died, either over there or shortly after they came home. Some of them are still dying because of it. Regardless of what we did over there, we all came home different than we were when we went over.

I flew helicopters for the 129th Assault Helicopter Company in II Corps in the central highlands in 1971. I spent over eleven months in the suffocating heat, humidity, and mildew that engulfed the country in a cloud of misery. I lived among mosquitoes that could carry off a small child, rats as big as opossums, and cockroaches that would laugh at a can of Raid. I endured the tedium of waking each day to the stress of flying, be it treacherous winds in the mountains, or into a hail of bullets, and the uncertainty of returning home, or just the monotony of routine resupply mission.

Most of us had never experienced such a hot, humid climate, and our bodies faltered under the stress. When I first saw Vietnam from fifteen hundred feet in the air looking out the door of a UH-1H helicopter, I remember thinking how beautiful it all was, how peaceful, inviting, like the travel photos I had seen in magazines touting the pleasures of tropical serenity. I also remember that after the first of many combat assault I lost that vision in the junkyard of my mind, the place where all of the things I wanted to forget were stowed away, camouflaged from the faux reality in which I had lived since I returned to the United States.

But then it was over, and I was only too glad to escape that unforgiving country and leave it all behind. I never wanted to return; never thought about it. Never.

Until Thomas Baca called.

I didn't know Tom Baca; had never met him. Well, only as a friend on Facebook through a common military connection. He was familiar with my book, *The Other Vietnam War*, a memoir of my eleven months in Vietnam, and even put a plug for it on Facebook. He told me that he and some other Vietnam vets were planning a trip back there in December. One of the members cancelled, and Tom asked me if I'd like to take his place.

I recall thinking, "Why in hell would I want to go back there? I was darned lucky to get out of it." After visions of thousands of dollars fluttering out of our bank account, and the thought that my family was due a vacation, I took a breath and brought the phone back near my mouth.

"I appreciate the offer, Tom," I said with reservation. "But I don't think I'll be going."

My wife, Bobbie, was listening and gave me a quick look. The kind that said, "What are you doing?"

"We've got issues with my wife's mother," I told him. "She's recovering from hip surgery and needs constant supervision."

Of course, that wasn't the real reason I declined the offer. For the past 44 years, I thought I had done a mighty fine job of laying the beast of Vietnam to rest in the back of my mind; all of the sordid memories, the fear, the anguish, the hatred I had felt for the Vietnamese. No, I had no intentions of returning to the country that leached oceans of sweat from my body and chewed off a part of my dignity.

"Well, I'd sure like to have you along" Tom said, disappointment in his voice. "We need a writer like you on the trip with us. And besides," in a humorous aside, "it would be nice to have another Liberal on the team. There's only two of us."

I never really thought of myself as a Liberal or a Conservative, but recently, I had found the Liberal face of the political muck to be the least offensive and the least hypocritical. I had responded to many of Tom's posts with positive signals. I guess he thought I was one of them.

"Wow," I said, laughing. "Hope you don't get beat up too bad."

"Oh, that's alright. We don't talk politics on these trips. This is the fourth time I will have been back."

I'm thinking here, why would he want to go back four times? I left him hanging with my indecision, and he told me I knew where he was if I changed my mind.

"Who was that?" asked Bobbie.

"Tom Baca," I said, hanging up the phone. "From Facebook. He invited me to go to Vietnam with his group."

She looked straight at me, another look that I read again as, "What are you doing?"

"You should go," she told me.

The words just hung there in the air as if waiting for an opening to get past my ears and into that mass of stubborn gray matter that often gets me into trouble. Then in a flash of surprise, it dawned on me what she had just said. I looked at her, wondering what had prompted that advice. We had been talking about a family get-away sometime during December or January. I was retired, we had a fixed income, and I wasn't sure that spending that much money on a frivolous trip to Vietnam was such a good idea. But notwithstanding my flawed logic when it came to matters of family and conscience, I know that somewhere deep within my wife's keen insight into my shortcomings, she probably had a good point.

I had read about some veterans who had returned to Vietnam, and I'd like to say that I understood what might have motivated many of them to do so. I had read of their accounts of the journeys back to the country that had milked them of the innocence and the youth that had been charged with awe in a place so different from what they had known. They extolled the beauty and charm of the country, a newer and more robust version of the one they had left behind so many years ago. I had never been able to see it that way, and that's most likely why I'd never had an inclination to return.

Bobbie's customary encouragement, more of a lecture really, bore on the idea that I should go back to see what had become of it, which I interpreted to mean that I should face my old ghosts and put them to rest. Not that I had that many, but I believe every soldier who served over there and survived has some albatross hidden away in the depths of his or her mind that, without a means to resolve, festers and becomes a liability to the future. I always wondered what kind of person I would have been without Vietnam. Not that I was unhappy with who I was, but there's still that nagging notion that I could have been a better person. But then again, perhaps Vietnam made me better than I would have been.

Then my daughter, Courtney, found out about the proposed trip.

"You should go," she said, as stolidly as her mother, as if no thought had been required, no consideration necessary for the impact on me or our family.

For the next day, I waffled on the notion, trying to think of how such a trip could be justified. Why would I want to go back and spend two weeks traipsing through a country I had tried to forget for such a long time? I had finally come to terms with my service there and even wrote about my experience in the book that Tom Baca had extolled. It was published in May of 2015, and I had received many emails from readers expressing their enjoyment of the book. Some even went so far as to compliment me on its unusual content, more to do with what went through my mind while I was there, rather than the white-knuckle adventures like so many other books about the Vietnam War. The book had been favorably received, and writing it seemed to divest me of the "ghosts" that I had long tried to deny.

As Bobbie told me in her cleverly honed wifely counsel, it all boiled down to the fact that if I didn't go back, I would always wonder if I should have, and what it would have been like, and what it would have done to me. What *had* happened to Vietnam after nearly 45 years? I had read accounts of a flourishing country, riding on the high tide of a successful capitalistic economy luring other countries to invest in its future. It hadn't fallen to decay and stolid Communist oppression as I had been led to believe would happen from the army's indoctrination I had endured so many years ago. Not so bad, I thought.

Then there was the question of me. What had I really become? What had Vietnam done for me or to me? In college, I had thought I was destined to be an architectural engineer. After all, that's why my wife had slaved during that last year and a half I was in college, so that I could earn that master's degree. Was I really better for the experience of Vietnam, or would I have become a successful entity in the world of architecture, renowned for the business and design acumen that I would have acquired, an award-winning engineer? Well, that was certainly doubtful. I never liked the limelight, and I'm sure there were many fellows who had a better handle on engineering than I.

But what it all came down to was my family. My wonderful, beautiful, intelligent, and tolerant wife. Who else could possibly put up with my stoical stubbornness and tendency to turn everything into a marvel of engineering? And my daughter, Courtney, who by all accounts, was a gem of a woman, smart as hell, beautiful, and independent. She was a tribute to my wife's undaunted skills as a mother. She had earned a doctorate degree in political science and was teaching in a nearby college. I couldn't be more proud of both of them. I realized that had it not been for Vietnam, I would never have met Bobbie, I would not be bragging about my daughter, and I would not be writing this book.

And besides, if I were any measure of a man, I would face my adversary and exact justice. I called Tom back and told him I was going.

CHAPTER 2

PREPARATIONS FOR THE JOURNEY

During my four years on active duty in the army, I had never encountered anyone I had known in any of my military assignments. Not officer's basic at Fort Belvoir, not Primary Rotary Wing Aviator School at Fort Wolters, Texas, not Advanced Rotary Wing Aviator School at Fort Rucker, Alabama, not in Vietnam. And not at Kaw Dam and Reservoir in Ponca City, Oklahoma. Most of the fellows I have talked to since then always had friends within reach, even in country. I never did.

It wasn't until after I returned to the United States and let the Vietnam War experience fester beneath my life for forty some odd years that I realized how isolated I had been. I started noticing books written about the Vietnam War and wondered what had motivated the authors to write them. After reading several of these books, I discovered what it was that they knew that I didn't.

It was that I had never tried to make sense of it all. I had just socked it away in hope of forgetting it. These authors, the fellows who had enough courage to pull their experiences out of the mothballs and face them, had found answers to the many questions that left us as enigmas to ourselves, uncertain of our station in the world, in the universe. Some questions would never have answers, but many of them did. I found some of them when I wrote of my own experiences in the war.

When I began researching veteran's organizations, I found a vast world out there calling to me. Facebook offered contact with Vietnam vets, as well as veterans from other wars, and I found comfort in just being a part of it all. These guys were fellow veterans, guys with whom I had shared adventures that few people taste. Fellow survivors.

When this trip offer came up, there was a new opportunity in front of me. The opportunity to meet eleven other guys who did what I did and felt what I felt. How could I have *not* agreed to take advantage of it?

As preparations neared completion, my anxiety approached an almost calming level, and worry became an idle pastime instead of a burden. I felt better about flying off to Vietnam and meeting fellow veterans.

I still had reservations about leaving my wife alone to deal with the daily issues at home, especially with her mother in the shape she was in, but I had to discover what it was about Vietnam that was now pulling me toward it; absolution, relief, guilt?

Something else was pulling me, too. Recent emails from Tom Baca touted the excellent food available over there. And beer. Craft beer was a booming business and countless varieties could be had for a pittance. Well, I was nearly quivering with excitement as I pictured myself, beer in hand, slurping a bowl of pho. And the list of hotels Tom sent me sharpened my curiosity. They were all modern and upscale, the kind of places I might balk at choosing for myself because of the expense. My philosophy was that if I'm renting space to sleep, that's pretty much what I'll be doing. I don't need a lot of luxurious accoutrements, or fancy furnishing, or conference centers. So, my wife and I commonly tend toward the middle of the road accommodations. Why shell out a small fortune for a room I'll see for only a few hours?

Tom had a friend in Vietnam, Dinh Ngoc Truc, whom he said had arranged everything for us. He emphasized the "everything." There would be a $1550 cost for the trip itself. This included all lodging with breakfasts, all transportation in country, and all admissions to events and features we would be enjoying. The only things I would be responsible for were my airfare to and from Vietnam, lunches and dinners, and any personal expenses I might incur. I did the math. For fourteen days, that was slightly over $100 per day. Could that be right?

Tom assured me that the amount was correct.

"Vietnam is really cheap," he said. "Things are not that expensive at all."

I was still doing calculations in my head.

"That's about a hundred dollars a day," he went on. "It's hard to beat that anywhere."

I was sold. I thought it odd that Tom's friend would go to so much trouble for a group of veterans who, except for Tom Baca and Jack Swickard, he had probably never met. And as for the cost he quoted us, I couldn't imagine that he would be profiting from it. I had to wonder what had prompted all of this.

I began receiving emails about weather in Vietnam, our itinerary, our transportation, hotel accommodations, schedules, and a list of fellow vets I would meet on the trip. I also received the entrance and exit visa forms, and other documents necessary for visiting the country. Truc had arranged all of this and the only thing I had to do was to reserve a hotel room in at DFW Airport for November 29, and my flight to DFW and Vietnam and back.

Tom arranged for my flights to and from Vietnam, along with his group of five others who would be meeting at DFW. He offered to do this for me because with his connections he was able to get more favorable airfares. I couldn't believe my good fortune at having Tom and Truc doing so much for us, and for me.

As isolated as I was in Sallisaw, Oklahoma, I had few close friends that lived anywhere near me. Any contact I made with any of them was a long distance matter, not conducive to flourishing friendships. I suppose that's one of the reasons that I was drawn to this opportunity. It would bring me closer to other veterans, men similar to me with a common sense of patriotism and the desire to connect with those who had seen military service. Men of the same ilk who could form a bond of friendship.

All arrangements for the trip had been made. I remember thinking that if I had been required to do all of this myself, I would never have made it to Vietnam, much less been able to take a two-week tour of the country. All for about $100 a day. The more I thought about it, the more overwhelmed I became with what Truc had managed to do for us.

Then there was the question of clothing I would need in Vietnam. The last time I was there, I didn't have to worry about that. Uncle Sam provided my wardrobe of jungle fatigues and Nomex flight suits, neither of which were comfortable in the stifling heat and humidity of the country. The heavy material served only to block the sun's damaging ultraviolet rays and did nothing to allow comfort. Ten minutes after dressing, sweat would be rolling down my body and into my boots. My clothing would be sopping wet and by the end of the day, I would reek of something akin to a goat. I knew the jeans and shirts I had were not going to be suitable for Vietnam.

I had never been farther north than Da Nang, where the weather cooled during December, and I knew that farther north in Hanoi the temperature dipped lower than the southern parts of Vietnam. So, I asked Tom for an idea of what to take.

He sent me a list of what he was packing, and it all seemed reasonable for tropical travel. I didn't have some of the things on it, like long-sleeve tropical shirts and comfortable tropical pants, so I went shopping. Eddie Bauer is one of my favorite clothing stores, and they didn't let me down. I found lightweight long-sleeve travel shirts with rollup sleeves and stretch pants that were suitable for tropical climates. I also invested in some long-sleeve knit shirts and lightweight shoes, as well as a hooded waterproof jacket. I remembered the rains over there that seemed as if they would never end. An RFID protected wallet was another investment I made.

I was all set, and two days before launch I started packing. I had a suitcase, a carryon bag, and a backpack. Oh, and a camera, my trusty Olympus SP-350, an old one, but reliable. I got the cash I would need for Truc when I arrived in Vietnam, and expense money. I was set to go.

My wife dropped me at the Fort Smith Airport Sunday afternoon, November 29. We said our goodbyes and I hated to leave her there. Our kiss was one I would remember. Then I was off on the hour-long trip to DFW.

The short flight afforded just enough time to think about Vietnam and what I would find there. The arranged tour would be stopping at Qui Nhon near where I had been stationed at Lane Army Airfield, a large post at the foot of Nui Hon Cha Mountain, about nine miles west. Almost all of the resurgence of memories had been about my time there; the guys I flew with, the hooches, the Koreans we supported, and of course, the missions I had flown. The small village of An Son was nearby, although I had never been there. The rest of the area was rice paddies and fields. I recalled looking down at the flat, green fields sectioned by dikes, the thatched houses and villages that dotted the land, and the conical hats that bobbed over the hoes in the paddies. Little else was around there except for cities like Qui Nhon and military facilities.

As I thought about what it all would look like now, a queer feeling spread across me, the kind that I recall experiencing just before my first mission ride in country. Just like it was then, I had no idea what I might encounter. I was filled with anticipation of a new experience, but at the same time, charged with dread. It's always the unknown entity that fires our imagination and lowers a veil of deceit over our minds, often leading us to think the worst, usually because we can't comprehend what the best might be. Suddenly I had reservations about getting on that plane.

On arrival at the Dallas-Fort Worth International Airport, I got a shuttle to the Hyatt Regency DFW and checked in. Tom Baca had told me that he and Sterling Essenmacher would be in the room next door to mine. Although I was tired, I dumped my bags in my room and knocked on their door.

I'd seen pictures of Tom on Facebook, so I knew what to expect. The round face smiled when he greeted me, his glasses shining in the soft light. It was nearly nine o'clock, and he and Sterling were getting ready for bed. In fact, Sterling was already *in* bed. Tom was shorter than I imagined and a bit plump, but pleasantly so. He always seemed chipper and upbeat whenever I talked with him on the phone, and there was little difference talking to him there in the room.

Sterling, with his manicured moustache, thinning hair, and discreet grin, was the utter portrait of aplomb. After introductions and a short discussion of plans for the morning, I left them to their beds and returned to my room to wait for Tom Horan, my roommate for the night.

I was catching up on some homework for the trip, reading Robert S. McNamara's book, *In Retrospect*. As part of my "making sense of it all" program, I wanted to learn more about the how and why of the Vietnam War. McNamara's book shed new light on my limited knowledge, and I began to understand how America got into that terrible situation and why it failed. The book also cast a different light on the Vietnamese people, contradicting the indoctrination that the U.S. Army had put its soldiers through. The more I read, the more I learned and the more confused I became. That was usually the case whenever I elected to study something I was unfamiliar with. It always takes a while for things like economics, politics, and military strategy to soak in. I was hoping that somewhere on this trip I would unlock the trove of answers that I had been looking for.

The door opened and a large man walked into the room, a smile beneath the white moustache.

"You must be Tom," I said first, before he could open his mouth.

"Tom Horan," he replied, in a forceful baritone voice. "And I guess you're Marc."

We shook hands, and he set about preparing for bed.

"I see you got checked into the room okay," I told him. "I wasn't sure what to expect after all the hoopla of changing the reservation to a double. At least we wound up with two beds."

When I had first booked the room, I was planning on staying by myself. But Tom Baca told me that Tom Horan had also booked a single room, and if we bunked together, we could save a small bundle. I mentioned it to Tom Horan, and he agreed. So I changed my booking to a double, and he canceled his.

He wasn't at all what I had expected. Tom was one of those fellows who showed the strain of aging, but not yet to the point of being old. Although he was not going to run any races, and at our age that's something we all aspire to, he seemed to get around pretty well. His balding, white hair that became sparser on top was balanced by a large, drooping moustache, also white. He was quite a bit taller than I and a bit heavier. A big man. We exchanged personal histories, and I found his knowing face to be inviting, like someone I would be comfortable talking to. He was the kind of fellow people would tend to trust.

He had flown with C Troop of the 3/17 Air Cavalry in 1969-70. He said he flew the OH-6, the Hughes Cayuse, as a scout. I had trouble picturing him bending his large frame into the cockpit of one of those little egg-shaped helicopters.

If you are not familiar with the Loach, or OH-6, it was a small craft used to scout out enemy locations. Tom had a good story about his time in this small helicopter:

Life changed on May 29, 1969, and has never been the same. I became a Scout pilot in C Troop, 3rd Squadron, 17th Air Cavalry, in Vietnam, flying the light observation helicopter, the OH-6A. A cavalry scout in the air is of the same lineage as Jeb Stuart and George Armstrong Custer, over a hundred years apart but bearing some of the same eccentric characteristics as those cavalrymen of yesterday. The major difference is we rode in the air and they used horses. Our mission was the same: to find the enemy so our army would know their position and be able to engage them, and we also wore cavalry hats, western style Stetsons.

In John Ford's western, "She Wore a Yellow Ribbon," circa 1949, filmed in Monument Valley in Arizona and Utah, Sergeant Tyree, a former Confederate cavalryman, was the eyes and ears of John Wayne,

"Captain Nathan Brittles," as he led his mounted troopers in the effort to return the Indian tribes to their reservations. Sergeant Tyree was gone for several days out of sight and without support of other American soldiers and reported on the whereabouts of the tribes of the Southwest that Brittles and his soldiers were seeking out. That was the role of the scout then and in Vietnam; to find the opposing forces.

But the Vietnam aero-scouts had reassuring support from the AH-1G Cobra attack helicopters [also known as Snakes] and from the platoon of infantry that was in the air or on close alert next to their transport, the UH-1H Huey helicopter.

The Huey, with its four-man crew, is the helicopter most associated with the Vietnam War, and the *whop-whop* rotor sounds still bring chills to many Vietnam veterans. In our case, its primary role was to rescue the LOH (OH-6A, sounds like Loach) crew, if we were shot down or crashed. The Hueys carried C Troop infantry to pull us out of the scrap. Due to the eternal mystery of Charlie's movements, if we were shot down, our infantry soldiers could find themselves in a battle in which they could easily be outnumbered, or if we crashed, we could be in some deep stuff.

The crash of an OH-6 could be caused by a mechanical failure or something as simple as an accident, hitting a tree or getting too curious and flying too slow, losing tail rotor control and spinning in. This was the most common incident.

The Cobra helicopters were flown by a crew of two, both pilots. They normally followed racetrack patterns in the sky at 1500 feet above the scout aircraft, watching and poised ready to strike with 2.75-inch rockets, 56 of them, and a mini gun with thousands of 7.62 millimeter rounds (a modern day airborne Gatling gun). Their primary role in the scouting mission was to cover the LOH and extricate it from any danger. That and teaming with another Cobra in a gunship mission providing air cover to ground troops.

Beginning in mid-June of 1969, I became a platoon leader. I had the responsibility for command of the scout platoon, with its 25 men and pilots and 7 OH6-A Hughes light observation helicopters, as if anyone could command or control scout pilots or scout crewmembers.

The scout pilot, by his nature, avocation, and the size of the helicopter, was a one-man show, assisted by their on-board crew of, at times, two enlisted men, the observer and the crew chief. In some units, the crew chief did not fly on all missions. The scout pilots viewed themselves as great warriors, but I always questioned the wisdom of those volunteer observers and crew chiefs who flew with us.

The Loach, also often called the Low Bird or Little Bird, since it flew so low to the ground and because of its small size, normally had a crew of two, a pilot and an observer. However, in our unit, C Troop, 3/17 Air Cav, we carried a crew of three. The pilot flew the aircraft from the right front seat and controlled the actions of the LOH's crew. He coordinated with the Cobra and reported what they had spotted on the ground.

The observer in the left front seat had a CAR 15, a smaller automatic version of the M16 rifle with a thirty round clip, and it could fire as many shots in a few seconds. The noise of the weapon firing made the observer feel better, but we are pretty sure the observer didn't hit that much except jungle.

The crew chief was in the compartment just behind the pilot armed with an M-60 machine gun. It fired 7.62 mm bullets at the rate of 500-600 rounds per minute. It was capable of causing considerably more damage than the CAR 15. The crew chief was responsible for throwing hand grenades at the enemy, including both normal hand grenades and white phosphorous, used for marking targets and burning targets like structures or vehicles.

The observer in the front seat carried a red smoke grenade with the pin pulled with the handle held down. The red smoke would alert the Cobra that the LOH was receiving fire and it was used to mark the locations of the enemy. Once the Cobra saw that red smoke or heard an excited radio transmission about enemy right under the aircraft or that the LOH was receiving fire, the Cobra would bank and begin a run firing rockets at that spot, while we in the LOH began to exit the area quickly as to avoid fire from both sources.

On a typical mission, the Cobra crew received the briefing on the mission and directed our LOH to the area we were to search. Upon arriving at the area at an altitude of 1500 feet, we began VR (visual reconnaissance), from a high speed spiraling, descending turn into the area, usually covered by triple canopy jungle. The high-speed descent was exhilarating but alarming since we did not know what to expect. We leveled off five feet above the trees and began to slow our speed to about ten to fifteen knots, and often to zero. At that height, we could see below the trees and into the jungle so we could find trails and fortification and most importantly, the enemy soldiers.

Over the jungle, I often flew at zero indicated airspeed, like a slow walk, just 5 feet above the jungle looking for signs of enemy or trails on the ground. I could get too absorbed in this and hear the rotor blade clip off small tree limbs or foliage. The Cobra pilots complained that my radio calls were garbled at times and had too much background noise, but that came with flying with my head out in the door in the wind stream that interfered with the microphone. Our whole crew had our heads out the door and on a swivel looking for the enemy. We were a team without rank in that tiny aircraft, just like the aircrews we saw in the movie theaters in the 1950's and 60's about World War II bomber crews.

LOH crews were happy for the Agent Orange defoliation that was sprayed on the jungle during the war, because we could see down through the foliage to the jungle floor. The call sign of the air force aircraft that flew those missions was "Ranch Hands." The twin engine transport planes, the Fairchild C-123 Providers, flew in low level formation flights of two to four aircraft, pushing out gallons of defoliant as a pretty white spray. They looked like firefighting aircraft that we have in the USA these days fighting forest fires. Agent Orange was a great tool for the American soldier, but who knew the consequences?

We would radio locations of enemy bunkers, foxholes, supplies, vehicles, or soldiers, to the Snakes (Cobra's), including description, quantity, in what direction the footprints were headed, or whatever else we found, like weapons or supplies. The Cobra would pass those along to American intelligence-gathering personnel.

If we found enemy soldiers shooting at us and we were in a free fire area, we fired our weapons. We often had strict limits on where and under what conditions we could fire, including no-fire areas, where we were prohibited from firing.

I did, on three or four occasions, tell my crew chief to fire and got reports of two kills on those occasions, though I did not personally see the bodies; however, that was not always the case and on one mission that I remember quite clearly we got over an enemy foxhole and my crew chief said, "I got a gook," indicating this was not a friendly South Vietnamese soldier but an NVA or VC soldier. I told him to fire, and I heard his M-60 fire one round and no more. This happened while I had our aircraft at a complete stop, at a hover about 15 feet above this fellow holding his AK-47, not a good place to be. My crew chief said, "My gun is jammed, sir." I exited the area quickly, getting about 50 meters away. He said he had he had his gun cleared, and we went back in and repeated the sequence. One round fired; jammed, still no fire received from the enemy soldier. We left him to fight another day, but not without leaving a memory in our crew and that enemy soldier on the ground

When we completed our missions, normally an hour and thirty to an hour and forty-five minutes, we flew as close to the ground or the top of the jungle as possible at the highest possible speed. Then I would pull the stick (cyclic for you helicopter folks) back toward my stomach and pull a roller coaster like climb up to about 500 feet above the terrain, and rejoin big brother, the Cobra, for our ride back to refuel or to our home base.

My life-changing mission came on July 9, 1969, the date my oldest son was born in the United States. An air force forward air controller had spotted a North Vietnamese truck near the Vietnam border concealed in the jungle. They had already put in one US air force airstrike on the truck with no results and asked us to go look for the truck so they could put in another strike.

It was getting near dusk, the time the NVA liked to shoot our helicopters down. Our soldiers would try to rescue the helicopter crew in the dark and the NVA could kill or capture them. We were in bad guys' territory and tensions were high. After quickly flying over the area, we slowed down, and we saturated the area with machine gun and Minigun fire from the LOH. There was no return fire. We were down low for about an hour reconning by fire, shooting our machine guns and dropping grenades and not seeing any sign of a truck or the enemy but found an old enemy trench line and bunkers they could bomb with their fighters. The planes were about five minutes out.

We were just starting to gain speed to exit the area and climb out when my crew chief said, "I got a gook." I radioed the Cobra and turned around, stopping the helicopter directly over the enemy soldier, and told the crew chief to open fire. Then the world went to crap. The whole woods opened up on us. Unfortunately for my crew and me, the stupid pilot (that would be me) had not only came back around and stopped, but I did it in an open area, 50 feet up, silhouetted against the sky, a great target for the bad guys. I started yelling in my microphone to the Cobra, wondering what he was doing because I heard no rockets going off. His words were, "Sorry 'bout that... I broke off on my gun run when you turned back around and stopped over that guy. Can't help you right now." Those were sad words to hear. We would have been in his line of fire.

I had to remember to pull power slowly and lower the nose slowly for us to get out of this mess I had caused. Had I put in a big pull of power and a quick lowering of the nose of the aircraft to get quickly out of this mess, which is exactly what my whole being wanted, those actions would likely have spun us in an ever tightening spin and put us crashing on the ground smack dab in the middle of those not too happy enemy soldiers.

It wasn't our day to die. Miraculously, we didn't even take any hits to our aircraft, though a lot of fire had been directed at us, but it sure got my adrenalin pumping about two minutes later, and that gave me the shakes.

That was my worst mission, even worse than the one a few weeks earlier in the same area. We had just begun our visual reconnaissance mission and found ourselves directly under one of our air force's B-52 strikes with 250- or 500-pound bombs dropping all around us. After that fiasco, we immediately went back and landed and stormed into the office of the Captain from the 25th Infantry Division, who had sent us on this mission without checking the status of the upcoming B-52 strikes. The Cobra pilot and I both had our pistols drawn and told him we were going to take the rest of the day off and proceeded directly to their officer's club for a beer at 10:00 in the morning. No more flying that day.

I said earlier my life was forever changed by becoming a scout pilot, which came about because I couldn't read a map very well. Being a Cobra pilot was out, as they had to be great map readers. I didn't like to fly in formation with rotor blades of the other helicopters so close to each other, and I worried about striking the rotor blades of another helicopter in making a formation landing or takeoff just because someone else made a mistake. Since our Hueys (UH-1Hs') flew a lot of formation flying that was also out for me. So I had to be a scout driver.

The OH6 was a great option for me, as I liked to be by myself as a pilot and make all the decisions and act quickly using common sense. My priority was the mission to find the enemy and second to get my crew and myself home safely.

We were not carrying American troops into battle like the Huey's in other units did, nor were we flying medical evacuation flights that the "Dustoff" pilots did, although I felt good once flying around and providing protection to a Dustoff pilot. He was hovering about 50 feet over the jungle bringing a casualty up on a hoist, his ship in a vulnerable position. They did that all the time. They were true heroes.

Scout pilots, me included, have brought that independence and bravado back with them to the "World," the USA. It still flows through almost all my decisions. I don't usually ask permission to act. I sometimes ask forgiveness afterward. It made me decisive and, unfortunately, impatient with those who have a slower pace in making decisions.

The plaque I brought home from Vietnam for my time with the C Troop Scouts reads, "After you've flown scouts, what else is there?" In truth, there is more, a lot more, but being a scout pilot in Vietnam sure changed me.

Tom had not yet retired, but was soon destined to join me in the ranks of the unemployed. Living in Albuquerque, New Mexico, he was a lobbyist with the state legislature, dealing mostly with the medical businesses. His son would soon be taking over, he told me, then he could actually retire. He only worked part time as it was. He was a close friend of Tom Baca's. I think Tom Baca was a close friend of just about everyone on this trip, except me, and our relationship had only been through posts on Facebook. Well, that and the book I wrote about my Vietnam experience, which Tom had read and recommended to the others.

I found sleep hard to come by for a while. I laid in the bed thinking about my first step back onto Vietnamese soil. The last time I was there, in 1971. It was not pleasant. My mind took off then and seemed to be doing its own thing. I recalled my first mission ride in country, something I hadn't thought about since I wrote that book:

I had been assigned to Cups. That was the call sign for James Massencups, a tall fellow, red hair, and an almost handlebar moustache.

He was the unit's instructor pilot on his second tour of Vietnam. The mission was an ARVN insertion on the hillside west of Lane toward Pleiku. Naturally, I was excited, but at the same time, not feeling so good about what might happen. As a naïve newbie, all I could think about were all of the stories I had been told about Charlie shooting the crap out of helicopters and the crews in them.

Cups seemed like it was just another day. I was busy worrying about what I didn't know. We loaded our first troops at the pickup zone, number two in trail formation. The landing zone was only big enough for one ship at a time. Off we went, and I tried to keep my mind on the mission, the instruments, the radios, and Cups. I remember clearly the exhilaration of going into combat. My first time. The army had spent two years brainwashing me to be able to do what I was expected to do that day. I figured, boy, were they suckers, because I had no idea what I was doing. I was merely going through the motions, or the ones I remembered, anyway. There was no way the army could let you practice actual warfare. Then Cups told me, "Keep your hands on the controls. If anything happens to me, you'll be able to take it." That's what woke me up.

We had the LZ in sight, and the radio was alive with chatter. I had no idea what they were saying. The first ship set down and a mortar exploded about hundred meters uphill from the LZ. The ship unloaded and took off and we were on short final for the LZ. I was thinking what the hell was I doing there? I know I was probably just worthless baggage because I had no idea what I would have done if anything had happened to Cups. I was still amazed that he could sit there so calmly and drive our ship into certain annihilation. Just before we touched down, a second mortar round hit below the LZ. Charlie was bracketing. I had figured that much out in spite of my frozen state of terror. I also remembered from my training that the third mortar round usually hit the target.

When the last ARVN was pushed out the door, Cups yanked pitch and we shot out of there like a bullet. About two seconds out we both heard it. When we made a slight turn to check it out, the LZ was gone. A direct hit from a mortar round. The radio was squawking like hell, and I was about to pee my pants.

We made several more trips to a new LZ to unload the rest of the troops. That night I didn't sleep a wink.

I know I had fallen asleep sometime during the night, because I didn't remember anything until I woke up in the morning, still thinking about that mortar round.

The sun rose the next morning over Texas the same as it did over Oklahoma. The eight of us checked in for our flight to Incheon and converged in the airport for breakfast. I met the other four vets I would traveling with: Ken Bartholomew from Lutherville, Maryland, Jack Swickard from Roswell, New Mexico, Ed Knighten from Broken Arrow, Oklahoma, almost a neighbor, and Pat Matheny from Shinnston, West Virginia. It would prove to be a good mix of personalities.

I felt comfortable there in that restaurant with the other seven vets. I felt as if I belonged; that I was one of them. That's a feeling I seldom got in Sallisaw. I had no close family left, and my wife's family was all there was. But it just wasn't the same as my own family. No shared history, no shared memories, and different affections. To me, that's what made a family. But with the fellows there with me, it began to feel like family.

The thought of a thirteen-hour trip to Seoul, South Korea, did not lift anyone's spirits except for the anticipation of being that much closer to Hanoi. The call came for boarding and off we went.

CHAPTER 3

HANOI, FIRST NIGHT

Monday, 1 December, 2015

The flight from the Dallas-Fort Worth Airport to Incheon International Airport in Seoul, South Korea, was uneventful, if you can call getting a sore butt a non-event. I sat next to Ken Bartholomew just behind the bulkhead in the exit row, oodles of leg room, and a restroom right in front of us. It was one of those wide body jets with two aisles. Our seats were a bank of two next to a window. We wouldn't have to scrounge for room and there was no stranger that would insist on dominating the center armrest. Most of the passengers were Asian, many of them probably Korean, since that's where the plane was going.

About a third of the way through the flight, people began congregating outside the restroom door in front of us with faces of boredom, anxiety, and what looked like pain. The line would grow short, then long, then short again. One lady, a middle-aged Korean, I guessed, stopped in the open space directly in front of us and started kicking her legs, one after the other, alternating with squats. I thought this poor woman must be really desperate. Ken commented to her about her spritely activity, to which she gave him a friendly smile.

"Exercise," she said. "It keeps blood going."

Several other folks had the same idea. Deep vein thrombosis is a threat to people on long plane rides, resulting in possible blood clots in the leg from lack of activity. Any kind of exercise for the legs helps avoid it. Having gotten our attention, the woman's regimen was resumed with renewed vigor and cheery glances in our direction. She might have been laughing at us.

Ken told me he was from Lutherville, Maryland. He had served two tours of duty in Vietnam. The first was in 1967-68 with the 1/9 Cavalry. The second was with the INFANT NETT (Iroquois Night Fighter and Night Tracker) in 1970-71. He and I had a lot in common. He was one of the first Vietnam vets I had ever talked with, just man-to-man,

21

bare bones talk. Being from Sallisaw, Oklahoma, the availability of fellow veterans was pretty much limited, or so I believed. At least I hadn't run across many, and those few that I had weren't exactly sociable. Of course, I wasn't a popular socialite either, but I will talk to people if I think there's something to talk about.

I believe Ken and I both felt the same about the war and our experiences there. We had mixed feelings about the whole thing, but we didn't let them dominate our lives. He admitted that he hadn't talked much about it and he also said that he still had moments of anxiety as a result. But more importantly, we both had a liking for single malt Scotch whisky. Ken was my kind of guy.

He told me he was reading my book about Vietnam. I was surprised to hear him mention it, although after what Tom Horan had told me, I shouldn't have been. That made three of them. I wondered if everyone else in the group had read it. Tom Baca *did* give the book a plug before the trip. I'm always a bit on edge when I talk to people who have read my books. There's always a nagging suspicion about their true feelings toward what they had read. I had received only a few negative comments about the books, but that could just be a ruse of politeness.

Ken was about a third of the way through the book and gave me a hearty compliment on its accuracy and the memories it rekindled. I figured that's what this trip was going to be about. I replayed in my mind some of the near misses I'd had in Vietnam. Like the time we impaled our helicopter on a rock:

I was flying with WO1 Cale, with SGT Icovitti as the crew chief and PFC Whittington Jr. as the gunner. We were chalk 3 (third position) in a diamond formation. We were the center ship of a 5-ship formation. That in itself was bad. Cale had just made AC and he drew a weak ship. We had six American troops on board and were to drop them at an LZ on the ridge of a mountain. It was hot that day. We had left LZ English and the density altitude there was 3500 feet, not good for 6 heavy GIs and an old, underpowered bird. Density altitude is the equivalent height above sea level due to temperature, atmospheric pressure, and humidity. Given that LZ English was only 98 feet above sea level, the heat and humidity made it seem like we were flying high in the mountains before we even took off from the LZ. On top of the mountains, the density altitude would be much higher that than 3800 feet. According to the book, the maximum density altitude for a *good* ship was 3800 feet. We were pushing the limit.

As we started the approach, the lead ship began his flare to slow down. This would have been okay for a flat and level LZ. But landing on an upslope, the trailing ships would be higher off the ground. Cale and I both realized we would be too high for a safe landing.

Chalk 4 and chalk 5, also realizing they were too high, broke off and went around for a second attempt. But we were surrounded with nowhere to go but down.

The ship started settling and Cale was pulling on the collective to slow our descent. Rotor RPM fell off and we continued our dive for the ground. When Cale had the collective up under his armpit, the needle on the torque gage passed 55 psi and the ship kept going down.

Cale alerted the crew chief to ensure that the GIs were prepared for a hard landing. Then we hit. But not as hard as I thought we would, more like a crunch instead of a bang.

I shut down the engine and turned off the fuel, then sat there and watched the blades swoop around. It seemed like they would never stop. I looked out the port side and saw nothing but blue sky. On the starboard side, the hillside rose steeply. I tilted the rotor to the right so any tendency they had to lift would be to force us into the slope instead of toppling us downhill.

The GIs began jumping out of the port door, and the aircraft listed that way. The damned thing was leaning downhill and I just knew we were going to roll down the mountainside. When they were all out, Whittington bailed out of the starboard door and took off running uphill. Icovitti lunged out after him and tackled him just before the blades hit the gunner in the head.

Cale told me to get the hell out while I could and I jumped out of the right door, keeping low and near the nose. We all met up aft of the aircraft and watched the poor thing teeter about on a huge rock protruding from the hillside.

If Cale had set the thing down a couple of inches either way, we would have been toast.

I knew exactly what he had felt during his tour. I guess all Vietnam vets who had been in combat felt it. I still get the feeling that Uncle

Sam lied to me, maybe not intentionally because much of the brass was misled by the government. As great as this nation has become and as much of a beacon of hope it had been and still is for millions of people around the world, I couldn't help but feel like our government was playing us all for fools.

Meals aboard the big airliner were not the greatest of choices, but then airline food rarely is anymore. We were offered Asian-inspired fare that would not win any awards, but it was better than the C-rations I had eaten in Vietnam. I don't mean to suggest that I don't like Asian food. I do, but I've sampled only those dishes served in American restaurants, even those with Asian names, prepared for the stale tastes of the overindulgent American populace. I was to learn that fine Asian cuisine lay beyond what I thought were my vast worldly experiences.

I'd had the foresight to pack a store of snack bars, nuts, and trail mix to get me through the wearisome ordeal. Ken was more than willing to help me consume part of it.

Several boring hours later, we started our approach to Incheon International Airport. The anticipation of getting out of that seat was cause for a quiet celebration within my own private world. My butt was sore as hell, and I knew I would have trouble just getting out of the seat. Whenever I sit for extended periods of time, my knees stiffen and a prankish nerve sent spears of pain through my right thigh. It was hell trying to stand up. That's one of the many changes I had noticed about my body as I have aged. Mentally, I still felt much like a young buck, temperamental at times and in a hurry to get things done, having little patience with annoyances. At 69 years of age, in my mind I was 26 with 43 years of experience. My body was still 69.

These large planes seemed to require forever for the crew to situate the thing so the passengers could disembark. Once that had started, it took another forever to get them all out of my way. Then I managed to stand up.

Incheon was a trouble-free stop. Our bags were checked through, and we only had to pass customs and security. It went smoothly and we soon boarded the Vietnam Airlines plane, an Airbus 350-900, a new wide-body aircraft with plenty of room and a hospitable staff. We departed on time for Hanoi.

The crew's uniforms, crisp and attractive, seemed more professional than other airlines, yet festive. The first order of business was to pass out warm, moist towels to all the passengers to freshen our tired faces and cleanse our hands. They did so with welcoming smiles on their faces. I'm sure that these folks had been vetted for fluency in the English language, but due to my hearing impairment, all I heard was a garble of words with that mysterious but annoying Asian accent.

My hearing aids help, but they can't restore my hearing to a normal state. That's one of the difficulties I have around other people. They aren't aware of the fact that I have hearing aids and I can't expect them to know about it. I don't want to broadcast the fact to the world, so I endure the troublesome task of trying to interpret what people say. I'm not a lip reader, so I rely entirely on my ability to distinguish various sounds in speech. Sometimes, especially with a foreign accent, it's nearly impossible. I resigned myself to look into getting new hearing aids when I got back.

As I would learn, most of the fellows in our group also had hearing aids. In fact, Ken told me that he had no hearing at all in his left ear, and the hearing in his right ear was far worse than mine. That explained why he was always replying with, "What?" to much of what I was saying to him.

The crewmembers were attentive, as I would come to expect from the Vietnamese. Courtesy and respect seemed to be at the foundation of their rearing. It was going to take awhile for me to become accustomed to such gracious bearing. It made the flight pleasant, the seats were reasonably comfortable and each with its own small monitor for movies.

We landed in Hanoi around nine o'clock in the evening, local time, on December 1. It seemed strange that in eighteen hours, an entire day had passed. The International Date Line really messed up my sense of time.

I had no idea what to expect from Hanoi, but the airport was a modern testament to the country's progress. It had been open less than a year and was an impressive piece of architecture. The soaring roofline and modern conveniences were a pleasant welcome to the country I had shunned as a foul reminder of a dark time in my life.

We collected our baggage, passed through customs, and waited for our tour guide, Truc, in front of the arrival doors. Tom Baca was on his phone trying to contact him.

The excruciating flights had left me with little energy and no sleep, much like everyone else in our group. Crossing the International Date Line had launched me a day into the future and half of a day off my body clock. One positive aspect of it all was that even though it was approaching my body's lunch time, it was nearing 10:00 at night and I had hoped that I would be able to get a good night's sleep.

Even though I was riddled with fatigue, anticipation was wearing at my patience. I could see it in the others, as well. Eyes wide with weary excitement, we all stood there wondering, is this really Vietnam? Are we really here? From the modern facility we had just processed through, it looked like any other international airport. Had it not been for the Vietnamese language on the signs and the abundance of Vietnamese people about, it could have been anywhere.

Dihn Ngoc Truc was a bit shorter that I and carried a little extra weight, but only the kind that made him a lovable character. His cordial smile put me at ease and he acted like an old friend. He met us there at the ground transportation area and introductions followed. Tom Baca, Jack Swickard, and Don Hooper had worked with Truc to organize the trip. I was to find out later that Truc worked for the Ministry of Information and Communications in the Operations Centre in Hanoi. A fellow like this is nice to have as a tour guide. I call him Truc, because Vietnamese names are reversed from American names. The surname is given first, followed by the given name. We loaded onto our shuttle bus and left for the Hanoi Pearl Hotel.

On the thirty-minute ride to the hotel through the bright lights of Hanoi, Truc introduced his oldest son, Hung, an attractive young man in his mid-twenties. He proudly announced that he had just married three days before. His honeymoon would be delayed until after our tour. I thought that was quite a concession for a son to make for the family.

The bus left Hanoi International Airport and bullied its way through the congested streets of the city, barely squeezing its bulk between sidewalks that seemed inches away. I fell out of my comfort zone. My mind fought with reason to make sense of the strange phenomenon occurring just beyond the windows.

Hanoi was nothing like what I had imagined. Actually, I'm not sure what I had imagined because I had no idea what Hanoi looked like. After all, it had been my good fortune to never have been there. I had seen recent photographs of it, but to see it first hand was a revelation to me. The tall buildings reached toward an overcast sky illuminated by the profusion of lights that seemed to veil the city in the glow electrical effervescence. I stared through the window of the bus at the remarkable beauty of it all.

When we reached the old town, people were everywhere. Motorbikes were everywhere. Cars were everywhere. It might have been just the narrow confines of the street, but it looked like we were trying to drive through a crowded room. When two cars met, even though most of them were compact models, one of the vehicles would pull as far to one side as possible, at times over the curb, and the other vehicle would creep by with inches to spare. It reminded me of fighting my way through the choked hallways at my school between classes.

I could only stare in awe at the throng of people and motor bikes. The sidewalks might have been six feet wide at the most and populated with bikes, tables set out in front of restaurants, and small kiosks. Street vendors were prolific, appearing every few feet, selling clothing, food, produce, fish and seafood, souvenirs, and crafts. The rest of the space was occupied by motor bikes parked at the storefronts. A person couldn't walk on the sidewalk without stepping onto the pavement and the oncoming traffic to bypass the obstacles.

The hotel was located in the old town amid even more narrow, crowded streets and sharp turns. The bus driver seemed to know what he was doing, although I thought he might have run over several people and sideswiped cars and motor scooters on the way. Even at this time of night, from my vantage point slightly above the surrounding traffic, I witnessed a throng of motor scooters and small cars traveling within inches of the bus, moving along with it like sticks thrown into a flowing river. Shops sat nearly on the street and what little sidewalks spanned between the shops and curbs were filled with people strolling past the storefronts, pausing to go around scooters parked in front of them. The strange aromas of Hanoi reached in through the windows and I got my first real whiff of the smell of Vietnam that I had forgotten; the rich blend of exhaust fumes, sour, musty air, pollen, seafood, and waste. My pulse might have accelerated slightly.

We unloaded at the hotel entrance and right away, we were waved off our bags. The wait staff in their pressed trousers, stark white shirts, and gleaming smiles, would do that for us, they said, as they opened the doors for us to pass through.

We would be spending three nights there, touring the city and nearby attractions. According to our itinerary, we would see the presidential palace, Ho Chi Minh's mausoleum, and Hoa Lo Prison, otherwise known as the "Hanoi Hilton." I had heard of all of these places but had never given them a second thought. After all, I hadn't really given Vietnam much thought after I had left the first time. The only thoughts I'd had up until now were of my own mortality and what had seemed to be an unusual run of luck when I was there.

I checked into my room and took stock of it. Well, after I figured out how the lights worked. It took some time feeling around in the narrow corridor of light from the open door until I saw the slot beside the doorframe. I inserted the key card and like magic, the room blazed with the sudden glare of fluorescent illumination.

It was a decent size, pleasantly furnished, the two beds good and firm. It was equivalent to a Marriot or Hyatt in America. I quickly reviewed my calculations on the $100 a day cost for this room, the breakfast to follow, and the bus transportation. I thought, what a frigging deal!

I got ready for bed and noticed the complimentary bottled water on the shelf in the bathroom. Then I recalled what 'they' say about foreign travel: "Don't drink the water." I didn't. I opened one of the bottles.

While I laid in bed catching up on McNamara's take on the Vietnam War, I took a break and reviewed the channel lineup for the television. After a few clicks, it was obvious that I didn't know what they were saying. All of the channels were Vietnamese stations. Well, what was I thinking? I went back to McNamara.

My roommate, Thomas Gilbert, had made his own travel arrangements and would show up later. It was nearly eleven when he walked through the door.

Thom was a tall dude, large frame, dark hair with a bit of gray becoming evident, and dark-rimmed glasses. He had one of those voices that you could hear across a football field. Deep, resonant, and forceful. Even though I had hearing aids, I knew I would have no trouble understanding him. His face had one of those mischievous smiles, the kind that makes you wonder what he had been doing.

"I'm from Sallisaw, Oklahoma," I told him. "I live out in the sticks."

"I've got a place in Sacramento," he said. "We live by a river. I do a lot of boating."

He tossed a Kindle onto the bed.

"Heavy reader?" I asked him.

"Yeah," he said. "I read a lot."

Conversation turned toward family.

"Right now, my oldest son is living with my wife and me," he volunteered. "I have a daughter living in Oakland and another son that also lives in the San Francisco Bay Area."

The daughter was involved in retail sales of medical marijuana. I had never met anyone who dealt with that. I'd had encounters with folks who used it, but I'd never given much thought to it. I'd never had the inclination to try it. Hell, when you've got a good bottle of Scotch at hand, what would be the point? I had read many articles about the beneficial effects of medical marijuana, and I felt some kind of satisfaction that people with harrowing conditions had some means of relief.

"I just finished reading your book," he said.

There was that spike in trepidation again.

"I was stationed at Lane, too."

"When were you there?"

"In 1968," he said. "The 498th Medevac."

The 498th was located across from my unit, the 129th, on the opposite side of the control tower. It was nice to meet someone who had seen service in the same area in II Corps in the central highlands. Even though it was late, I found it easy to stay awake and get acquainted with Thom.

I had noticed that instead of Thomas, he used Thom, with an "h," and I asked him about that.

"I got tired of Thomas," he said. "I just dropped the ass and started using Thom."

I had already made up my mind to like this fellow.

Thom was another of the guys who hadn't retired. He was a CPA and active in several civic organizations. A busy fellow, I guessed. In spite of all of the jobs I had now that I didn't have time to do when I was working, he was probably busier than I was.

We finally wound down and turned off the lights. It took a moment for my mind to stop wondering what I would face in the morning.

Here I was, back in Vietnam, a place to which I had never dreamed of returning and oddly enough I felt no fear, no curse; just anticipation. Still, there was an unremitting feeling that something wasn't right. I didn't' know what it was, and I didn't know why it was there, feeding on my anxiety. I managed to keep it at bay.

Meeting the other vets gave me a euphoric feeling, as if I were coming home. The feeling that I belonged, that I was a part of something bigger than myself. But then I thought, what was I doing here? What did I hope to find? What *would* I find? And would it help or…?

Well, sleep prevented me from thinking about the rest of it.

CHAPTER 4

HANOI, SECOND NIGHT

Wednesday, 2 December, 2015

Breakfast is a big deal to the Vietnamese; they take it seriously. When I walked into the restaurant of the Hanoi Pearl Hotel, I found no less than 50 feet of buffet line with every imaginable kind of food one could eat for breakfast, or any other meal for that matter. The creative breakfast offerings included noodles, loads of vegetables, fruit, soup, sausages, bacon, potatoes, cereal, breads, rolls, and an egg station for custom cooked eggs and omelets. Oh, and a variety of juices. An army of waitresses was on hand to take care of refilling coffee cups, removing dirty plates from the tables, and anything else that needed attention. The girls were pleasant, gracious, and eager to please, smiles always on their faces. I've never been in any restaurant with a waitstaff so attentive. It put American restaurants to shame, especially the hotels where you find waitstaff only if your credit card bounces.

And the coffee. Well, you must understand my position on coffee. My daughter calls me a coffee snob. I suppose I am. I prefer Arabica coffee, bold and strong. I even purchase whole-bean coffee, the darker roast variety, and grind it myself every morning before I brew it. I gave up the cheap Robusta supermarket coffee years ago after I found there were better things in life.

Vietnamese coffee was outstanding, bold, strong, and a hint of chocolate. Like army joe, you could almost stand a spoon in it. I later discovered, from our resident wizard, Don Hooper, that Vietnam is the second largest exporter of coffee in the world after Brazil. Rice is its largest export. I didn't even know Vietnam produced coffee. I did have one complaint about the coffee, though; those dinky cups were ridiculous. My finger didn't fit through the hole, and after two or three sips, it was time to refill.

Thom came down about the time I had finished. I was still talking with Jack Swickard and Tom Baca, who had joined me at the table. Jack's hair and beard, like most of the others, had nearly completed their transformation into that touchstone of age that gives one an aura of wisdom. His smile was bold and infectious, the kind that made me want to smile with him. I could imagine him at the controls of his slick, reveling in the mastery of the mechanical beast known as a Huey.

Both of them had been back to Vietnam before and had taken a liking to Vietnamese food. I never saw Jack at a table without a pair of chopsticks. I'm not sure he knew how to use a fork.

When we all had finished, it was only about 8:30 and we weren't due to meet at the bus for an hour. Thom and I wanted to find a phone store and get pre-paid sim cards for our cell phones so we could call home without the outrageous fees charged for roaming.

The night before, I had talked with two of the fellows who had arrived earlier, Dennis Gulich and Duane Speirs. They had already explored the local area around the town. Dennis and Duane were two of the most easygoing, brash, amusing characters I'd ever met. Their eccentric behavior endeared them to me immediately. Thom and I met them as we stepped from the lobby onto the sidewalk outside.

"Where you guys heading?" Dennis asked in his jovial manner. He had one of those smiles that would make you think he had just pulled off the biggest heist in history.

"We're off to find a phone store," I told them. "We want to get sim cards."

Dennis's eyes lit up, almost proudly. "We got some last night." He turned around and pointed down the street between the rows of shops. "If you go straight down that street then turn right, you'll run right into it."

"So, do your phones work?" I asked.

"Mine works good," Dennis said.

"Mine didn't work the first time," Duane mumbled through his scruffy beard, that reminded me of Papa Smurf. "They had to put another one in. It works fine, now."

Duane's gray crew cut gave the impression of serious but entertaining man, if you subscribed to wry humor.

"Don't use the little stores," Dennis cautioned. "That's where we went. You'll probably have better luck at the big one down the street, there."

"How much did the cards cost?" I asked.

"I gave them twenty bucks and they fixed me right up."

Thom and I looked at each other and nodded. We thanked Dennis and we were off down the street.

The first thing I noticed about the old town was the smell, stronger than it had been on the bus. There was an odd blend of cooking food, and a whiff of something beneath a layer of exhaust fumes, overtones of fish, and the sweet-sour miasma of what seemed like an open sewer. It reminded me somewhat of the French Quarter in New Orleans on a sultry day.

I had seen the narrow streets from the window of our bus, but looking at them from curbside, it seemed like we were in a time warp. The street was just wide enough for two small cars to pass, providing the hundreds of motor bikes parked to the sides weren't there. Yes, there were hundreds of the things. The motor scooter was the primary means of transportation in Vietnamese cities. Mass transit systems were largely unknown in the country, except for a few buses. No subways, not many taxis, and no big cars. Well, I did see a few Mercedes and BMWs, but they could only manage to squeeze through the narrow streets with extreme care.

Noise echoed off the two and three-story buildings that were crammed together like townhouses, much like you might see on a small prosperous town's main street in America. The Vietnamese flag, a yellow star on a red field, flew everywhere that a pole or staff could be attached. The stores, only about twelve or fourteen-feet wide, huddled next to each other forming a kind of variegated wall, the fronts open to the morning air, already steamy. Trees that appeared to have grown there for a century or more sprouted from holes in the concrete sidewalks and leaned out over the street shading the roadway between the colorful facades that reached to the far corners of the blocks. The buzzing and purring of motor bikes reverberated down the gallery of stores and the high-pitched nasal twang of the local dialects pierced my ears, some in casual conversation and others with raised voices in discord, giving orders, or in jest, it being hard to tell.

The street was alive this early in the morning and had been for some time, I gathered. Child-sized plastic tables and chairs filled the sidewalks in front eating establishments. Being small of stature, the Vietnamese apparently found little discomfort in this inexpensive furniture, since patrons occupied many of the tables and were partaking of specialties of the shops.

Thom and I walked carefully, which is what you do when your eyes are looking everywhere except where you're going. The streets were cluttered with signs, bright colors, and a multitude of merchandise. Even though I had to stop several times to avoid collisions, the local people did not seem flustered by it and, instead, smiled and nodded. Everyone I saw smiled at me and nodded, acknowledging my presence. Individuals I met head-on on the sidewalk graciously moved aside to allow me to pass before I could manage to do so for them, and they were always grinning. Many of them spoke to me, not that I had any idea what they were saying.

My entire concept of Vietnam had just been challenged. I had lugged with me the old memories of hooch maids and workers that were indifferent much of the time toward us soldiers. And along with that, I had retained the distrust I had learned to nurture during my tour of duty. None of that seemed appropriate now. It was a different world. The effect of the narrow, bordered lane was one of intimacy, a closeness to humanity I had not seen for a long time. I'm not sure how I actually felt about it then. I do know that somehow I felt safer there than I would have felt in any large American city.

Thom and I found the Viattel phone store easily enough. We went in and told the lady what we wanted. After explaining the options, each of us selected the 30-minute voice plan with 1 gigabyte of data. She took our phones and expertly installed the chips, tested them, and returned them. The cost was VND 400,000, or dong, the Vietnamese dollar, or about $20 U. S. We hadn't exchanged our U. S. currency yet, but she gladly accepted our American dollars. We left with new phone numbers and the anticipation of texting and calling our wives.

We returned to the hotel in time to grab our gear from the room and meet outside the lobby by the bus that was parked in front, crowding the narrow street. While waiting to board the bus, I met the remaining member of the tour group, Don Hooper. I was to learn later that Don was not a veteran, but he was a close friend of Tom Baca and was widely traveled. He had assisted with planning for the trip.

I was overwhelmed to be surrounded by fellow Vietnam vets, my extended family. The ones who I knew had gone through pretty much what I had; ones I'd had never had the opportunity to meet.

I was surprised that they all looked so normal. After all of the books and articles I had read about the effects of the Vietnam War on soldiers, I had wondered just how deeply the injuries, handicaps, trauma, and disenchantment with America had sliced into the fabric of patriotism and the life that civilians might consider to be normal. In these eleven men, I saw no evidence of any of it. Only the effects of aging that had lightened or removed their hair, slowed their gait, and swelled their stomachs. What it had not done, though, was to erase the smiles of optimism from their faces.

The bus was a beauty. A 32-passenger coach, gleaming in the muted sunlight reaching down through the congested buildings, filtered through leaden clouds. Truc had really come through on our transportation. We all stepped on board and settled into the large seats surrounded by walls of windows. Off we went, weaving our way through the glut of motor bikes and cars that challenged us to the right of way within the confines of the constricted pavement.

Our destination was the Ho Chi Minh Mausoleum. It was located in the Ba Dinh Square area along with the presidential palace and Ho Chi Minh's residence. I was familiar with Ho Chi Minh but had never studied the man in any detail, nor what his impact on Vietnam had been, other than the fact that he was considered the "Father of the Democratic Republic of Vietnam." He had been President of North Vietnam during the war. Well, I would have the opportunity to learn more.

Once we fought our way out of the strangled mess of narrow streets of the old town, a more modern Hanoi erupted with broad avenues and a horrendous barrage of traffic going every which way. Our bus driver was good. That's all I can say. In spite of the onslaught of vehicles passing by the intersection, he carefully prodded the bus into the storm of motor bikes and small cars and as if by a magician's magic wand, the stream of metal and glass seemed to redirect itself to flow around the bus as it nudged its way into the current. The flow caught the bus and sucked it into the surge of traffic like a boat pulled into the torrent of a flood.

Our bus cruised down the streets a mere breath away from surrounding motor bikes and cars. I felt safe in the fact that the bus was much larger than anything else on the road. I could not even compare it to the confusion and congestion I had witnessed in Los Angeles the last time I was there. But unlike the traffic in L. A., the spectacle around me was a harmonious dance of vehicles, each visibly tolerant of all the others, and orchestrated by some unknown entity that allowed it to function flawlessly.

We arrived at the avenue that fronted the Ho Chi Minh Mausoleum. The barricade across it allowed us to park in the middle of the street for disembarkation. The mausoleum was an unmistakable landmark, visible from several blocks away. And even from a hazy distance, I could make out the dreary chill that seemed to suck all of the happiness from the environment. Sitting upon a tall foundation, it looked like a concrete blockhouse surrounded by a colonnade and topped with a three-tier concrete slab. The thing was a homely hulk in the midst of a verdant expanse. It sat across the street, vacant of traffic, from a line of government building as stark and lifeless as the mausoleum. Only tourists and guards populated the street's edge.

Military guards greeted us with solemn faces, no joy there. We made our way to toward the gray hulk of stone with idle chatter and carefree attitudes. Only a short distance into our walk, a guard approached us with authority and gravely motioned us out of the street and toward the edge of the sidewalk where white lines marked the path we were to follow.

"Twos," the guard called out sharply, and held his arms straight in front of him, I suppose to replicate parallel lines. "Twos," he repeated.

So, we paired up and proceeded along the designated path like schoolchildren on a field trip. A couple of the fellows let their minds wander a bit too much, straying from the white confines, and the guard immediately hollered a warning to them and motioned them back onto the trail. It was obvious that the military escorts meant business. The guards gave me an uneasy feeling, but then I realized that Vietnam *was* a Communist country, and the fleeting images of Communist oppression I had been indoctrinated with in school blew through my mind. I was careful to watch my step, although I had mixed feelings about the situation.

After a block-long walk under the watchful eyes of the guards, we arrived at a small building where Truc purchased tickets for the group. Before we made our way toward the mausoleum, however, one of the attendants told us that no cameras or videos were allowed. And no smoking, eating or drinking. Visitors were faced with a number of rules. Legs must be covered (no shorts), no talking, hands visible, not in pockets or crossed arms. I wondered what all the hubbub was about. Hell, Ho Chi Minh was dead. How would he know? Truc agreed to stay behind and take care of our cameras, since he had already seen the exhibit. He would meet us at the exit.

Another block-long walk took us by manicured plots of bonsai trees and other species that looked like something I might see in a gardening magazine. The plaza surrounding the mausoleum was divided into 240 squares, displaying plants and flowers from all the regions of Vietnam. Not a leaf was out of place. The closer I got to the mausoleum, the more the air seemed to lose part of its energy, as if a brisk wind had just died. It was one of those eerie feelings I got when I was about to experience something unknown to me, fearful, even.

We turned at the walk leading to the steps of the massive structure and approached the huge doors that stood open at the top where honor guards in stark white uniforms with red trim and gold hardware were stationed at the entrance, replete with chrome-plated weapons, sabers, and all of the formal military regalia. It was all quite impressive. More solemn looks greeted us as we carefully passed through the blast of cool air whooshing out of the doors.

As stark and austere as the exterior façade was, the interior was even more so, smelling of cold, hard stone. In the presence of white-uniformed guards at every corner, silence prevailed as we ventured forth into the depths of the cold, inert tomb, a place where people wouldn't think about how happy they might have been. I remember a very uneasy feeling overtaking me as I followed my footsteps along the red-carpeted hallway, up step after step, corner after corner. The illumination waned with each step until we were in near darkness. Even the bright red carpet runner beneath our feet lost its color and several of us lost our footing, stumbling to find purchase on the steps. A guard would suddenly lunge forward to assist, I suppose, to prevent injury to the innocent victim of the desolate gloom.

I was surprised at having to travel upward, since I had expected to be descending into the depths of solemnity. We reached what appeared to be the uppermost level, and by that time, the temperature seemed to have dropped into what could have been suitable for a refrigerator, and

I was thankful for my foresight to wear a long-sleeved shirt. It was as if the life had been sucked out of everything.

We turned the final corner and it sprang out of nowhere. A glass enclosure beneath spotlights contained the embalmed body of Ho Chi Minh. I suppose that explained why we were all shivering. The mausoleum really *was* a refrigerator.

We maintained our formation of twos, or single file, as we slowly passed around the glass case, gawking at the figure inside, amazed at how well preserved he was. Since Ho Chi Minh died in 1969, some maintenance was required from time to time to keep things presentable. While our eyes were on Ho Chi Minh's body, the guards' eyes were on us, naïve tourists that stumbled around the carpeted pathway.

As the founder of modern Vietnam, Ho Chi Minh was held in high esteem by the Vietnamese people, even reverently. I have seldom seen such respect given to any head of state. The best we seemed to be able to do was a flame that burned at President John F. Kennedy's grave. Even the Tomb of the Unknown Soldier at Arlington National Cemetery receives more respect than our heads of state, but I understand the reason for that.

We gladly exited the mausoleum and wandered toward the vendor's area where we met Truc and retrieved our cameras. We set out to view the President's mansion, a large and imposing yellow-gold structure built by the French. Ho Chi Minh refused to inhabit it, preferring instead, the more modest house on stilts nearby. He had felt that such luxury was pretentious, far removed from the common people of his country.

The grounds were alive with ancient trees, plants and flowers that thrived in the carefully tended park. Ho Chi Minh's residence was a small, two-story structure, open across the bottom where meetings were held. The upper floor contained his office and bedroom and personal areas. The residence overlooked a large fishpond, and behind the house was an L-shaped row of what I suppose was the staff's quarters. I found the magnificent park relaxing, the entire grounds a fitting tribute to Ho Chi Minh.

We ventured farther into the park to the old Citadel where the North Vietnamese Army, the People's Army of Vietnam, placed their headquarters during the war. A part of it had been destroyed long ago and was under excavation and renovation. We toured the offices of General Vo Nguyen Giap, Minister of Defense, and General Van Tien Dung, Chief of the General Staff. The modest complex of single-story buildings was built of thick walls and flat roofs with a layer of sand to prevent the intrusion of shrapnel into the interior. I was amused to see that the placards describing the exhibits referred to the Vietnam War as the "American War." The underground bunker contained equipment essential to the combat operations. It was surprising to learn that the war was conducted from such a humble environment. It gave me new respect for the North Vietnamese.

Looking at the war maps on the walls, I noticed that the names of provinces and towns were split into two or more words, such as Viet Nam and Ha Noi. Truc informed us that this was the actual spelling of the Vietnamese names. Viet Nam means people of the south, the people living at that time in southern China and Viet Nam. Ha Noi means river within or inside. It was taken from the Red River that runs through Hanoi.

During the war, correspondents reported back to their offices using teletype machines on expensive communication networks, usually at a charge per word. To reduce costs, many words were contracted into single words, especially the names of Vietnamese towns. The single-word monikers became standard usage in America.

We returned the bus to travel to the Qua'n An Hgon Restaurant. Not exactly posh, but not crude either, it presented a casual ambience not too far removed from street-side dining in some areas and typical blue-collar dining I had seen in America. We were led through a throng of hungry diners to a large room upstairs where we occupied a long table. After scanning the lengthy and all-inclusive menu, someone suggested that Truc order for all of us. By then, I was convinced that Truc knew his business and letting him order seemed the logical thing to do. I didn't know what most of the stuff on the menu was. Beers were also ordered and passed around to whoever wanted one; Tiger Beer, a popular one in Vietnam. A variety of dishes were passed along the table and most of us sampled whatever was on them. However, Pat Matheny was not so inclined. If it didn't look like a cheeseburger, he wouldn't have it. I'm not sure what he ate for lunch that day, but I suspect he was ravenous by the time we returned to the hotel that evening.

Fried spring rolls, fish, chicken, and assorted vegetables gave us all a taste of Vietnam. The food, although some of it new to me, was excellent, at least to those of us who ate it. The beer continued to flow freely. By the end of the meal, we were properly stuffed and some of us a bit more jovial than usual.

Then back onto the bus for a trip to the War Museum where vehicles, aircraft, and weapons used in the Vietnam War were on display, including Vietnamese, American, Russian, and French pieces. The wide variety of equipment and weapons surprised me and illustrated the scarcity of weapons and tools available to the North Vietnamese.

The next stop would be Hoa Lo Prison. I wasn't sure what to expect there, since I had only seen photos from documentaries and stories on television. When the bus stopped at the curbside of what looked like a nondescript beige building in the middle of the block with the words "MAISON CENTRAL" on the gray archway over the entrance, I was surprised to learn that this was Hoa Lo Prison.

Once through the doors, its function as an official building became evident due to the stark, inhospitable interior, small spaces, thick beige walls, narrow doors, and practically no windows. Farther into the depths of the structure, the color changed from a mundane beige stucco-type finish to taller spaces, the corridors narrow and the wall painted a depressing gray at the top changing about mid-height to a sickly greenish-gray at the bottom that could easily induce queasiness. The floors were finished in rustic bare concrete. The prison was built by the French in the 1940s. A number of cells lined the walls and sturdy iron-barred doors covered some, solid steel doors on others.

I'm not sure I can adequately describe the feeling that wrenched my body into a tense and unsettled agitation. I knew it was only an old prison and even though no danger was present, I couldn't shake my uneasiness. The American prisoners of war that had been kept there, among whom was Senator John McCain after his capture, had dubbed the prison the "Hanoi Hilton." High profile prisoners, like pilots, had been kept in small cells apart from the main population. Others had been jailed in larger rooms with only benches on which to sit and sleep. Most cells had been equipped with leg shackles to restrain prisoners, restricting their mobility and making escape nearly impossible. Other cells contained shackles suspended from the ceiling, intended to keep one's feet from touching the floor. One large room contained an old guillotine left behind by the French. Life-sized dioramas gave the visitor some sense of what it might have been like as a prisoner of war, but I'm sure that did nothing to impart the real misery of it all. Even the prison itself was little more than a gruesome hellhole that would lead anyone to think he would never leave alive.

As we wandered through the concrete corridors, what little subdued conversation escaped hesitant lips echoed between the hard, concrete walls. There was little joking or silliness, just the niggling from the atmosphere inside this dismal place.

I thought of all of the close calls I'd had when flying in Vietnam, and how many bullet holes in our aircraft the crew chiefs had patched up. Any one of those bullets could have come through the cockpit or engine instead of the tail boom. And I could have had a forced landing anytime in the middle of Charlie's ranks. I thought about one time in particular that my own stupidity could have landed me in the Hanoi Hilton, or a coffin:

I was a new AC (aircraft commander) flying resupply to the Korean Tiger Division outposts. It was autumn, the time of year when monsoons start raging in the central highlands. We had stayed on mission late for an "emergency" sortie, the RTO had said (radio/telephone operator). He was a Korean soldier, our guide and interpreter for the resupply missions. We had just taken off very late in the afternoon in hopes of making it back to Lane before the sky opened up with its customary torrential rainfall. All of the blue had already disappeared and the clouds had become these huge gray monsters that had sucked all of the moisture out of the air and land below. We were about halfway back to the airfield when, without even a sprinkle or other sign of the impending rain, it was like a thousand fire hoses opened up aimed right at us. The rain was so heavy I couldn't see crap.

In a miraculous feat of visionary magic, the crew chief spotted a field below.

"Sir, I think there's an empty field at ten o'clock next to the ROK (Republic of Korea) outpost. We could probably set down there."

I looked out my side window where the rain caused only marginal blindness, and I saw it. I made a beeline for it and set down just outside the fence that surrounded the Korean compound. As we were shutting down to weather out the rain, a group of Korean soldiers surrounded the ship. We had ditched our RTO at the Regimental Command Post, our last stop, so we had no idea what the fellows outside were saying. The gunner opened his door and one of the Koreans jumped on board, his face in a rare expression of puzzlement.

"Weather," I tried to tell him.

The crew chief tried as well. The poor fellow looked just as perplexed. I pointed outside and wiggle my fingers upside down to mimic rain falling. He finally nodded his head, then made a call on his radio. Another soldier came up behind and talked to him. Then he told us, "You stay here tonight," pointing toward the outpost. "You come."

Well, I tried to explain that we would stay with the ship to guard it.

"No," he shook his head, pointing again outside. "They guard," he nodded his head.

Sure enough, when I looked around outside the helicopter it was surrounded by soldiers in ponchos standing at port arms in the pouring rain, rifles at the ready.

"You come," he insisted.

We jumped out and the guide motioned with arms parallel and moving up and down. My assumption was that, for some reason, he wanted us to follow single file. We did. He led us into a bunker with a couple of dozen Koreans sitting around in their baggy boxers looking at us with that innocent look the Koreans give you when they don't understand something. The guide pointed to four empty beds.

"You sleep," he said. He announced something to the men in the room then turned back to me.

"We radio you headquarters. Tell them you here" Then he left.

The guys in the room started to smile and nod their heads. One of them opened a box, pulled out four beers, and passed them to us. Warm beer. I'd never drunk a warm beer. Considering that we hadn't had anything to eat since the C-rations at lunch, it was pretty darned good. It would have to last until breakfast.

I asked the Korean in the bed next to me whose bed I was sitting on. After bridging the language barrier, I finally learned that the beds belonged to the men out guarding our ship. I had never felt so low in my life. Taking a man's bed while he did something I should have been doing. Boy, did they get screwed.

After a restless night's sleep, the crew gathered at the door where the guide had come back to get us. He asked if we wanted breakfast. We told him no, we just wanted to get back to Lane.

"I show you way," he said, turning around to leave.

"You don't' have to," I told him. "I think we can find that big hunk of helicopter by ourselves."

He looked at me with that puzzled look again.

"No," he said, "you follow."

"It's okay," I told him. "We can find it."

"No, no" he said adamantly. "I show you way through mines."

"What mines?" I asked.

"The ones around helicopter."

`My body stood there in spite of what my mind told it to do. Then a chill raced through me just before the adrenaline started pumping. You know how you feel when you unexpectedly find out that you've just screwed up. Then the embarrassment hit, kind of like farting at a royal tea. Holy Hell! I had landed in a frigging minefield!

The dismal gray walls seemed to close in on me and I thought what if I had landed in Charlie's back yard instead of that Korean compound? Or if only one of the tracers that streaked toward the ship actually tracked right for my head, or any one of the crew? But even in the throes of anxiety, there is always a bit of levity, and then I wondered why in hell the NVA had such bad aim?

I can't say I was disappointed to leave the prison. I'm glad I had to opportunity to see it and experience the exhibits, but it was not on my list of favorites.

Just before we got back on the bus, Truc was there to convert our U. S. dollars to dong. This fellow was quite efficient. I had taken a liking to him when I first met him at the airport. My fondness for him was growing.

We returned to the hotel to prepare for dinner that evening. Truc had arranged for us to dine with Senior Police Colonel Nguyen Thanh Hung (Asst Police Chief of Hanoi), with the official title of Deputy Division Chief, Hanoi Metropolitan Police Department. The Vietnamese are fond of titles. He was a friend of Jack Swickard, who had met him at the International Law Enforcement Academy in Roswell, New Mexico, a state department program for senior law enforcement officers. We were Colonel Hung's guests for the evening at Opera Open, an upscale restaurant in downtown Hanoi.

We were shown to the upper floor of the restaurant where one long table was set for dinner. The rest of the floor was empty. Jack and Tom Baca sat near the Colonel, since they had known each other for some time. Just before the dinner officially began, we all presented the Colonel with small gifts from our home states. It was customary in Vietnam to offer gifts to your host, wrapped in bright colors, anything but black.

Dinner consisted of at least seven courses, but I really wasn't counting. We started with cream of chicken soup with salad and bread, followed by fried clams, then fried spring rolls, rice sheets and vegetables. Rice sheets are super thin sheets of rice paper to wrap the vegetables in. Then prawns, each of which was nearly as large as my hand, then steak and potatoes, and finally fried rice. Oh, and a plentiful supply of wine. The waitresses never let a glass become empty. It was all finished off with bananas.

It became customary for Truc to lead a toast about every four or five minutes, with his, "Yo...yo...yo!" Then we all clinked glasses and threw back a good swallow of wine, or water, like a couple of the fellows chose to do. The frivolity increased as the evening wore on and the toasts became more frequent and more robust. I have no idea how many bottles of wine were consumed that night, but I'm sure it put the Colonel in good stead with the restaurant's owner. The dinner would have cost him a small fortune.

It was time for the hotel and bed. Back in the room, I tried out the sim chip and called my wife. She seemed surprised to hear from me. I had sent her texts earlier, but that's not the same as hearing someone's voice. She had just gotten her mother situated for the morning and we had a nice chat. Having heard little but the high-pitched nasal twang of the Vietnamese, it sounded so good to me to hear her voice, real and robust. I hadn't realized how much I missed her light-hearted humor.

Ha Long Bay awaited our visit the next day. I'm not sure what we were going to see there, but I was game for anything by then. We would travel by bus to the bay, a three-hour drive, then we would have to return to Hanoi.

I had talked to my wife, my stomach was still full, and I was getting sleepy. It would be a restful night. But before than happened, I thought about what I had seen during the day, especially Hoa Lo Prison.

I have tried to imagine what it might have been like there during the war, but if someone has never experienced it, I don't think it is possible to understand. Much like serving in the Vietnam War. If you weren't there, you will find it difficult to comprehend what it was like. Then I thought about the fact that I could very well have been a resident at the Hanoi Hilton had my helicopter been shot down on a combat assault. During my tour of duty, I had always thought about being captured, but I never considered it to be probable, and that might explain the casual attitude we had toward it. We never realize how lucky we are much of the time.

CHAPTER 5

HANOI, THIRD NIGHT

Thursday, 3 December, 2015

Thom and I awoke early and after breakfast went for a walk toward Hoan Kiem Lake, about a block away from the hotel, a focal point of the old town. Once past the narrow confines of the old businesses, the streets opened up into a four-lane one-way thoroughfare filled with a flood of motor scooters and small cars. Many of the women drivers wore white masks, I supposed for protection against pollution, exhaust fumes, and pollen. However, I eventually learned that women wore masks to prevent burning or tanning of the face.

As we tried to cross the incessant tide of vehicles, we found that the drivers were not so accommodating to pedestrians as they were to other traffic. No one slowed or showed any inclination to avoid ramming our bodies unless they were within a foot of us. Not that the traffic was moving that fast, perhaps 20 miles per hour. So, we patiently waited for the tide of traffic to ebb before scurrying across. There was little else we could do.

Although safety conscious, since the law required bike operators and passenger to wear helmets, little thought must have been given to pedestrian safety. I guess you weren't supposed to walk there. However, I never saw anyone run down by a vehicle, and maybe that was because of the excellent reflexes apparently developed as small children as passengers on the determined motor bikes that navigated the sea of vehicles.

The lake was fairly large, stretching three or four blocks from one end to the other, and surrounded by a walkway of pavers bordering gardens and more walkways, some of which had been installed recently, and others under construction. It seemed as though everything was under construction there. Many old trees stood proudly against the dull and cool morning, their shade lost in the overcast sky. The sidewalk adjacent to the roadway ran beneath a web of lights festooned across the pavers. At night, the illumination bathed the park in a festive glow.

Beds of freshly trimmed grass, flowers, and perfectly pruned shrubbery filled the park, and hundreds of people had taken advantage of the mild weather to exercise in the fresh morning air, fresh and un-tainted by fumes and the odor of fish. As we strolled around the lake, we saw Tai Chi, yoga, badminton, jogging, power walking, stretching, calisthenics, and even dance classes. It was strange to see a Vietnamese couple doing the Foxtrot. I assumed that fitness must have been a prior-ity for many of the locals. The park *was* a grand place for it.

Then I thought about America, where one must have a gigantic SUV to so much as retrieve the mail from a box at the end of a long driveway. And then there were the hulking buses that transported chil-dren to and from school, where in Vietnam, there were no buses. It sad-dened me to think that we had become so spoiled and lazy, squandering energy as if it were sand poured down a hole.

The pavement was clean, no litter, and the garden areas and trees were immaculately maintained. It looked as if an army of gardeners had just finished sprucing it up. The people we met on the walk graciously moved out of our path and smiled as we passed by, most of them nod-ding. What we didn't see was any hint of altercations, arguments, or confrontations. These people just seemed content to be among others, happily cohabitating and sharing the resources the city offered. They all seemed to be in tune with nature and their places in the universe.

That thought erased all of the ill feelings I had harbored for the Vietnamese people that I hadn't even realized I'd had. Indoctrination by the army had made a huge difference in my perception of others, taint-ing it with the need to be alert for signs of danger. Complacency will kill you, they had told us. You must be alert to survive, they said. But that was in preparation for war and in that case, there is little room for compassion or humility. Only the instinct to fight.

So, again I considered the last 44 years in which I had lugged around the baggage of suspicion and aversion toward the Vietnamese, all because that's what I had been trained to do. I thought, how funny that I was walking among the very people I had learned to avoid, and that I should become aware now of the serenity that greeted me in that park, the throngs of the Vietnamese people who smiled at me and treat-ed me kindly, neighborly, as if delighted to see me, a foreigner in their land. I doubt that we Americans would be so considerate of them when visiting or living in our country. There is abundant evidence of that in the news media I had watched on television and read in the newspapers and periodicals. A sad testament to the "Land of the Free," since most of us are descended from immigrants.

As Thom and I returned to the hotel, I couldn't help but notice the spotless streets, unblemished by cracks, stains, or unsightly gaps. It was as if this part of the city had been recently constructed, provided one didn't look at the facades of aged buildings that bordered the pristine pavement. Walking in a similar town in Oklahoma I would have been kicking papers, Styrofoam cups, and other trash out of my way.

Later in the morning, the bus pulled out of Hanoi bound for Ha Long Bay, about three hours to the east, on the coast of the South China Sea. Truc was unable to join us that day, so his two sons, Hung and Thinh, and his niece, Tram, accompanied us to act as tour guides. Hung, recently married, was knowledgeable about Hanoi but not all that fluent in English, being more attuned to Japanese. But his brother, Thinh, provided adequate translation.

The use of Agent Orange in Vietnam by American troops was an attempt to defoliate the forests in order to deprive the NVA and VC of concealing their presence beneath the heavy canopied trees. As it turned out, it was bad for us and bad for them. Vietnam veterans still suffer from the effects of the deadly herbicide, and untold numbers of Vietnamese still endure the suffering from exposure to it, including the following generations that inherited its effects. The result of Operation Ranchhand had left those people debilitated and unable to find suitable employment in the ranks of normal occupations. The Vietnamese government had taken a creative approach to dealing with the problem. Instead of handing money over the victims of Agent Orange, as we do in our welfare programs, the people were given education and training in vocations and crafts. The market place at Hoang Tan was one of the places where these folks sold their products. In this way, they became productive citizens and could earn a decent living for their families.

The complex had three large buildings, each catering to different ethnic groups. The staff in each building was versed in the language of the expected clientele. One building was for American tourists, one for Korean, and one for Japanese, the three most popular. The outside area was filled with sculptures of all sizes and genres. It was not uncommon for a tourist to purchase one and have it shipped to his home, which could be anywhere around the world. The goods included jewelry, clothing, art, and a host of other crafts. After wandering through the staggering variety of merchandise, we took a break and had tea and coffee and a snack in the restaurant. I purchased a silk scarf for my daughter there, for 67,500 dong, or about $33.50. A beautiful thing. I have seen nothing like it anywhere else. It was my contribution to the Agent Orange victims.

Once back on the road, Hung and Thinh provided information about the countryside and Tram graciously made sure we had water or anything else we needed. The overcast sky left a misty haze that followed us to our destination.

We unloaded at Ha Long Bay in the Gulf of Tonkin and headed for the wharf. The water echoed the gray, looming clouds, but with an emerald glaze, ripples from the cool, stout breeze trickling across the surface. We were directed to one of many tour boats moored side by side, awaiting their fares. Each of the boats was about 60 feet long with a two-story pilothouse in the rear overlooking a dining area. The tables inside were already set for lunch and we made ourselves at home.

The boat cast off and we settled down to a meal that was delivered in courses, a tradition in many Asian countries. Much to Pat's disappointment, we started with shrimp, then crabs, then fried spring rolls, which seemed to be standard meal fare. I'm sure Pat was still looking for that cheeseburger. Next came a vegetable slaw, rice, fish, and it was all polished off with a ripe banana. Bananas there are remarkably good, sweet with a just right meaty texture, a more robust flavor when ripened on the tree. I couldn't help but notice Pat's long face, disappointed again.

Following lunch, we went out on deck to view the bay and the unusual rock formations that broke from its depths like gnarls growing from the roots of trees. The rocky protrusions were everywhere, about 2,000 if, it was possible to count them, jutting out of the water in steep and craggy slopes, the brown gray and white limestone crusts peeking through dense vegetation. I didn't count them, but there could easily have been nearly a hundred tour boats in the bay, all filled with gawking tourists reveling in the wondrous sights.

Legend has it that the setting there in the bay was created by the charge of a mountain dragon into the coast, its thrashing tail sweeping aside the ground to form valleys and crevasses. The dragon plunged into the sea leaving it to fill with water, only pinnacles of the limestone pillars visible. Intriguing, as is much of Asian lore.

Cameras were clicking while we all scattered over the deck, pointing at this and that, and relaying tired jokes to one another. It was the light rain that finally drove us back into the cabin.

We docked at the steps to Thien Cung Cave, one of many located in the bay area. Not as large as Carlsbad Caverns, but big on charm and features. The attraction was well adapted to tourism, although the steep steps gave some members of our group cause to slow down and take things easy. Lighting inside the cave was arranged to highlight many of the unusual features of the rock formations. Our guides, Hung and Thinh, explained some of them that resembled animals and characters from Vietnamese legends. In spite of the underground ambience, I warmed quickly, droplets of sweat beading on my back. Some of the others removed their jackets. I've not seen many caves, but I can say that this one was fascinating in its character and ease of traversing. We stopped in the central cavern for a group photo shoot and each of us received a print.

As we left to walk back to the pier, more tour boats had arrived and they were docked side by side, as if something had pushed them all together like pigs at a long trough. Another boat made its way into the group, aiming for a narrow gap between two of the craft. It slowly pushed its way in, forcing all the other vessels to either side.

We boarded our boat to return to the harbor and our bus. We each laid out $15 for the lunch and were on our way back to Hanoi. That evening we were to have dinner with Truc and his family in honor of our veterans group, and also to honor his oldest son's wedding.

The bus unloaded at the door to the restaurant and Truc and his wife, a gracious woman with that look that made me think of a cover model, welcomed us. We were directed to a table just inside the door, a long one set with better than average dishes, an expanse of silverware, and, what would come to be expected at every dinner, wine glasses. These folks are fond of wine. It has a place of distinction on every dining table nearly every meal, except breakfast.

As expected, the dinner came in several courses: traditional fried spring rolls, vegetables, chicken, fish, rice, and others, of course. Wine flowed freely and so did our spirits and the many toasts that sprang up every third or fourth bite. The meal was monitored by a group of waitresses that seemed to be there to assist before any on us realized we needed it. The dining experience in Vietnam was magnificent, something I have rarely encountered in America.

We presented gifts to the married couple and Truc's wife, tokens of gratitude from our home states. Truc surprised us with a gift for each of us, as well. I opened my bag to find a pictorial biography of General Vo Nguyen Giap, obviously one of Truc's heroes. Fortunately, it was written in both Vietnamese and English.

Each of us pulled from our gift bag a tee shirt, red with a giant yellow star on the chest, a likeness of the Vietnamese flag. A red hat, similar to the shirt, completed the ensemble. Oh, we were also presented with three small dispensers of bamboo toothpicks. Picking teeth is customary following a meal; however, protocol dictates that a hand must cover the mouth to conceal the fact that it is taking place.

The shirts and hats brought forth series of whoops and hollers, along with another toast.

"Yo...yo...yo!" Truc would say, as he lifted his glass high and clinking began at one end of the table and worked its way to the other.

"Yo...yo...yo!" again.

Then it was time for pictures. In the short time I had been in Vietnam, I was puzzled by the attraction of the Vietnamese to the camera. It was as if it provided a source of sustenance to their existence. Whenever we stopped to take a group photograph, one of the locals would invariably step forward and offer to take the picture of us so that we could all be included in the shot. And they would also seem delighted if we offered to take their pictures, as well. They were all a bunch of sweet hams.

Of course, Truc encouraged us to don our new "VC" outfits, as he called them, for the pictures. The jocular mood had infected everyone and we soon became Truc's "VC Platoon." We would long refer to ourselves as members of the revered "VC Platoon."

We were to leave in the morning on a flight to Dong Hoi, about an hour and a half south by air. We would have to be at the Hanoi airport in time to catch the 8:20 flight. So, it was going to be early to bed for most of us.

Best wishes were extended to Truc's son and his bride, and to Truc's wife. We left the restaurant with a newfound sense of fellowship, a closeness to the Vietnamese people that few of us had ever experienced. With the humorous gifts of shirts and hats we felt as if we had become closer as a group, veterans of a war that up until recently had had little place in the scheme of honor and prestige in our own country. However, in Vietnam, the place we were all so eager to leave behind and forget, we had not been forgotten. Nor had we been buried in the detritus of censure. Americans seemed to be a source of delight and interest to these folks. I'm not sure I can describe how that made me feel at the time, but I now consider Truc's family to be among my dear friends.

I looked forward to the next day when we would explore the DMZ, or the Demilitarized Zone. It was one of those places I was all too familiar with but never gave much thought to, except that I was darned glad that I hadn't been stationed that closely to it in the war. Of course, the DMZ was a thing of the past, but we would see the monuments that were there as reminders of the terrible conflict that consumed America in a divisive and bitter gulf of patriotism.

CHAPTER 6

FROM HANOI TO DONG HOI

4 December, 2015

Five-thirty came earlier than I wanted it to. In spite of the darkness engulfing the room, Thom and I toppled out of bed, took our turns in the bathroom, and went down for chow early. Even though the restaurant was not officially open until 6:00, a petite girl in a waitstaff uniform, a smile across her adorable Asian face, met us at the door and motioned us in.

It hadn't taken long the previous morning for me to gage the locations of the best foods on the breakfast bar, so I made quick work of the bountiful offerings, consuming more than I otherwise would have. We were going to be traveling and had no idea when our next meal might be.

My stuffed gut made the elevator ride seem longer than usual. We fetched our bags form the room and returned to the lobby where the bellhops ferried them to the bus. I suppose the other guys were affected by the early morning hours too, because no one was moving with the buoyant spirit that had started our adventure. Truc was perceptive enough to leave well enough alone and let us crawl out of our sleepy reveries at our own paces.

At 6:30, with everyone on board, the bus dove into the throng of scooters and cars, forcing some of them to the curbs that defined the narrow streets. The old town was alive even at that early hour, people milling about, eating breakfast at the sidewalk tables, and delivering food stuffs to the shops, others merely on their way to their jobs. The gray sky clutched a dreary presence, a slight mist drifting through the soggy air.

On the way to the airport, I called my wife again. She and her mother were watching television and she was hoping the old soul would get sleepy soon so she would go to bed. I thought about how boring it must have been for her there, repeating the same instructions to her mother, whose aging mind seemed to lose words like a leaking bucket. I knew I would be of little help to her if I were there, but a tinge of guilt stayed the keenness I'd had for the day. Still, hearing her voice rejuvenated me and I was ready to face new adventures.

We arrived at the domestic terminal of the airport about thirty minutes later. The flight was to leave at 8:20 on a high wing twin turboprop plane, small but roomy. The 350-mile trip to Dong Hoi would take only an hour and a half, and I felt confident that I could endure that better than the 15-hour trip over the Pacific. Dong Hoi was just north of the 17th parallel, formerly the DMZ, that had separated North and South Vietnam during the Vietnam War. I had never been there and thought back to my first month in country. That was when I had realized that II Corps might have been more secure than I Corps at the DMZ, and the overwhelming feeling of doom had subsided to a mere fear of tragedy. It was one of the many times I had felt lucky over there.

It was in Dong Hoi that we boarded the bus we would be using for the remainder of our 500-mile trip to Ho Chi Minh City, previously known as Saigon. The bus was a Thaco 32-passenger orange and white coach outfitted with large windows and wide, comfortable seats. Our luggage was stowed in the compartments beneath and we had plenty of room inside. The bus driver, Nguyen Thanh Phong, seemed like a typical Vietnamese man, small stature, trim, dark hair, an easygoing look on his face, but like most Vietnamese, with vigilant eyes. They might look as if they held no emotion, but behind them was an ever-present awareness of what is going on around them.

I have to say that the transportation provided by Truc was first class. He had really done his homework. In fact, it would turn out that every little detail on this trip had been planned with extraordinary care. The man was a dynamite tour guide.

The highway could have been any American road. Vibrations lost themselves in the seat cushions and bumps were tempered by the mass of the bus. We had started our drive under the effects of too much food and inadequate sleep, leaving a pitiful band of old men to weather the effects of indigestion, flatulence, and perplexity at what passed by the windows. A round of the clock was enough to allay our overindulgence and murmuring grew more robust, spirits sharpened, and eventually the group was back to its boisterous form, tales flying across the aisles evocative of the narrators' previous experiences in Vietnam so long ago.

Highway QL1 was the principal route between Hanoi and Ho Chi Minh City. Our course took us through small towns and villages that seemed to pop up everywhere. The larger ones resembled the old town section of Hanoi, a cacophony of buildings painted with the patina of age, bevies of motor scooters parked on sidewalks, a few people in casual trousers and shirts milling about. Small trees lined the streets, appearing to have been there for only a decade or two. Unlike Hanoi, traffic was lighter and fewer people populated the narrow sidewalks that were just as clean. The pavement seemed a bit wider, some separated by medians, rich with shrubbery and flowers.

I wondered if these people spent a lot of their time cleaning. I suppose in a slower mode of life, one would have ample opportunity to do that. I also figured cleanliness must have been important to them. I sure wished it was more important to the folks back in America.

The variety of storefronts, some old, some newer, exhibited an intriguing degree of design and disarray. Had it not been for the Vietnamese language on the signs, I could very well have been riding down the main street of small town America.

As I studied the stores, I found that they appeared to be mom and pop type businesses, each with a specialty line of merchandise. Clothing shops sold clothing, plumbing supply shops sold plumbing supplies, and if you wanted a hat, you found a store that sold hats. Repair shops for motors, scooters, and other mechanical equipment, squeezed themselves between other shops, the repair work being performed on the sidewalks in front of the business, machine parts, tools, oil, and grease spread across the concrete. I don't know if they actually had a workshop inside or not.

The entire picture was that of an unassuming town, a concoction of colors, facades, old and new. It was the pre-war Vietnam and the contemporary one, mingling in a complex dichotomy of tradition and technology that emanated charm, mystery, and amusement. As our bus rolled through it all, heads leaned into windows and cameras clicked, their lenses sweeping their targets like shotguns tracking ducks. I imagined the tens of thousands of photographs that would make their way back to the States to be sorted through, pointed at, and printed or posted in photo archives. Some of them had already found their way to Facebook from those on the bus with iPads and smart phones.

We had discovered by then that the bus was equipped with Wi-Fi. In fact, I leaned that most buses in Vietnam were similarly equipped. This new revelation sent everyone to their iPads and phones to connect to the Internet, heads down, fingers on keypads. Silence drifted over the bus.

The country was no stranger to technology, as I found by looking out the window of the at the myriad strands of wire stretched between utility poles that marched down the main streets. One pole in particular was draped with no less than a hundred wires, radiating in several directions, and three large coils of cable hung precariously in their midst, as if a tornado had blown through and left them dangling where they had fallen. The technology seemed to work fine there, although seeing the jumble of cables on the pole, it escaped me as to how that might have been possible.

Between the larger towns, the highway raced past rural Vietnam, leaving behind the shops, gardens, and miles of wires that adorned the roads and highway. Out in the "country," as I would refer to it in Oklahoma, houses dotted the landscape, plopped in the middle of small trees and lush grasses. The buildings had little to compare to the picturesque settings of the towns. Instead, their petite and nondescript facades squatted in their humble surroundings, mute and detached from the march of progress across the country. However, the rural areas had not been overlooked as far as utilities as shown by the electrical lines that paralleled the highway and reached into each tiny abode.

Conversation never seemed to stop on the bus, Dennis Gulich, Jack Swickard, and Duane Speirs, providing most of it in between narrations by Truc about the places we passed by. I found comfort in just listening to the banter that passed between seats, the friendly exchange of insults and caustic criticism that coaxed the humor and camaraderie between men. It dawned on me then that I had seldom participated in such an exchange since my year in Vietnam. I had forgotten what it was like to trade barbs with the fellow that had shared my misery there.

I knew about rubber plantations from books I had read about the Vietnam War, especially in southern regions, although I had never seen one. Some of the U. S. forces were prohibited from firing into them for fear of damaging the trees, for which the owner of the plantation would be compensated at an inflated rate. Needless to say, the NVA and the VC would use the plantations as a refuge, safe from enemy fire. Just one of the many stupid rules of engagement that our politicians thought more important than actually winning the war.

The rubber plantations were nothing like I had imagined. The spindly trees were top-heavy with foliage and resembled the scrawny rubber plant I'd had in my apartment in college. I looked at the matrix of trees and wondered how on earth one could extract rubber from the seemingly anorexic trunks.

Much of what we saw from the windows of the roving bus was an expanse of rice paddies, the furrows filled with water silvered by the dull, steel-gray clouds that hung from the sky. The rich, green shoots of the young rice plants were just beginning to emerge from the dark, fertile earth. Mountains beyond stood guard with their craggy peaks and walls of stone covered with a billowing blanket of vegetation. Even the overcast sky could not hide the beauty of it all.

We stopped at a small town along the way in front of a market to procure a supply of wine. Most of us ventured out of the bus in search of snacks and alcohol. I was surprised to find a healthy supply of about anything one could want. I grabbed a bottle of Johnnie Walker Red. VND 320,000, or about $16 U. S. I was liking this country more than ever.

We arrived at the Saigon Phongnha Hotel in Phong Nha, Just outside of Dong Hoi. It was on the banks of the Son River that ran through the Ke Bang National Park. The stark, white building with teal-green trim and accents had a tropical flavor to it, very different from the Pearl Hotel in Hanoi. The three-story L-shaped structure wrapped around an inviting terrace with the central desk, a bar, and tables and chairs. The lack of an enclosure to the area reminded me of Lane, as did the lack of glass in windows in the small dwellings we had passed along the highway. My hooch at the Lane airfield had only screens and canvas tarps on the sides for windows. Such a luxury as glass was unnecessary, as was air conditioning. I still remember my days of grade school when windows were opened to moderate the heat emanated from a room full of preadolescent boys and girls with unbridled metabolisms. Even the houses I lived in as a boy had no air conditioning like we all think we have to have today, but only evaporative coolers that did little more than increase the relative humidity inside the house. Even that was a luxury.

Thom and I walked along the gallery to our room on the second floor and took stock of the amenities. Not as posh as the Pearl Hotel, but it had a more casual air, much like what I would expect to find in a small vacation spot, quiet, remote, almost a sleepy mien. The small bath area allowed access to a lavatory and a separate area for the toilet and shower. Not luxurious by any means, but comfortable. When I went past the desk downstairs, I picked up a brochure for the hotel. According to the rate schedule, a suite could be had for as little as VND 1,500,000 a night, or about $75. Something like that in America would run at least $150. Internet service was available, as we would find in all of the hotels we stayed in, as well as laundry service and cable television. But I darned sure wasn't there to watch television. I wouldn't be able to understand it, anyway.

The hotel faced the Son River, which flowed about 150 feet from the terrace. The reflection of trees on the opposite bank of the river was muddled by the barely rippling emerald green water. The river, only about 300 feet wide at this point, calmly drifted by in harmony with the patient lifestyle of the Vietnamese people.

We made our way to the terrace where we sat at one of the tables, the large red umbrella above us wavering in the soft breeze. The white tile floor grew wet from the light rain that had started moments before.

I was thinking about how lucky I was to be there, enjoying the agreeable weather and the beautiful bounty of the country. With all of the busy work I had at home, it was such a pleasure to be able to sit and relish the peace and quiet and the fresh scents that wafted through on invigorating air. Everywhere I looked, I saw untroubled life going about its business, which it would do whether I was there or not. I guess that's what embossed itself on my mind the most. The folks there seemed to have it all together. There was no race to keep up with the neighbor's new car, because few people had a car. There was no competition, no display of the hierarchy of status that I could see, and no stress to finish work before a deadline. There didn't seem to be any deadlines. What a way to live. But, of course, that was only what I could see from where I was.

A mere ten minutes later, the rain stopped and cool air drifted across the terrace. Out of curiosity, I checked my phone for the local temperature. The low 70s; perfect. Then the shiny tiles on the floor reflected the glare of the sun that would come and go throughout the morning.

Three small boys from about five to seven years of age kept vigil around the terrace for signs of new guests. They had met our bus on its arrival, leaving their bicycles on the ground while they had displayed their wares on trays hung from cords around their necks, post cards mostly. We all politely declined.

This was not to be an uncommon occurrence in Vietnam. Children and women would flock to tourists, offering anything from jewelry, trinkets, rain ponchos, hats, and anything else that could be taken home as a souvenir by an overwhelmed tourist. It would have been impractical to purchase something from all of them, so most of us chose not to purchase anything. Those of our group who did, bartered to find the best deal.

Lunch was a plate of fried noodles with beef and vegetables. Of all the Asian restaurants I have patronized in America, nothing came close to the savory aroma and flavor of this dish. The firm and chewy texture of the noodles blended well with the mixed vegetables and beef, and the sauce was delectable. Not being a fan of beef, I have to admit that it was delicious. We chased it with fresh bananas, one of the tastiest I had eaten. I guess that's the advantage of tree-ripened bananas. Most of the fellow enjoyed it. Some, however, were not at all excited by Asian cuisine. Pat was still looking for that cheeseburger. But at $7, the lunch was a bargain.

Pat Matheny had joined Thom and me at our table, leaning back in his chair, enjoying the day. Pat had been stationed at Bien Hoa during 1965-66 as a crew chief with the 118th AHC, call sign Thunderbirds. He was from Pine Bluff, a small community near Shinnston, WV. I asked Pat about his time in the army.

"So you were one of the early ones over here?" I asked.

"Yeah," he said. "Everything was getting built up. More troops were on the way."

"So, what did you do?"

"I was a crew chief. Ed was a gunner. We had the B model Huey until September. Then we got D models."

"You were with the 118th?"

"The Thunderbirds," he said. "Gunships were called the Bandits. We were at Bien Hoa, and our job was to carry troops. My ship was Thunderbird 7. I named her SUZY-Q, after my girl back home."

"What do you do in Shinnston?" I asked him.

"I was a coal mine supervisor. We worked underground. I'm retired, now."

"Tom Baca told me you were a writer, but he never said what you wrote."

He almost laughed. "I write a column for Pine Bluff News. It's just a community paper, population of about 200. Not a real big circulation."

"How long you been doing that?"

"My mom started in the 50s and I took over. Been doing it ever since. I keep a journal of everywhere I've been. I like to write about things like that."

"I'd like to read some of those articles," I said.

"Give me your email address and I'll send some to you."

Ed Knighten drifted by about that time. I asked him about his time in the service.

Ed was the kind of guy who liked to talk, and his bellowing voice would command your attention. He reared back on his heels and it started.

"Well, I went to Germany, first. Stuttgart. I was a clerk in the Signal Section. Then a letter came around asking for volunteers for Vietnam. I signed up."

He paused to take a deep breath, I suppose the story, however brief so far, was taking its toll on his endurance.

"When I got there, I was assigned to the 120th in Saigon. But something big started up at Bien Hoa and I was sent there. I wound up in Operations. It was pretty boring, but then they started looking for replacements for door gunners. Just a temporary kind of thing. Anyway, I volunteered and got to fly several missions. I loved working that M-60," he said with gusto. Of course, about everything he said was with gusto, but I'm sure he meant to emphasize the part about the M-60.

"What kind of missions did you fly?" I asked.

At this prompt, he stood at ease and leaned back a bit more before he resumed talking.

I was very lucky to make it thru without anything major happing to me other than a few scratches. There was one mission where we were going back to see what movement there was after three days of psy-war.

There was a Buddhist monk walking down a road. We had a Vietnamese officer with us, and he said to take him out. There were three firing passes made on him, and the last time we saw him; he was walking off into the trees. Makes a person stop and think. Then there was the day we were out picking up troops from a hot LZ. While flying cover for the slicks and making a turn to come around, I thought I had leaned out too far and unplugged my helmet. I reached up to plug it back in and found out that I only had about four inches of cord left on my helmet. Lots of luck on my part. I was getting short.

His story brought a round of laughter to the table. Someone called to Ed, and he wandered off. I exchanged information with Pat and I looked at him with new respect. Crew chiefs and gunners seemed to fall short of the respect and notoriety given to pilots. I knew that without the crew chiefs and gunners, the pilots would seldom have gotten so much praise. I wished I had given them more respect when I flew with them.

Like some of the other guys, Pat was keeping a journal. Of all the vets I had talked to, few of them did this and their experiences will probably be lost forever when they pass away. I thought it sad that so much violence, fear, and misfortune had consumed the military men and women of this country and little of it will truly be known, except for those of us who recorded it and wrote about it. That's the only way people would ever learn the truth about what happened in Vietnam and how terrible war really is.

Conversation grew louder as the fellows got wound up with anecdotes of their adventures both in Vietnam and other places. Whenever a group of veterans meet, a host of war stories follows, and tales blew across the terrace, mingling with the refreshing breezes.

We watched as other tourists arrived by bus, the boys at hand ready to hawk their wares. As I sat there with Thom and Pat, I became aware of a pattern that would repeat itself along our journey. I had witnessed no boisterous or obnoxious behavior other than the spirited conversations within our group. There were no petty squabbles or disagreements among guests, and everyone kept a polite demeanor. I thought back to the last few times I had stayed in hotels in America. The wild and disrespectful children, the arrogance of some of the guests, and the disregard for the presence of other people made it seem like such an uncivilized country. I wondered if it would be possible to require all new parents to live in Vietnam for a year. Boy, would that solve a lot of problems.

The call to assembly came soon after lunch, and we boarded the bus for a trip down the Ho Chi Minh Trail. We traveled what seemed like quite a few miles to the west before we reached the part of the Ho Chi Minh Trail that Truc had selected for our tour.

The trail ran about 1000 kilometers between what used to be North Vietnam and South Vietnam along the Laos-Cambodia-Vietnam border. Having been originally a dirt-packed track, since the war, it had been paved and in many places, complete with concrete gutters for water drainage. Although narrow in places, it was easily traveled by bus, even through the twists and turns that wound around the encompassing mountains. In forested areas, the foliage was deep and even though much had been cleared to widen the trail, a heavy canopy hung overhead dappling the road in shade. The steep, craggy mountains would challenge most climbers with their rocky faces covered in trees and brush that grew out of the cracks between the rocks. I tried to imagine grunts scrambling up the hillsides, battling the brush and trees, slipping on the steep slope and fighting for every inch of progress. That was when I was glad I had been a pilot.

The Ho Chi Minh Trail was used by the North Vietnamese to move troops and supplies to the south. The trail was begun in 1959 when the NVA sent 300 soldiers south to blaze an infiltration route to South Vietnam through Laos and Cambodia. Once it had opened, about six months had been required to traverse the trail from start to finish.

Our bus stopped on a bridge about 50 meters from the Laotian border. We all got off to explore the incredible scenery around the valley that seemed to embrace us with its verdant carpet of trees and vegetation. Even the overcast sky did not erode the beauty of the lush, rough slopes climbing toward ragged peaks that nudged the clouds. The river that drifted by under the bridge wove its way through the rugged terrain, and like other bodies of water in Vietnam, it had a soft, translucent emerald glow that seemed to reflect the dense vegetation hugging it as the river crept between its banks. We were surrounded by almost solid green.

The sun, then retreating toward the horizon, cast a soft light beneath the clouds that filtered distant mountains through a haze, like sheer curtains might disperse the harsh light from a window. We took advantage of the many photo ops and Phong, our bus driver, humored us with group photos with each of our cameras.

The road was reasonably well maintained. Truc told us that nearly 300,000 people were required to keep the road in good form: doctors, laborers, engineers, and others. We noticed a bit further down the road just past the far end of the bridge, a lone worker that was trimming overhanging vines with a gas-powered string trimmer. It was just him out there in the middle of nowhere, no vehicle or gas can in sight. We all wondered how he got there and how he would get back to wherever he came from.

We all met for dinner that evening on the terrace restaurant, ready for the stimulating banter. Truc broke out a box of wine and the party began. I took my own glass of Johnnie Walker to the table. We started with pumpkin soup, then fish, followed by rice. Then pork and eggs, vegetables, and bread. Another marvelous meal that endeared Vietnam to me. Again, $7 paid for it all. Just incredible. Still no cheeseburgers.

Back in the room, Thom and I took stock of what it had to offer. The lingering bouquet of mildew charged the air, and once again, memories flooded back from the wet Nomex flight suit I would pull onto me each morning because the incessant rain of the monsoons left little room in the air for anything to dry. When I returned home, my mother threw most of the clothes I had brought back away rather than wearing out the washing machine trying to remove the smell

Like the other hotels, the key card activated the lights in the room. A slot by the door accepted the card and acted as a switch for everything electrical. I noticed two other switches in the bath area, one of which provided instructions to turn it on in order to get hot water. I found that this needed to be done well in advance of using it. I didn't object to the cold shower, but a warm one would have been more pleasant. It was as if I was back in that tiny corrugate tin shower in my hooch hurriedly rinsing myself in the cold water because the heater in the hooch next door was inoperable.

We were provided only with bath towels, no washcloths or hand towels, not that I needed them. I had spent many years of my life before

I was married without those luxuries. I never saw the need until my wife demanded that we have them. The one small bar of soap seemed to satisfy our needs. I suppose had we stayed there longer, we might have been given more. The beds, though, were comfortable and we had no complaints as we settled in for the night.

We would have much of the morning to explore the area, since we planned on a late departure. We would be passing by the DMZ on our way to Quang Tri. I was anxious to see the ancient Citadel there, a hallmark of Vietnamese history.

CHAPTER 7

DONG HOI TO QUANG TRI

Saturday, 5 December, 2015

My plate, already burdened with a load of fried eggs and noodles, got a lot heavier by the time I reached the end of the buffet. That didn't stop me from adding a bread roll and fresh fruit from the other side of the tables. Oh, and of course, coffee. I passed up the sausage, potatoes, and biscuits that some of the other guys heaped onto their plates. Breakfast was my favorite meal and I suppose I might have fit right in with the Vietnamese lifestyle, as far as breakfast goes. Some of the guys relished the Asian fare, others, like Pat, avoided it.

Truc had asked us to wear our red tee shirts and caps that day. He told us he had been a private in the North Vietnamese Army assigned to an anti-aircraft unit. That wasn't until 1974, after all of us had left the country. It was comforting to know that he hadn't been shooting at any of us, since we had all left country by then. I believe it was Dennis who suggested promoting him to honorary colonel, and we all agreed. Colonel Truc called us his "VC platoon."

After lunch, Thom and I ambled over to the park adjacent to the hotel. We strolled through a marketplace along the riverfront that offered clothing, souvenirs, and food. Not a lot going on that morning; only the delightful singing of birds and the slapping of water against the hulls of tour boats moored to the dock drifted through the calm, heavy air. I could smell the water, not fishy, but fresh, almost aromatic The blue canvas tops of the boats bobbed with the gentle rippling waves, the tour guides congregated at one end, deep in discussion of local issues of the day, I suppose. The terrace, covered in the familiar concrete pavers, was punctuated by palm trees, sculptures, benches, and tables beneath umbrellas, an inviting place for contemplation or just watching people. The overcast sky still spit mist occasionally, but it was not disagreeable. Only when rain threatened did we retreat to the hotel's veranda.

The bus was not due to leave for a few hours, so Thom and I spent the rest of the time beneath the red umbrella, him reading and me writing part of this journal. Blissful solitude surrounded us with the sporadic yells of the boys at play with a soccer ball on the sidewalk just outside the terrace's rail; some of the same boys that had greeted our arrival. No fancy clothes, no shoes, no squabbles, and no worries.

"You know," I said, "I could live here."

Thom looked at me with a quizzical eye, as if he were either entertained by my musing or uncertain of what I had said.

"I mean, look at this place." I swept my hand across the view. "Sunshine, rain, great temperature, everything is green, water everywhere, and the food…"

He shook his head. "Yeah, it's nice, all right. But would you actually move here?"

There, he had me. I sank in my chair a bit, my dreams deflated by reality. I didn't think there was any way in hell my wife would move there. My daughter, well that was something else.

After a huge sigh, I had to have the last word. "It's just so damned perfect."

Beyond the walk, water buffalo grazed on the grass by the river, and another boy had set about gathering sticks from the ground and hauling a bundle of them on his shoulder. I suppose he was taking them to his home for crafting into whatever they made with sticks. The folks there seemed to be self-sufficient for the most part, making do with whatever they could find at hand. They seemed content with what they had. No luxuries, and apparently, little desire for them. It was a refreshing thought.

It occurred to me that the Vietnam I was seeing then was nothing like the Vietnam I had left 44 years earlier. The country was no longer full of little men in black pajamas and hooch maids in those conical hats, flap-flap-flapping in their rubber thong shoes. The people there were congenial, generous, and delighted to be in our company. Then I wondered if Hanoi had been merely an anomaly, some bizarre sect of the population conditioned for the benefit of tourists. That might seem to be a cruel thought, but when you consider all of the nasty things about Vietnam our army leaders had told us during our training, it isn't that difficult to see how one could be molded into an eternal skeptic.

Time had come to check out and board the bus. All of us, in our VC uniforms, trampled up the steps and settled in for the ride to Hue, stopping at the 17th Parallel, or the DMZ, the area between North and

South Vietnam during the war. We would also be visiting the childhood home of General Vo Nguyen Giap, Commander in Chief of the North Vietnamese Army during the war. Then on to Quang Tri and the ancient Citadel.

We left the hotel in the mist that hung in the air like a pall of tiny bubbles. The low-slung clouds hovered overhead and the peaks of mountains in the distance beyond the buildings disappeared into the steel-gray sheets spanning the horizons. The weather did not dampen the vivacity of the town, though. The small shops were open for the parade of shoppers, selling everything from food to tires. It was like a mini-Walmart strung out in a strip shopping mall. Armies of motor bikes were clustered in front of some of the buildings. Even after a hearty breakfast, my mouth still watered as we passed by the fresh fruit vendors at the curbside offering bananas, papaya, passion fruit, mangos, pineapple, and other things I didn't recognize, all to be had for a pittance. Every now and then we passed by a three-story house, large windows facing the street with newly varnished or painted doors opened to the porches, and laundry strung out on wires to dry.

We worked our way through the small town back toward Highway QL1 over the rough road, the bus undulating with the heaves in the pavement, like a boat hurdling the waves. As we turned onto the wider roadway and continued south, the wet asphalt stretched past rice paddies and villages scattered along its route like a patchwork quilt laid out on the sopping earth. I watched the locals work the paddies, some with water buffalo drawing metal shares, and a few with small combine harvesters, where the operator sat on a seat behind the contraption and guided it along the rows of the rice plants. Progress seemed to have halted at the invisible demarcation between town and country. It was like watching an Oklahoma farmer plod behind a plow pulled by a team of horses in scenes from early documentaries on television.

Although the cities had been brought into a modern era with the mechanization of daily routines, many of the fields were still worked by hand. The nearby houses, more akin to hovels, looked like the tarpaper shacks I remembered from travels through rural Mississippi and Alabama, only smaller and without the charm. Roofs were tile, corrugated metal, or thatch. Most of the small dwellings had no glass in the windows, as many building there didn't, and few had doors, but merely a hinged flap covered with corrugated metal that was lifted and propped up during the day, or a rustic slab of boards that folded over the opening. Of course, with the moderate temperatures, why would you want glass in the windows and weatherproof doors? I'm thinking they didn't lock their houses at night.

The rural areas had few luxuries, and I imagine the people who lived in the small houses and labored in the fields rarely left home. There was no need. I never saw a Laundromat; clothes hung from lines stretched between poles or houses. Most of the food they consumed was raised or caught by them. During my tour of duty there, thatch huts populated the countryside. About the only difference I saw now was a slight improvement in the quality of houses and the electric lines that connected them to a bit of progress. Time seemed to have nearly stopped for that part of Vietnam, stuck in a perpetual cycle of unassuming existence that might well stretch in the next several decades.

Sprinkled between the small huts I saw more elaborate structures built of concrete or concrete blocks, usually two or three stories in height, some taller. I think it was Don Hooper, a well-travelled sort, that told us a person can only own so much land in Vietnam. You can't really own the land, just the use of it. The land itself belongs to the collective population, or essentially, the state. The amount of land you could use determined how large the house could be. Nearly all of the houses of this type were about 16 feet wide and 48 feet deep. If that didn't afford enough room, additional stories expanded the living space. The red, blue, yellow, and green facades almost glowed through the clouded air. The sides had been left as the natural gray of the concrete or whitewashed. I'm guessing paint might have been a luxury for the average homeowner.

Many of the smaller houses, most likely one-room affairs with no plumbing, did not appear to be well kept. Paint was probably not considered important. Since no one was keeping up with the Jones's, what would be the point? Building materials probably were hard to come by anyway. Large trees weren't that plentiful nearby, and I hadn't noticed any sources of lumber, so I doubt that repairs could be made frequently. In contrast, most of the concrete houses were better maintained, but then they wouldn't have needed much maintenance.

Since family was an integral part of life in Vietnam, it was not unusual for several generations to cohabit a house. Oddly enough, though, I rarely saw a lot of people around any of the houses, except for children.

Conversation on the bus never seemed to stop and whenever we passed something of interest, Truc was on his feet explaining what it was. Driving through towns and villages brought out the cameras. Some of us busied ourselves with jotting down notes about what we saw. Others just enjoyed the scenery as it slid by the windows. The fellows in front, Ken, Jack, and Dennis, were the principal source of chatter while others worked at their phones, following our route on a map, or surfing the Internet. Sterling occupied the seat in front of me and seemed content to just enjoy the scenery. Behind me, Pat was busy taking photos with his iPad, and Tom Baca was doing everything with *his* iPad: photos, phone calls, videos, and whatever else he could do with the thing. Ed, Tom Horan, and Don kept a low profile while watching the landscape slide by. Thom had his nose buried in his Kindle.

From all of the power and communication lines that paralleled the highway. I assumed that electric service reached to nearly all of the rural areas of Vietnam, but I had only seen the eastern part of it, away from the mountainous interior that bordered Laos and Cambodia, where communication access might not have been so widespread.

I also saw much construction along the way, be it roads, buildings, or housing. Pockets of it were everywhere, most of it incomplete, as if work had been abandoned, unlike the municipal areas where every effort seemed to be geared toward beautifying the urban landscape. Just like America, most of the resources were directed toward population centers, and the rural areas were left to wallow in what was left.

By that time the road narrowed, traffic was sparse, and Phong had to find lay-by areas to allow opposing vehicles to pass. Water buffalo and cattle roamed the fields surrounding the mountain ranges that cast a dramatic backdrop for the villages squatting in front of them.

Roads ran in sections from good to poor with construction popping up in unexpected places. Large wheelbarrows, that I assumed to be trash buggies, sat alongside the road, overflowing with deposits from the local population. I supposed that at some time trash would be collected, but the rubbish spilling over the sides brought doubt to that assumption.

We traveled along the Kien Giang River for several miles on a narrow route that hugged the river's bank and left little room for the bus. Opposing traffic was forced to dive into the bordering trees and brush to allow our beast to pass by. Houses lined the road and riverfront for miles, apparently part of a large community comprised of a series of villages. We finally stopped at An Xa village in the Loc Thuy commune, Le Thuy district in Quang Binh, the childhood home of General Giap.

He was born in 1911, and by the age of 14, he had been indoctrinated into revolutionary activities against the French Occupation. As a star student of President Ho Chi Minh, he eventually became the commander in chief of the North Vietnamese Army. He is considered to be one of the greatest military geniuses of the twentieth century.

The small house, a simple frame structure with a shingled roof and thatched porch, had become a shrine to the general's memory. Since the rural areas of Vietnam were generally of modest means, the few rooms inside contained only necessities, what I would consider minimal requirements for a brief stay, not an entire lifetime.

Prominent figures, such as Ho Chi Minh and many of the generals that commanded troops in wars, are revered by the Vietnamese. Many had come to the house to pay homage to General Giap and light an incense stick, placing it into a vase in front of his portrait. It appeared that a full-time staff was on hand to greet the visitors as they solemnly paid their respects. The entire scene played out as a humbling influence, somewhat different from our so-called shrines in America. Our attempt at reverence seems inundated with grandiose backdrops and crass commercialization. It's still all about the almighty dollar.

After a flurry of camera shutters clicking, we were back on the road. When we reached Highway QL1, we turned south again past the unceasing rows of villages and towns. This section of the country seemed to have a more complete electrical infrastructure. More power and communication lines ran along the roads, sometimes on two and three rows of poles. The paving was rough, but no more so than most highways in America.

Truc had stopped at a store near the last hotel to purchase our VC lunches, he called them. I learned that these were called Banh mi sandwiches. They were filled with a combination of meats and vegetables with chili sauce, chilies, mayonnaise, and cheese.

When we stopped at the DMZ monument, we swarmed the tables at a small outdoor eating establishment beneath a simple shed roof, and Truc passed out the sandwiches. He told us that was what the VC soldiers traditionally ate for lunch in the field. A few of the guys thought the sandwiches were too spicy, their faces askew with grimaces. Others smiled while they chewed, obviously enjoying the new treat. And some were indifferent. I found the sandwiches to be tasty and even took a second one, although they weren't as filled out as the Subway sandwiches I got back home.

The new experiences we encountered on this trip kept our interest alive, in spite of the long bus rides and early mornings. Everywhere I looked, I saw something new, different. I expected to hear a lot of grumpy souls moaning and bitching from long spells of bending their bodies to fit into the bus seats and long stretches between pit stops. The fact that my bladder could endure several hours without flaring into a painful emergency startled me when I realized it had been nearly three hours since our last stop. It was amazing what we old codgers were capable of.

Some people tend to avoid new things; that old fear of the unknown. I had even done that myself on occasion. But there in Vietnam, a place to which I had never thought I would want to return, I relished everything I had seen and done. It aroused my curiosity for more.

We sat there under that shed roof, enjoying the pleasant weather and digesting our banh mi sandwiches. There was the obligatory banana for desert. By this time, the mist had turned to light rain that started and stopped of its own accord.

All of us had lived through the drenching downpours of the monsoons, so a little sprinkle wasn't going to hurt us. We sauntered across the parking area toward the DMZ flag tower with its giant red flag and yellow star majestically waving in the slight breeze. It sat upon a square, trapezoidal base that rested on a round single-story structure encircled with a mosaic mural that portrayed the history of Vietnamese struggles. I wondered how long it must have taken to complete such an extensive project. Like everything else I had seen there, the craftsmanship was exceptional. I could almost picture the small-boned local artisan, squatting on a pallet, and poking each tile into cement with a precise and deliberate technique. I'm not sure I would have the patience for that kind of thing.

Beside the flag monument was the building where the Geneva Accords was issued under the supervision of United Nations representatives at the close of the French-Indochina War in 1954. The agreement separated North Vietnam, under the Communist leadership of Ho Chi Minh, from South Vietnam under Bao Dai. The north came to be known as the Democratic Republic of Vietnam; the south, the Republic of Vietnam. The DMZ extended 5 kilometers to either side of the Ben Hai River, and ran from the South China Sea to the Laotian border. A diorama inside the building depicted the famous meeting. It struck me as peculiar, as it did at the Hoa Lo Prison, that they would go to so much trouble to manufacture mannequins for the occasion and outfit them with such accuracy. They wanted visitors to see it, perhaps as an appeal to them to understand what it was all about.

We all walked with some urgency across the highway to avoid the oncoming traffic that showed no signed of giving way for pedestrians, a common hazard there. A museum stood serenely at the end of a red and gray paved walk; the concrete pavers again.

Two giant loudspeakers about as tall as I was flanked the door. They had been used for propaganda during the war, voices blasting across rice paddies and fields in an attempt to cajole the enemy to lay down arms and surrender. Inside, exhibits displayed scenes from the Vietnam war, which they again referred to as the "American War." Dioramas illustrated life in the tunnels dug during the French-Indonesian War. By the time of the Vietnam War, they had evolved into complex, sophisticated networks that spread for several hundred kilometers underground and could be as many as eight levels deep. I think we were all surprised at the complexity of the networks of tunnels with intricate interconnecting burrows, and how the NVA and VC were able to live in them for any length of time. It made me realize how determined the North Vietnamese were.

Another display showed the capture of an America pilot, the images reminiscent of documentaries broadcast on television. Other artifacts included weapons, pieces of aircraft and vehicles used in the war. I was surprised at the ingenuity of the Vietnamese when I saw an operating table that has been crafted from parts of an American airplane. The museum was remarkably eloquent, expressing the romance and glamour that the Vietnamese placed on the war. After all, it was their fight for unification of the country.

This was the second museum I had visited. The War Museum in Hanoi I had passed off as a propaganda tool for the Communist government. But as I walked around the DMZ Museum, I began to recognize the theme, one that revealed my foolish ignorance. It was only proper that the Vietnamese would be represented in a victorious light, their feats and conquests embellished for posterity, just like we Americans do with our own historical institutions. It was about the country and its people. There in Vietnam, it was about them, not about us.

I laughed at myself for thinking how corny the exhibits had seemed up until then. When seen from their perspective, they weren't corny at all. I realized that I was merely looking at the historical accounts of the victor of the final days of the Vietnam War. What else could I have expected? I'm sure, like in my own country, the exhibits were enhanced with their own twist on history, and I began to understand the dignity of the Vietnamese people there in that museum. They had made considerable achievements and had much to be proud of. And besides, the victor writes the history.

A narrow bridge for foot traffic, built by the French, spanned the Ben Hai River and led to the Reunification Monument on the south side. We had loaded in the bus to travel to the opposite bank and disembarked to take in the monument. The artistic structure was an outcropping of six feather-like projections rising at least a hundred feet into the air behind a sculpture of a woman holding a child. The captivating scene was dramatic, a fitting tribute to the reunification of Vietnam.

While we were looking at the monument, a local fellow on a motor scooter stopped at the side of the road and, in an aggressive gait, marched over to our group. The serious looking fellow faced off in front of one our guys then let loose with a barrage of what we figured was something less than cordial, his body bent forward, irate and assertive, his arms slapping the air to his sides. Truc stepped in and, following a brief exchange of curt and hostile words, sent the man reluctantly on his way.

We asked Truc what the man had said. He only replied that he was drunk. We assumed that he had taken offense to Americans wearing our VC shirts and hats. Someone said, "I guess he's never seen an American VC before."

We broke down in laughter.

Then we were on our way again, reliving the brash encounter with the strange fellow on the motorbike and riding the waves of the rough pavement past villages and towns that illustrated a familiar departure from urban life, another reminder of the contrast with rural American roads. In this country, a more reticent lifestyle enabled the residents to go about their daily tasks without the bustle of busy streets; instead, tending rice paddies and their livestock that provided for their sustenance. In America, if the house was not part of a farm, you could bet everyone there had his or her own vehicle, at least one satellite antenna would be on the roof, and not a soul would be seen outside. I wondered how we had ever become such materialistic, self-serving people.

The southern part of the country possessed a different nature. The infrastructure seemed to be more contemporary and widespread, structures along the highway tidier, showing signs of a more affluent population. Houses were more ornate and adorned with colors on the sides as well as the front. I also noticed more trucks and heavy construction equipment on the roadways.

While cruising through larger cities, I noticed scores of manufacturing facilities that I hadn't seen in the north. The south seemed to have been influenced more by the French, Russian, and American presence, and the more heavily populated areas provided a good labor force.

We passed by Da Nang, one of the hot spots in the war. I had flown missions up there a couple of times, neither of which were pleasant experiences. Sterling hadn't had a particularly good time there, either, as he explained:

I was assigned to the 281st Assault Helicopter Company, and later I was assigned to the 5th Special Forces Group at Nha Trang, Vietnam. From there I was sent to the Special Forces C Team in Pleiku. My first aircraft commander was First Lieutenant Leon Flanders. We flew to the Special Forces camp of Tan Rhi. While in the team house, a short round landed in the place and he was killed in action. My next aircraft commander was Warrant Officer Jerry Golden. He was from the First Cavalry Division. He was a damn good teacher and taught me all the tricks of the trade, Thanks, Jerry.

I was appointed aircraft commander after Jerry returned to the United States. I picked up a new copilot, First Lieutenant Robert Reynolds and returned to Pleiku. We were a very good match. We were together until October 1966.

On November 1966, we got into a little scrape near the Special

Forces camp at Du Co. A Mike force was under fire and needed a medical evacuation and ammunition. We made several trips and evacuated all of the casualties and brought more forces into the landing zone. On the last trip in, as we were ready for the last load to get on, when a VC got up about 70 yards away and opened fire on us with an AK 47. I still can't figure out how he missed, but a tank solved the problem.

For this action, we both received the Distinguished Flying Cross.

In October, I was transferred to Nha Trang. I was assigned to Special Forces B–52 project Delta, which was a long-range patrol operation. I was to take a UH-1D to Pleiku and exchange it for their UH-1D. As we landed at Pleiku, Lieutenant Reynolds came up to the ship and told me not to take the emergency mission to resupply the Mike force unit. He tried and had two men killed, and his Huey was shot all to hell when he landed in the LZ in the middle of a firefight. I was asked to make the medical evacuation and was loaded up with ammunition and two medics. At this time, my copilot was Major Pat Sheely. This was his first operational flight. We took off and headed for the landing zone. While in route, I heard the sound of the Viet Cong 12.7 mm anti-aircraft gun shooting at me. We landed and the Mike force had control of one-half of the LZ. The supplies were unloaded and the injured loaded. There were 14 injured on board. There was heavy contact underway. We made this trip four more times until all wounded were evacuated. On the last trip, I saw a UH-1C gunship crash a little way from the landing zone. I hovered to its location to look for survivors when it exploded under my helicopter. There were mortar rounds going all around the crash site. When I contacted the air force forward air control ship, he informed me that the mortar rounds were not friendly. On the last trip from the landing zone to Pleiku, I heard the anti-aircraft gun firing again. I called the forward air controller and gave him the location of the gun he called in napalm strike, and that was all over with. We were awarded the air medal for valor.

Then off to Khe Sanh for the project delta operation. We returned to Nha Trang at the end of December. Training was continued for new pilots at Nha Trang and Bong Son. Since I had under 100 days left and country (we called it the double digit fidgets), I was pulled off the riskier flying and was used for training and routine administrative flights. My date to return from overseas was May 23, 1967.

In early May I had an administrative flight to take some officers from Nha Trang to Da Nang, where we spent the night. The next morning, I was asked to fly to Con Thien. They had lost some radios during an attack and like a dumb ass, I accepted the mission. I flew to Dong Hoi to refuel. While there, I asked several marine gunships to escort me into the Special Forces camp. They said okay. I landed and there was a large group of marine infantry there between two large amphibian vehicles. After my passengers got off, a marine asked me to evacuate wounded, and of course, I agreed. The marine gunships we're circling at 2000 feet above me. I made three more trips into Con Thien. There I was, with two weeks before going home, and look at all the crap I just got into. I received a Distinguished Flying Cross with Oak leaf cluster.

Shortly before 2:00, we reached Quang Tri. As the bus rolled through the city, I couldn't help but notice that the buildings seemed elegant compared to other parts of the country. Cleanliness, ornate facades, and a semblance of order predominated, and traffic was heavier, more cars and trucks on the streets; and buses, which I took to be tour buses like ours, only larger.

We parked near the Citadel among the crowd of cars and other tour buses and hiked to the bridge that spanned the moat encircling the ancient walled city. Each side of the Citadel had gates that had at one time been guarded by fortresses that projected from each corner. The Citadel had protected the town palace where the king lived and worshiped. During the Vietnam War, the NVA had overtaken it and occupied it until the 81-day war of 1972. That's when American and South Vietnamese forces recaptured the Citadel after heavy bombing by U. S. planes. Much of the Citadel was destroyed, included the four fortresses at the corners, as well as, the palace.

As I started across the bridge, two ancient cannons beside the gate came into view. They looked more like ancient mortars, short but large in diameter; I could almost have crawled inside one of them. The bases had an aged, red patina embellished with an Asian relief. Ornate and primitive, they would have provided ample defense against attacks.

The massive walls, blackened from centuries of weather and pockmarked from bullets during the Vietnam War, bore arched openings beneath a hefty rampart that passed overhead. The enormous wooden doors that hung from the side of the archway had been restored and welcomed us to the interior.

The courtyard inside, like most other public spaces, was pristine and free of any litter. It was covered in colorful red pavers (yes, the same kind) in the center leading toward a memorial that stood toward the rear as a tribute to the many soldiers who died there defending their country. It was a popular tourist attraction and a place to pay homage to Vietnam's defenders, especially between March and September.

Tourists filled the tree-lined walks and nodded or spoke when we passed by, a very pleasant welcome. Even children, playing on the pavement, were curious and also acknowledged our presence with a quick look and a smile. If we spoke to them, they always returned the greeting.

As we congregated inside the gate, we noticed a group of about ten locals in military uniforms sitting on a bench. They immediately saw us and some of them approached our group. Apprehension gnawed at me, kind of like it did when I first saw my orders for Vietnam. Thinking about the incident at the DMZ, I wondered if we might become involved in another unfortunate exchange. I was relieved when Truc met them and friendly dialog ensued. I imagine the men were most likely wondering why we Americans were wearing shirts with the Vietnamese flag on them. I, and the other guys, were wondering why they were wearing their military uniforms.

We learned that they were veterans of Khmer Rouge War, 1976-79, and had come to lay a wreath at the monument inside the Citadel. They seemed to be taken with us, surprised and curious, as we were with them. They all mingled among us and fragments of questions flew back and forth. They all seemed determined to shake each of our hands. We exchanged greetings with broad smiles, not that any of us knew what the other was saying, but the expressions and gestures were enough to understand our mutual delight at the chance meeting. Once the cameras came out, naturally a group picture was required. So there we were in our "VC uniforms" side-by-side with veterans of a Vietnamese war in their uniforms, smiling at the camera as if we were long lost friends. As I look back on that day, I honestly think we were.

I believe everyone in our group gained some respect for the Vietnamese as we deepened our friendships with people of that country. The veterans were delighted to meet us as we were them. Their curiosity about Americans surprised me, and I felt a sense of gratification because of that. I had always thought there might be some animosity toward

Americans in the country where so many of us fought for things we were never sure of. It was comforting to learn that they didn't hate us.

The museum was well stocked with relics of the war. Most of the exhibits' placards were printed in Vietnamese, and English captions were rare; it really wasn't necessary. I could understand the messages of what I saw there.

The portico outside was occupied by children and their coloring books. Lying on the concrete surface, crayons in hand, oblivious to anything going on around them, they were absorbed in bringing the black and white figures in their books to life. A couple of them looked up at me and smiled, then returned to their tasks.

I continued to be puzzled that children in Vietnam, or at least the ones I had seen, were so well behaved. Even the adults seemed to coexist in pleasant harmony, as if they had a common purpose in being there. This behavior would continue to baffle me for the remainder of the trip. I couldn't help thinking about all of the rude, selfish, and insensitive people back home. I wondered how the Vietnamese did it. Was it our penchant for accumulating possessions that led us toward our arrogance and disregard for diverse ethnic groups? Or was it our notion of working ourselves to death to be able to accumulate those things we desired? Or maybe just having so much more than other countries has spoiled us? I figured that I would continue to think about this phenomenon for the rest of my life.

We exited the museum in time to watch the veterans march to the monument to lay their wreath, a simple tribute to courageous souls without any materialistic or political spectacle to undermine its meaning. Another source of inspiration for me, as again, I thought about the callous nature of America's frequent lack of homage to our own champions and heroes except in a commercial vein. It seemed like everything had to be about money. How cheap it made it all seem.

I think we all left the citadel feeling more secure about our choices we had made in life and about our service in Vietnam. I then thought about McNamara's book, *In Retrospect.* Something suddenly became very clear to me. To think that I had at one time been so naive as to believe the worst about the Vietnamese people, only to find that the indoctrination by our military had been designed with no in-depth knowledge of the Vietnamese and their traditions and had been manufactured to make us soldiers, and to want to distrust them, to kill them. I suppose that's what every country's military machine does. It would be of little use to have an army that sympathized with the enemy. The soldiers must actually believe that the opponent *is* the enemy. My mind drifted to the Middle East situation and I suddenly thought about the similarities of the Iraq War and our troops in Afghanistan with the war in Vietnam. And then I realized that Al Qaeda and Isis were doing the same thing to their recruits that we do to ours, although with a more sinister purpose. Every war in history had followed the same pattern. War does more than just kill and injure people; it changes them.

I know that if someone tried to tell me that kind of thing now, at this stage of my life, I would certainly do my homework before I took his word for it. But we were all so young then, and not as wise as I like to think we are now. The Citadel visit opened my eyes and my mind. It was one of what would be many revelations I would experience on this trip.

When we left Quang Tri, we finished this leg of our trip in the city of Hue. The bus stopped in front of the Muong Thanh Hue Hotel. It had been a long day and I think everyone was glad to be somewhere that we could kick back.

The room was upscale, comfortable, and smartly furnished with contemporary pieces. Thom and I walked through the room toward the door at the rear of the room, which opened onto small balcony. A nice touch. Then we turned around and saw it right away: the see-through bathroom.

We stood there gawking for a moment before we both laughed. In the wall between the bathroom and the sleeping area, a large window rested on the tub ledge and offered a striking view of the toilet, sink, and bathtub. I had never seen an architectural feature such as this, at least not in a hotel.

"Well," I said. "What do you think?"

"This could be fun," he said, going in to check it out.

"Why the hell would you want a window like that in your bathroom?" I wondered out loud. I stood by one of the beds looking through the window at Thom in the bathroom looking through the window, smiling at me.

"Exhibitionism?" he said.

"Or to see the view out the window, there," I said, pointing toward the balcony door.

Then I saw him pull down a large shade that covered the entire window. How clever, I thought. It still didn't make sense to me.

We were driven to a restaurant somewhere in the depths of the many streets of Hue for a dinner of Vietnamese fare consisting of the standard fried spring roll, noodles, assorted vegetables, and such. For $20 and a $5 tip, I thought it was well worth it. Pat didn't. No cheeseburgers.

Unlike the north, especially Hanoi, the streets in Hue seemed cleaner and wider. The city appeared to be better developed and less crowded. Restaurants and clubs proliferated and were busy well into the night. Considering their mild manner, I wondered if the Vietnamese were really night owls at heart, or if it was just a contingent of them that had that disposition. Before I knew it, we were back at the hotel.

"When did you say you were in Vietnam?" I asked Thom.

"I was there in 1968," he said. "Eight months."

"The 129th was just on the other side of the control tower from you guys. You were all pretty tame, or it seemed like that."

"We were on call for Medevac, so we had to stay sober most of the time. We didn't get a lot of hours flying. And I was laid up in the hospital for a few weeks."

"What happened?"

Thom casually relayed to me his harrowing experience. The official version is:

"Chief Warrant Officer Gilbert ... on 27 September 1968 while serving as commander of an ambulance helicopter during a rescue mission west of Landing Zone Uplift. A ground unit had incurred twenty casualties during combat with an enemy force, and Mister Gilbert immediately flew to the pickup site located on the slope of a wooded ridgeline. In order to clear an extraction site, he hovered above a small opening in the forest to lower several chain saws to soldiers below. Suddenly hostile fire erupted, raking the aircraft and wounding several of the crew, including Mister Gilbert. When the damaged engine began to fail, he maneuvered his craft away from the soldiers on the ground below and crashed into the trees a short distance away. ...the crew members survived the crash and were rescued the following morning."

He then explained the rest of the story:

Some of the details not included: there were five of us as crew on the mission, myself, the co-pilot, a medic and two crew chiefs, one of them along for the ride; the aircraft Crew-chief, James Granville "Granny," was the one hanging out the door operating the hoist. He took several body hits and died shortly after the crash; we were lightly armed (I had an M-1 carbine with two clips and a 38 revolver); and we had no radio contact or water. An air force "Pedro" rescue helicopter tried to extract us shortly after the crash and was nearly shot down, taking close to 100 hits that killed the aircraft commander, Major David Pittard. The rescue helicopter barely made it back to the Phu Cat Air Force Base. It was dusk and, based on the direction of the contact, we moved away from the enemy and downhill, leaving Granny in the aircraft. Another crewmember, Marshall Kidder, had a gunshot wound in the leg and had to be carried. I was the least wounded and carried Marshall as we crawled through thick jungle forest. My co-pilot became separated from us after dark, looking for an open area for us to be picked-up. At first light, I located a potential pick-up sight, we were spotted and three of us were picked-up by another helicopter. The co-pilot was rescued later that morning a short distance from our pick-up site.

Glad to be alive, I was in the hospital in Qui Nhon when my CO interviewed me to complete the "after action report." He noted that when the ground troops reached the aircraft they found two KIA's. I never found out where the other KIA came from, but suspect it was one of the ground troops we were trying to rescue.

After 10 days off, during which I had an in-country rest and recuperation (R&R) trip to Tuy Hoa, I returned to flight status. My tour ended on December 7, 1968 when I was shot in the leg during another rescue mission. I fully expected to come home in a body bag or on a stretcher and was happy to be on a stretcher for my flight out of country. After a month in a hospital in Japan, I arrived at Letterman hospital in San Francisco. Nine months later, I received a medical discharge and started my life again finishing college on the GI Bill and becoming a CPA in Sacramento California.

When he told me that, my mind jerked itself backward, reliving for an instant one the fears I had lived with back then. Had my ship ever been shot down, I had always wondered what I would have done. I'd never had an answer.

"Well," I said, "I guess I'm lucky as hell I never took a round. Just lucky I got out of it at all."

The night passed quietly as Thom and I listened to Christmas music blaring from the restaurant across the street from the hotel. Christmas music in Vietnam. I had never thought about how they might have celebrated Christmas. We Americans take so much for granted and think little about other cultures and how they live. I guess I just assumed that since we celebrated Christmas with carols and such, everyone else did too. The familiar tunes made my glass of Johnnie Walker Red taste better, but a slight pang of nostalgia wafted over me. I thought about my wife and my daughter. What were they doing right then?

And I thought about the tour of Hue tomorrow. I would get to see the big Citadel there, the last one in the chain of Vietnamese dynasties.

CHAPTER 8

HUE TO AN HOA

Sunday, 6 December, 2015

Breakfast in the morning was another culinary adventure filled with dried beef salad, pickled figs, cucumber, boiled potatoes, sticky rice, fried rice with egg, pâté, noodles, passion fruit, bacon, sausage, grilled vegetables, assorted breads, boiled eggs, omelets, fruits, pastries, juices, coffee, tea, cereal, and a host of other things. So many good choices and such a small stomach. Life was just not fair.

The bus left at about 9:00 in the morning for Hoi An, about three and a half hours south. We drove beneath dull clouds that dampened the lively colors of the buildings, and through light rain that didn't seem to faze the local people. Even on motor scooters, they had donned plastic ponchos and zipped along the streets as if it were no different from a sunny day, although the rain brought cooler temperatures in the low 70s.

Hue used to be the imperial capital of Vietnam until 1945 when Ho Chi Minh assumed power. The 19th century imperial Citadel enclosed the Imperial City. Within it were palaces and shrines. The emperor's home was also located within the massive stone walls, as well as a replica of the Royal Theater. The Citadel marked the end of the last dynasty in Vietnam.

The gray sky spit rain and we donned our inclement weather gear and stepped into the drizzle among the throng of vendors that were poised to greet us, mostly women who swarmed new arrivals hoping to sell plastic ponchos, umbrellas, and pictures. We also saw cyclos (bicycle rickshaws) for hire.

Much of the Citadel was under restoration but most of it was intact. In spite of the renovation, there was no mistaking its grandeur, similar to the Citadel at Quang Tri, but on a much grander scale. The massive outer walls bore that blackened patina that masonry acquires after centuries of weather. The walls and gates were pockmarked with bullet holes from the NVA attack that led to its capture near the end of the Vietnam War.

The outermost wall, about two kilometers on a side, enclosed the Imperial Citadel belt, one of three sections of the complex. A moat and thick stone walls encompassed the ancient city. Ten gates penetrating the perimeter allowed access. I thought about the great pyramids in Egypt and wondered how they could have built such a colossal structure without modern construction equipment. Compared to the rustic culture of our ancestors that set foot on Plymouth Rock, nothing in early American history rivaled what I had seen there in Vietnam.

As we walked across the bridge that spanned the moat, my eyes were on the massive ancient brick walls, the mottled colors of rusty beige and black, a mural of the past. I kept wondering how they did it. Labor must have been cheap and plentiful to have undertaken such a task. The walk through the entry archway must have been at least 30 feet long, all encased with bricks, undoubtedly placed by artisans one at a time. It was an odd feeling walking through a portal that had once been traveled by ancient royalty. Like the vast spaces of early Byzantine and Romanesque cathedrals, one would feel small, insignificant, as if in the presence of a deity, although I imagine it would have been the monarch that assumed such role. It was impressive, nonetheless.

The arched gateway, some 8 or 9 meters in height, was one of four gates that led to the Royal Citadel within, a much smaller compound. The Thai Hoa Palace, where grand ceremonies were held, sat within this belt, along with several temples, storehouses, workshops and gardens. In the palace, the gilded emperor's throne stood proudly among the ornate Asian architecture. Taking photographs was forbidden there, but we had plenty of photo ops elsewhere in the complex. As infatuated as they were with the camera, it seemed odd that they would ban them at such important historical locations. It would make sense to tease the spectators with the spectacle so they would attempt to relay what they had seen to others, which never approaches any degree of accuracy, and those others would be inclined to want to see it for themselves.

Beyond this section was the Purple Forbidden Citadel. This area was the royal family's residence. It had been restricted to the royal family and its entourage.

Having been the site of one of the major battles during the Tet Offensive of 1968, the fighting had reduced much of the Citadel to barren fields. At the rear stood pagodas and a large gold dragon, about 12 feet high, atop a series of steps. It was there that our small group encountered a family from Australia, a couple and their daughter. We asked them to take our picture with the dragon. In return, we took their picture. They were just one of many international families we encountered. Again, cameras seem to bring out the best in people, affability and altruism.

Our platoon had split up into smaller groups, and I wandered through the ancient temples and structures with Don. We didn't say much; there was no need. What little we did say was out of astonishment.

The ancient wood and masonry had endured the centuries well, still intact with the intricate joinery, carvings, and reliefs. As an engineer, I couldn't help but notice the still perfect alignment of the buildings' structures. All of the columns were plumb and the beams level. A building that old would normally tend to settle over such a period of time and things would not appear to be so orderly. I wondered what kind of foundation had been used to thwart such a calamity.

"How long do you think it took to build all of this stuff?" I asked Don.

His head swiveled around once with that perpetual smile of his. "Too long," he said.

"Can you imagine building something like this?" I mused. "The artistry and craftsmanship....I just can't believe it."

"Yeah," he sighed. "Kind of makes you feel useless."

Such wisdom, he spoke. It was a startling thought that a person could love his craft so much that he created beauty, as well as, something useful. I tried to deduce the sum total of my efforts during my lifetime. In the face of this Citadel, that didn't amount to much.

"You know," I said, "I've built some pretty neat stuff, but how the hell do you build something like this?"

"I guess we'll never know for sure."

"No," I said, shaking my head. "No, we won't."

I tried to imagine an artisan working there, using his hands to craft such beauty, such perfection. Whenever I try to do something like that, it seems to take forever, and being the impatient guy that I am, I get frustrated and tend to forget about the quality of my work; I just want to get the darned thing finished. How different life must have been back then for these people to spend months, or years, creating the things I saw there, with not a flaw or error.

When I was there before, in 1971, I had heard talk of the Citadels and their magnificence. Because of the thread of aesthetic awareness that I had acquired from the study of architecture, I had thought what a shame that those ancient masterpieces might be damaged or destroyed, like so many other artifacts and structures that were be being decimated by wars. But, that was only a flash in my mind as the threat of Vietnam bore down on me with fervor. Any thoughts of aesthetics had suddenly been rammed to the back of my mind, and I thought, so what? I was so young, then.

I passed through doors and frames that glistened from their bright red paint and gilded designs. I admired the intricate carvings on the doorjambs, and ran my hands over the dragon handrails and concrete light posts cast with what looked like serpents crawling up them. It was exhilarating to touch something that an ancient master craftsman's hands had created with probably months of painstaking patience. My hands caressed what those primitive hands had formed. The round columns and beams in perfect circular form painted bright red almost glowed, finished to a glassy smoothness, and all of the other woodwork handcrafted to exacting standards. How did they do it? How long did it take them? How many workers were required?

I had seen nothing like it. Of course, I knew that the Asian cultures put much importance on artistry and skill. But the scale of it all surpassed anything I could have imagined in America. It seems like we are too eager to be done with a task to care about the perfection of it. I know, I have fallen to the same level of mediocrity. We are only too glad to finish the job and grab our paychecks. We have little pride in much of what we do or try to accomplish. About the only worth we deem precious is the income that is constantly measured against our rivals, and the only ambition is the free time to be entertained by so called "heroes" that are paid millions of dollars a year just to play games, like children, and contribute little to society. But yet we watch and pay for the privilege. While Vietnam has busy rebuilding their country and their culture and heritage, we have been busy collecting possessions, building financial empires, colossal sports complexes, and entertainment networks. And where has it gotten us?

We left Hue at 11:22 headed for Hoi An. We passed by Phu Bai Airport where some of the fellows had flown frequent missions. It had been one of the major airfields in Vietnam during the war. We got a group picture at the gate, but we were not allowed inside, a disappointment for some. At least we knew that the airport was still there.

Back on Highway QL1, we cruised on rain-slick pavement past lush countryside and the road ambled toward the beaches. Our bus followed the sandy shores for miles. It was not uncommon to see numerous men stopped along the side of the road taking a whiz. I thought that was a little odd, given the conservative customs of the Vietnamese. I have seen guys take care of business along Oklahoma roads, but they were a bit more discreet.

We reached the Khyber pass at about 1:00. Unlike the highway during the years of the Vietnam War that climbed over the mountains, we passed through a tunnel that had since been constructed, saving time. A few minutes later, we found ourselves near Da Nang, where the first American troops in the Vietnam War landed on the beach in 1965. From there the American presence spread throughout South Vietnam.

Lunch was taken at a pleasant resort area just outside of the city. The restaurant was a round building, with a tall conical roof. A landscaped pond in front gave it a tropical ambience. Truc arranged the meals for us, seafood noodles for $6 a head. And a "333" beer at $1 a can. Such a deal.

We stopped for diesel at a station and I happened to look out of the bus's window at the pump. Diesel was VND 13,300 per liter, about 66 cents. At nearly four liters per gallon, that would be $2.64 per gallon.

We reached An Hoa at 3:40. The bus left the highway and crept through narrow lanes and turned down what looked like a residential street, almost an alley. When it stopped, we saw the Ancient House Village Hotel.

As with the other hotels we had stayed, this one was friendly and accommodating, but with a more casual ambience. We were greeted with warm, moist towels and watermelon coolers. I'm not particularly fond of watermelon, but this drink had a sweet smoothness that pleased the palate. The folks there were all smiles and eager to please.

It was one of these places that could have been on a travel poster. The complex consisted of a main reception building, a restaurant, a recreation building, and a series of two and three story units that looked like upscale condominiums seated in lush tropical trees, plants, and flowers.

The hotel was quiet and peaceful; the rich smell of fresh earth filled the air. Even the sidewalks seemed to have emerged from between the rich plant life that populated the fertile ground, and overhanging fronds and branches brushed my head as I walked beneath them.

The hotel touted its ecological mission, using organic fertilizers and sanitized water to provide a green environment for the hotel and its guests. The rooms were spectacular with spacious, open plans and soaring ceilings covered in what appeared to be red clay tiles held up with dark wood runners. The bathtub sat on the raised bathroom floor in a field of white gravel just behind a low wall that separated it from the sleeping area. And then Thom and I noticed it. There was the picture window shower. I'm not sure what it was with the Vietnamese that favored exhibitionism, if that's what it was, or just to afford a view while taking a shower.

Our room had complimentary water bottles, instant coffee, cocoa, and tea. I also noticed what looked like small green bundles the size of golf balls on the coffee table between the chairs. When I got up enough courage to try one, I loosened the banana leaf wrapping that revealed a bon-bon-type lump. It had the texture of a pear and a flavor akin to figs. I couldn't place it, but it was delicious.

The furnishings were dark wood and white fabric, comfortable but the number of pieces required that they be squashed together in a compact arrangement. We had a second floor end unit with three doors that opened onto green fields and wooded lots. As was customary, there were no screens. This time of year, insects were not a problem.

I thought the hotel reflected the soul of Vietnam; the craftsmanship, the rich wood and fabrics, the simple furnishings and décor. There was no glitz and glamour I would find in many of the American hotels that preferred superficial sparkle over beauty. There was only the simple elegance of materials and construction native to the area. Of all the hotels I had patronized, this was the most beautiful I had seen, and by beautiful I mean an honest, natural beauty, not the supercilious icons of mediocrity that adorn American cities. Those are more suited for the unappreciative masses that think more is better.

Dinner that evening was held in the hotel's restaurant where Truc had arranged for our fare. We found many of the same traditional dishes we had tasted before, but with variation in the preparation. Asian cuisine is like American pot roast. Every region has its own way of preparing it. The culinary experience was well worth the $20 each of us paid. I would expect to shell out at least $40 at home for a comparable meal.

Truc was fond of wine and we had plenty to go around the dinner table. It was every few minutes that he stood holding his glass in the air and said, "Yo...yo...yo!" That was our cue to clink glasses and take a drink.

When we had stopped at the liquor store earlier, someone had purchased a bottle of Ruou Hoang De Minh Mang. It was professed to be an elixir for many ailments of the body. Apparently favored by Minh Mang, the second emperor of the Nguyen dynasty, it was used as a drug to prolong his health. Due to his many wives, he had fathered up to 142 children. The common inference was that Ruou Hoang de Minh Mang was an aphrodisiac.

Glasses were passed around and a small portion of the golden liquor poured into each. A toast followed as I tipped the glass to my lips and swallowed. I wished I hadn't. The vile liquid cut through my innards like a stream of lava. At 37% ethanol, it wasn't as potent as vodka or whiskey, but it still had quite a kick. It must have been the other stuff in it, whatever it was, that lit the fire. If I'd had a bottle of it, I'd have poured it into my car's gas tank. I darned sure wouldn't be drinking it.

After dinner, Thom felt compelled to go for a swim in the large pool.

"You're really hard core, aren't you?" I asked him.

"Hey," he almost laughed. "I live by a river. I love the water."

He modestly went up the steps into the bath area to change into his swim trunks, not that it did much for modesty when there was only a short knee wall to block the view. I still afforded him all the privacy he wanted by looking out the front door. The palms had been brilliant green earlier, even in the muted light of the overcast sky. They had since slipped into a hunter green, still evident in the twilight. Later, they would become nearly black, but not without that unmistakable iridescent hue.

"It isn't too cold?" I asked him.

"Nah," he said, waving off my comment. "Just about right."

"You're tough," I told him.

He grinned, that rustic, sly spread of his lips in the shadow of brushy eyebrows.

"It's invigorating," he said. "You ought to come."

"You're kidding."

"Well, I won't swim for long. Just a quick dip."

Then he was gone. I darned sure wasn't going to freeze my ass off, so I stayed in the room with a glass of Johnnie Walker and read and jotted notes in my journal. As comfortable as the seats in the bus had been when we started this journey, somehow it felt as if the cushion had begun leaving an impression in my butt. I hoped it would go away before morning.

I spent a good deal of time thinking about our journey to Qui Nhon the next day. Thom and I had been stationed at Lane Army Airfield, about nine miles west of there. Back then, I had made frequent trips to Qui Nhon, a dirty city inundated with slum-like housing that sat atop the green slime of the bay. I was anticipating what my return would reveal. If it was like everything else I had seen and heard the other fellows talk about, I had doubts that I would be able to recognize anything around there. Still, the memories swarmed my brain. I fell asleep reliving the time in my hooch.

CHAPTER 9

AN HOA TO QUI NHON

Monday, 7 December, 2015

I awoke shortly after 5:00 to rain; not a downpour, but a light, soaking rain, the kind that taps softly on a tin roof. I got up to open the doors to a healthy breeze. Thom had also found it hard to sleep and was sitting up in bed reading. It was so peaceful and quiet; I opened my book and dived in. Watching the palm fronds outside wave in the puffs of moist air, and hearing the raindrops tapping on the broad leaves was like paradise. Another hour until breakfast, but that didn't bother me at all.

The buffet that morning was more extensive than I'd seen, offering American, Vietnamese, and Korean dishes. I had stepped on a set of scales recently and was surprised to find that in spite of all of the food I'd consumed lately, I'd not gained weight. I lost count of my trips back to the buffet.

When 8:15 rolled around, we were on the bus bound for the five-hour drive to Qui Nhon, with a few stops planned along the way, the first of which would be Chu Lai. Truc made one stop on the way out of An Hoa to load up on "VC lunches."

The last two phone calls I had made to my wife had lasted longer than I thought, and the time on my sim card was about depleted. I planned to look for a Viattele store when we reached the hotel.

It was 9:00 before we turned onto Highway QL1, and everyone had discovered and enabled instant messaging on his phone. The things were pinging all over the bus. I suppose that was easier than yelling from one end to the other.

At 9:12, it was still raining and the temperature was in the low 70s, and the phones were still pinging. Even with the rain, it was a pleasant day, as were most days there. The road was decent, even with the occasional bumps. When fog replaced the rain, the windows bore a film of water droplets. Not a day for pictures. The bus was quiet except for the fellows up front who kept a constant chatter in the air and, of course the pinging of the phones.

Highway QL1 changed appearances frequently during our drive, one minute being a pristine, smoothly surfaced roadway, then becoming a graveled surface, filled with holes and dips, and later it turned into something like a patchwork of asphalt.

I wondered where the Vietnamese obtained their building materials. I saw few trees in the area that could be harvested for lumber. I suppose most of those might have been in the mountainous areas. I leaned that in the early 90s, it became obvious to the Vietnamese that their forests were being harvested at an unsustainable rate. Laws were put into place to control logging, requiring that timber be imported from other countries.

What I did see was a bevy of small-trunked trees, short and spindly. Many of the smaller ones were used as shoring and structural supports for buildings during construction. The innovative spirit of these folks continued to amaze me. I thought about some of the expediencies I had used over the years when building things, but I had never imagined using natural resources like that. Except for the handrails on my porch that spanned the front of my log house, the trees in the woods around my acreage had been safe due to my shortsightedness. That and the avoidance of harvesting trees and working them into logs suitable for building. It had been easier and faster to buy them cured and milled.

The road, like in the northern part of the country, was flanked by a series of shops, some in groups, some alone, most being little more that slender wooden poles supporting a tarp for a roof. I imagine the rural population found these small markets to be convenient, the only alternative being a long march into the nearest town or village. Few of the rural residents had cars or scooters that I could see, and I still suspected that that many of them never left their homes except to frequent the small shops nearby.

I was certain there were no zoning laws in Vietnam. In fact, I doubt that there was such a thing as an easement. Sidewalks hugged the paving of the highway separated by little more than five feet from the edge of the road.

It took less than an hour to reach Tam Ky, capital of Quang Tin province, and another 30 minutes to Chu Lai Air Base. The facility was built as a U. S. Marine air base during the launch of our involvement in the Vietnam War and eventually became a major air base for conduct of war operations. In 1970, it was turned over to the U. S. Army. It now is the Chu Lai International Airport.

We continued south to Quang Ngai, capital of Quang Ngai province. Just south of town we made a pit stop for lunch at the Sa Huynh Resort. Truc broke out the "VC lunches" and we drank our beer while wolfing down the so-called delicacy. I still found it odd that we could stop at a restaurant, occupy their tables, and bring our own food. Had we tried that in America, we would have been thrown out. What an odd country.

The highway ran alongside the shoreline of the South China Sea, and the resort sat on a beachfront. The expanse of sandy shore stretched into the steely water that echoed the dull gray of the overcast sky and the mist that peppered our glasses, only the white tops of gentle waves giving contrast to the tranquil scene. The temperature, in the mid-70s, was agreeable, but the humidity lent a bit of stuffiness. After group photos on the beach, it was back onto the bus and on the road.

The rice paddies I remembered from long ago popped up frequently as we neared Qui Nhon, the green stalks of rice plants poking through the water that flooded the fields. Little had changed since the war when the mama-sans in their conical hats bent over the rows, thinning out the seedlings. At that time, I had paid little attention to the daily routines of the local people, other than how their behavior might be a threat. Now it all seemed so picturesque and serene.

The smoky blue sea drifted past the windows and numerous islands in the murky distance seemed to grow out of the water like brownish-gray icebergs floating off shore. The beauty of it remained intact even in the drab gray of the clouds and mist that saturated the air.

We passed by Highway 19, the main route between Qui Nhon and the Cambodian border to the west, and Truc had Phuc stopped the bus in the next town. Thom and I got off and hiked over a short distance to get a better look at Nui Hon Cha Mountain that had bordered Lane Army Airfield where Thom and I had been stationed. He had been there in 1968 with the 498th Medevac, and I had been there in 1971 with the 129th AHC, the 7/17 Armored Cav. Back then, there were only small villages, open pasture, and rice paddies around Lane. Now, in place of the airfield, an entire town occupied much of the space. Had I not seen the mountain, I would never have known Lane used to be there.

"Do you recognize anything?" I asked Thom.

His head swiveled from side to side. "Not a thing," he told me. "Is this really it?"

"Yeah, recognize the mountain. I just don't see anything else I know."

"Where was Lane?"

I pointed to the base of the mountain. "There at the base. From here, about right in the middle of it."

He looked again. "If you say so."

I used to know this country like the back streets and roads around Stillwater, Oklahoma. Seven and half years of college does that to you. But now, looking at where I had lived for a year, I couldn't identify a thing.

I recalled some of the missions I had flown out of Lane, and the many times I'd flown by or into Phu Cat Air Force Base, just northwest of Lane. In fact, Ken had also spent some time up in this area. This is his account of one of his missions:

I found Vietnam a bit of everything; beauty, terror, boredom, comradery, happiness and sadness. My first example occurred after 3 weeks in country. I was assigned to the gun platoon of B Company, 1/9 Cav, and was in the early days of really learning to fly; you know, how to shoot a rocket, do a hammerhead turn at the end of the gun run, how to fly through your own shrapnel and other stuff they didn't teach in flight school.

We had just completed a mission very late in the day. The aircraft commander got out of the aircraft with the crew chief and said, "You and the door gunner take the aircraft to Phu Cat Air Force Base to logger overnight." We flew out of Two Bits, which was a small compound just to the west of Bong Son and near the mouth of the An Lo Valley. The "higher-ups" thought the compound might get mortared overnight, so they got the aircraft out of the area. I had made this flight with an overnight stay a few days before with the AC (aircraft commander), apparently as part of my training. The door gunner climbed into the left seat; he was now my copilot. The sun was setting as we took off. We were a flight of two. I was in the lead in a UH-1B Hog with 48 rockets. WO1 Godfrey was following me. He had been "in country" a few weeks more than I had. Does the phrase "the blind leading the blind" come to mind? With the sun setting behind the mountains to the west, it gets very dark early in that part of Vietnam. We had flown about 30 minutes down Route 1 when I started to see the runway lights of Phu Cat. I lined myself up for a very long straight-in and final. At this point of the flight, I was only scared a little. Night flying in Vietnam is significantly different than flight school. I had the runway at 5 miles and was almost sure I could land without crashing. I had dropped my altitude down to about 500 feet for a nice smooth, shallow approach.

That's when all hell breaks loose, the instrument panel lights up with warning lights and the low RPM audio starts whooping in my ears. The flight school training paid off when I slammed the collective to the floor. I could kiss all of those Flight School Instructors who rolled that throttle off at absolutely the worst time. I made a quick check that the throttle had not been rolled off. It was okay. "Holy@#$%^&"!!!! The first thought that went through my head was maybe I had a governor failure, but there was no way I could find the right switch in the dark with a VSI (vertical speed indicator) at 1100 fpm. I'm not actually thinking I've got 15 or 20 seconds till I reach the ground. It's more like, "I'm Going to die!"

At this point, I'm thinking how nice it would be if I could move my hand off the collective and turn on the landing and searchlights. No way; I can't move my hand; I'm too close to the ground. For some reason, never to be explained, I turn the aircraft about 30 degrees to left, level it, then I sense the presence of trees out the right side of the aircraft. I didn't actually see them. So, I'm going into the trees and act accordingly. I pull the cyclic back to the stop to reduce airspeed and pull the collective up to my armpit! From this point on, I feel I am surrounded or encased in black Jell-O. I hear no sound; I feel no motion; I do not feel the aircraft hit the rice paddy. Yes, a dry rice paddy. As I become aware of my surroundings, I reach down and pop the quick release on my safety harness and reach up to the back of my head wiping blood away. Only later do I wonder where my flight helmet went or why it was gone. I speculate on two possible scenarios. First, we had two M-60 machine guns mounted on bungee cords for the door gunner and crew chief. Did the gun behind me swing forward and hit me in the head? Second, did the blade flex through the cockpit taking my helmet but not my head?

Now that I have determined that I, in fact, did not die; it might be a good time to exit the aircraft. This is another great mystery to me.

My immediate recollection tells me I went out through the chin bubble of the aircraft. Logic tells me that is not possible, since after hard landing and skids ripped off, Houdini couldn't get by the pedals and out the chin bubble. With this in mind, I have decided that I went out over the instrument panel. This is also a vote for the rotor blade flexing through the cockpit. I crawled straight out of the aircraft and am now standing in front of it.

At this point, I need to digress a week or so. One of our pilots received an all-expense paid trip to Hong Cong on R & R. He asked if anyone wanted him to bring back anything. I wanted one of those fancy Seiko self-winding day-date watches. I got it the day before this flight! Now, back to the action.

I'm standing in front of the aircraft, and I have to know if I hurt my new watch. I hold my arm up so I can see my watch by the light behind me. What light is that you ask? It is really supposed to be pitch dark. About this time, the door gunner comes around to the front of the aircraft and says, "Sir, this thing is going to blow up." Sure enough, there are flames all over the engine compartment. Hence the light. I always wanted to do a commercial. "Seiko takes a lickin' but keeps on tickin'." But I guess Timex got it first.

We take off running and get about 50 feet from the aircraft when it blows up. Lying on the ground, I look back at the burning aircraft and quickly note that I am looking down the barrels of 48 rocket tubes. I'm really not the sharpest tack on the planet at this moment, but I tell my partner that I think we should move. We run to the northeast to get away from the aircraft and more behind it out of the aim of the rockets, still in the pods. We find a nice dry rice paddy ditch. It was just like the 4th of July. A rocket would launch, flash, boom. Another rocket and the beautiful arcing of white phosphorus. The LZ was lit by 24 HE (high explosive) and 24 willie pete (white phosphorous) and a burning Huey.

The aircraft flown by W01 Godfrey did not come down to get us. It was reported to me the next day that he thought my aircraft was on fire on the way down and exploded on impact. He climbed to altitude to call for help. Very close to the crash site was another Cav unit. It was the 227th or the 229th. They saw the crash and launched a helicopter immediately. All the rockets had launched but 7.62 ammo was still going off when they landed. The door gunner and I start running towards the flyable aircraft in the rice paddy. It was at this time I recognized that I might be hurt. I could not run; I could barely walk. I told my comrade to run ahead and don't let them leave without us. When I reached the UH-1D, I climbed up on the skid and hollered at the pilot, "There are only two of us! Get out of here!" Their crew chief was running around my burning aircraft trying to find two more people. 7.62 ammo was still going off. Their crew chief was retrieved and I climbed into the back of the lift ship. I tried to sit on the bench seat but screamed in pain. At that point, I don't remember much of the flight to Qui Nhon Medivac Hospital.

Upon arrival at the pad, they came and got me with a floppy-wheeled cart, rolled me into an emergency room and start sewing up the back of my head. It was at this point I realized there was a very pretty Army Nurse assisting. Okay, maybe I'll live. Then I was taken for x-rays. The doctor, with his best bedside manner, came in and said, "You have a broken back. You will be going home." The memories of being in the Medevac Hospital are the worst of this entire experience. I was in a large room with 30 or 40 other guys who were much worse off than me. The room seemed a constant 90 degrees F. I was miserable and in pain and still filthy from the crash. The staff was so undermanned and over worked they only stopped by my bed to give a pain killer. After two and a half days, I think it was, I was put on a C-123, hanging from the ceiling on a stretcher, and flown to Japan through Clark Air Force Base. At Clark, I was cleaned up and told I had a compression fracture. I stayed 5 weeks in the Hospital at Camp Zama, Japan, and then sent to the BOQ (bachelor officer quarters) for the next 7 weeks of recovery before being sent back to my unit in Vietnam. Some people have heard me make the statement as I got on the plane to return to Vietnam, "I would crash another helicopter for this trip."

I stood there with Thom, staring at the mountain. Even through the mist and heavy air, I recognized her. I looked at the giant hunk of earth and remembered the craggy and rugged surface, steep and imposing. The setting sun had lost itself early from Lane's viewpoint, helping to relive the furnace effect of the heat, but only marginally. I could still envision the gunnies diving toward it and unleashing a barrage of missiles into it during practice. Truc yelled, and I came around to the present for a photo op with Thom, Nui Hon Cha standing proudly in the background. Thom, I believe, was still in some state of astonishment.

You know how it is when you see a picture or some sight that that was prominent in your past and your mind erupts in memories you didn't know you had, and your body stops for moment, suspended in time that seems to have gotten lost somewhere and you just stumbled across it as if tripping across a crack in the sidewalk. I don't remember getting back on the bus.

We pulled away and as I looked at Nui Hon Cha Mountain through the beads of water on the glass and the haze that, like my mind, had wanted to keep it all hidden, I was still recalling the relief I had felt whenever I saw that mountain through the windscreen of a Huey. It meant that I was back "home," so to speak, safe from the impending danger of Charlie placing a round or two through the helicopter, or a .51 cal or RPG blasting us out of the sky. It meant a stop at the piss tube, a hot meal, beer and camaraderie, and finally, bed. Sleep that would somehow embed the day's stress into the back of my mind so I could do it all again the next day. I still felt that after all of those years.

Truc announced that we would be making a brief stop at a garage. A knocking sound beneath the bus had alerted Phong to the possibility that something might be wrong. So we pulled into the lot of a large garage outfit, and a fellow directed the bus into one of the bays. The mechanics seemed to be busy with a slew of other vehicles, but that didn't delay our repairs. We stayed on the bus while a mechanic opened a luggage compartment beneath and a series of knocks and clangs reverberated through the cabin. A clamp of some kind had come loose and was repaired quickly. We were soon on our way to Qui Nhon.

As we left the garage, I marveled at how expeditiously our problem was resolved. We show up at the doorstep, no appointment, we receive immediate attention, and the problem is fixed. That would be unheard of in America. Whenever I take one of my cars in for service, it's always, "Do you have an appointment?" or "We're pretty backed up, it might be awhile." With all of the unconventional things I had encountered in Vietnam, my mind had never been so soundly challenged to consider why things had to be the way they were in America.

We made it to the Muong Thanh Quy Nhon Hotel a little after 4:00. Several stories tall, the modern building stood near the beachfront of the South China Sea. The lobby was tastefully contemporary, but lacked that sparkle that gave it any individuality; a typical upscale hotel. The rooms were, as expected, comfortably furnished and pleasant, but unexciting. I anticipated a less than impressive staff.

After we checked in, I inquired at the desk about the nearest Viattel store. After some quibbling because of language, I finally was able to explain what I needed. I showed the woman at the desk the brochure I had taken from the last phone store and pointed to what I wanted. She asked if I would wait for a few minutes, then she asked if I had the cash for the transaction. The lady motioned to one of the bellboys and instructed him to go to the Viattel store. He nodded, while smiling, of course, and took the brochure, my phone number, and VND500,000 from my hand, then raced off with my money. It was less than 15 minutes before he returned with a receipt and confirmation that my card had been recharged with 50 minutes of voice and 8 gigabytes of data. I thanked the fellow and the lady profusely.

Ed Knighten strode to the counter and asked where he might purchase a pack of cigarettes. He was a tall and serious looking man with one of those mustache-beard combo things that looked like a furry ring around his mouth. I'm not sure it was his appearance that intimidated the lady, or just the nature of his question. His request did not seem to go as well as mine had. The language barrier got in the way. I don't know if he ever found any cigarettes.

Sterling and Tom Baca also happened by while I was gloating over my success and asked where the bar was located. The lady told them it was inside the restaurant, and they disappeared through the door. When they came out, Tom told me that they had ordered two Cokes and that they would be delivered to their room, no extra charge.

Notwithstanding Ed's disappointment, I could not believe the service that they had provided to a total stranger, even though I was a guest of the hotel. Even with what I had seen of the Vietnamese so far, I was still astonished at their amiability, all done with the characteristic smiles. It wasn't just the smiles; it was the look of unselfishness on their faces, as if they were glad to have been of assistance. I just wasn't used to that kind of treatment. I doubt that any of us were.

Anything the hotel lacked in physical attractiveness, it made up for in the courteous and helpful staff. The folks there were just too good to be true. Was Vietnam a great country or what?

Dinner that evening took us to the Houng Viet Restaurant. The aroma of Vietnamese food, although disagreeable to some, was like a magic elixir to me. Around Hanoi, the hundreds of varieties of noodles found their way into soups and other dishes. It reminded me of the Chinese food I had eaten at home, although the stuff we eat in the States is Americanized to our tastes What I got in Vietnam was on an entirely different plane of flavor and aroma. As we ventured south, I noticed more soups, called pho, like I'd had in Hanoi, and the dishes had a sweeter flavor.

The restaurant provided as fabulous meal of a flat bread cracker thing, fried seafood spring rolls, a beef and vegetable dish, a round of greens sliced in long shoots, beef ribs, rice, and fish. The food in Vietnam had been incredible. Unlike the Americanized Asian dishes in restaurants at home, Vietnamese dishes were more robust with a subtle mingling of flavors that teased my mouth with the combination of sweet, salt, and sour taste that made me forget about anything else but eating. The seasonings, the variety, and the flavors they impart to the food. I could get used to it.

That evening I lay in bed and thought about the day's events. It was still surprising to me that the Vietnamese people could be so accommodating. Even when sightseeing, invariably one of them would approach our group and offer to take our picture with our cameras. All of them. We didn't even have to ask.

While I was writing these notes in my journal, Thom was writing in his own journal about the memories rekindled by Nui Hon Cha Mountain, I suppose. He was writing much slower, but I imagine with much better penmanship. He had endeavored to write about something every day. So far, he was honoring his intentions.

Tourism was a major industry there, and I can see how it has been so successful. Expenses are less than most other countries and the folks here seem to go out of their way to make you feel welcome and valued as a guest. They were proud of their country and wanted to show it off. I was also surprised to see that the Vietnamese manage to overlook the crass and overbearing behavior of Americans and other nationalities. I'm not sure I could have done that. I have to admire these people for their integrity and humility.

The next day we would be headed for Nha Trang. I had never flown into that city, but had flown over it many times when I was there before. I had usually been on my way to Tuy Hoa or Cam Ranh Bay. I tried to remember what the country had looked like from the air, not that I had paid much attention to it then. The only vision that came to mind was rice paddies and villages and hamlets. And a lot of green. It looked so much different through the windows of a bus. I would try to make more sense of what I saw tomorrow.

CHAPTER 10

QUI NHON TO NHA TRANG

Tuesday, 8 December, 2015

The Muong Thanh Quy Nhon Hotel was the least favorite, so far. Although the staff was helpful, the accommodations were, in spite of the smart and comfortable appointments, unremarkable, almost mundane. The lobby mirrored commercialism manifested in modernistic design, a flat and uninspiring ambience. Though the breakfast buffet was loaded with a good variety of foods, fell short of the others we had sampled.

When I looked through the window of our room toward the South China Sea, I could barely see the expanse of gray water through the morning rain and haze. The weather had been unusually wet for this time of year, but it had kept the oppressive heat at bay.

From the hotel window, I followed the expanse of the city stretching as far as I could see. New buildings, their facades glossy from the precipitation, crowded together along streets no longer in the embarrassment of rag-tag huts and hovels that I remembered along their routes. Qui Nhon had exploded since I was last there. I recognized nothing. Even the older buildings which had been at most two or three stories in height were no longer noticeable among the taller, modern structures that predominated the city. I didn't see the jumble of shacks that hovered over the raw, polluted water as we flew over the shoreline back in 1971. None of that. Many of the streets were still narrow, but other wide thoroughfares now reached through the city with swarms of traffic. I tried to find the naval officers club with its landing pad on the beach. Couldn't see it. There was no longer any trace of PAE (Pacific Architects and Engineers) there in Qui Nhon, the construction company that had a complex on the shore. I recalled one trip I had made when we had flown the Korean Tiger Division General, Major General Myung Shin Chae, there for a meeting:

WO2 Applebee set Tiger Wagon down as soft as a feather hitting the ground. Tiger Wagon was a spit-shined UH-1H that was dedicated to the Korean general's use. Only short-timer ACs of the 1ˢᵗ Platoon of the 129ᵗʰ AHC flew it.

The general was meeting with the big wigs of PAE, a construction company that supported the ROK (Republic of Korea) Tiger Division troops in Vietnam. While there, the helicopter's crew was invited to the general's lunch. Although we ate in a room separate from the general and his entourage, the food was outstanding. It was my first taste of Boolkoki, and my first exposure to food that was not American. I was hooked. Oh, I'd eaten the typical Asian food sold in run of the mill restaurants and the canned "Oriental" food from the market that my mother prepared. It was nothing like this. From then on, I decided to be more adventurous; one of the good things to come out of the war.

On the way through the city, our bus passed by what I would have recognized had it still been there. The Qui Nhon Airfield, a major military airbase, served the II Corps area with its runways, fuel points, supplies, and a host of other services. Truc pointed out the bus window to a length of sodded ground that ran between two roadways.

"Air field," he said. "Used to be air field."

We all jerked our heads toward it and I marveled at seeing nothing but grass. No runways, no control tower, no hangars, no operations building, no fuel bladders, nothing but grass.

I didn't' think much about it the day before when we made our way to the hotel, but standing now at the window, thinking about what I had and had not seen, it began to sink in to my mind how much Vietnam had changed in 44 years. But why shouldn't it have changed? That's what things do. That what places do. That's what most people do. Change. Something we all take for granted.

At 7:00 that morning, we checked out of the hotel and left for Nha Trang, another 5-hour drive south. I studied the street as the bus glided along with the gaggle of motor scooters, plastic ponchos flapping around the drivers who seemed to give no mind to the weather. Tally Ho!

The bus went on and on down Highway QL1 over asphalt, concrete, and gravel sections, parallel to the coast of the South China Sea, or the South Sea, as the Vietnamese call it. China was not a word in good standing in Vietnam, nor were its people. The fewer references to

China, the better. Even the assistance of the Chinese to North Vietnam during the war did not temper the animosity held for the Chinese.

Construction projects dotted the roadside, some of them in progress, and many of them apparently abandoned. Houses and buildings half built surrounded by scaffolding made of bamboo and tree trunks cut from nearby wooded areas showed no signs of recent work. Looking at the spindly supports and questionable bracing, little care seemed to be given to safety. If this were done in America, the folks at OSHA would be weathering coronaries and anxiety attacks just to keep up with all of the infractions of safety rules and regulations.

And traffic laws? Merely foolish fantasies of visiting foreigners who had expected to see some semblance of control among the glut of vehicles that seem to roam the country at will. Stop signs and signals were scarce and the idea of right-of-way was completely unknown there. Phong just aimed our bus in the direction he wanted it to go and eased it into the stream of traffic where the other drivers miraculously allowed the big beast enough space to pull the rest of itself into the flow with minimal effect on anything else. There actually was order; it just wasn't discernible to the tourist.

The blue-gray water of the sea, still visible from the window, reached to the far edge of the clouds, the surf roiling through the fog and rain and breaking in white foamy spray at the rocky shore. Boats dotted the bay, bobbing in the water like corks on fishing lines. Distant hills erupted from the surface, rugged islands held down by the heavy sky that seemed to smother the horizon.

I tried to remember what the area near Qui Nhon had looked like in 1971, recalling old photos I had taken, but things looked so much different from a bus window than they did from 1500 feet above. I know that I had never looked for any redeeming qualities of Vietnam, instead looking for possible ambush sites, a copse with a .51 cal hidden within, a hamlet hiding VC, or something black on the ground with a rifle. I had never tried to appreciate the country. I didn't want to. I just wanted to leave it.

The highway hugged the mountains as it wrapped itself around the ragged slopes. Waterfalls from above spilled downhill toward the road, cascading into the vegetation and rocks before disappearing beneath the pavement.

The bus stopped at a turnout and we all got off to stretch and view the scenery. Small trees and shrubbery covered the hillside where we walked and paused to take pictures of the rippling carpet of what could have been liquid steel. The stark greenness of the vegetation, even in the dull glare of the luminous clouds, seemed to glow against the sea.

"Hell of a place, isn't it?" I said to Thom, admiring the view.

He stood with hands on hips, surveying the expanse of blue water like a captain at the helm of his ship. "Wish I had my boat."

"Yeah," I said. "You would. I never realized how beautiful it was here."

He looked at, tilting his head slightly. "What?"

"I just never took time to notice. Or wanted to. Don't forget; I didn't really want to be here."

"I don't' know many who did," he said.

"Would it have made any difference?" I asked, but by then he had wandered off through the brush. I was talking to myself.

Back on the bus, we turned inland, the pavement reaching away from the sandy soil that spread over the dunes to the beaches beyond. Even though our path was toward the mountains, they appeared no nearer than they had an hour before. It was 10:00 before the rain had stopped, and looking up at the sky, it appeared that the sun might break through. It never did.

We left the highway a short time later and found ourselves in the midst of villages bisected by the narrow road that snaked through them. Phong often found it necessary to pull off the road to let oncoming traffic pass by.

Rice paddies spread across the land as far as I could see, a vast network of agricultural subsistence. No industry other than that was as visible in the rural areas of the country. Agriculture was the livelihood of these people, and they had probably known nothing else for generations. Even though technology in the form of electricity had found its way into their lives, little else seemed have changed for decades or longer.

The rain came again at around 11:00. By that time, we had arrived at Ganh Da Dia rock formation near Tuy Hoa. Commonly called the Sea Cliff of Stone Plates, a bed of basalt columns had formed itself along the shore into a series of interlocking geometric plates, the result of the rapid cooling of volcanic eruptions. The blackened rocks covered the beach in tiers of what looked like scales that climbed up the slope to the plateau that overlooked the spectacle. A stone stairway led down to the rocks, bordered by a handrail ingeniously crafted of concrete, sculpted and painted green to resemble bamboo. Since the rain had stopped, several of us ventured down to join other thrill-seekers on the rocks to examine them firsthand. Much thought had been given to the attraction and it seemed to be popular with the other tourists who were there along with us.

At one point, the rocks seemed to have lain on their sides and their columnar structure was evident, like a giant pieces of black hexagonal chalk. Others a pentagon shape, all stacked like firewood neatly arranged in the rack.

I had never known this formation was there, although I'm sure I must have flown over it several times on my trips to and from Tuy Hoa. I just never took the time to look.

On the opposite side of the peninsula lay a barren area filled with boulders, rocks, and prickly pear cacti looking out over the South China Sea beyond. I had not expected to see such a familiar plant in the drenching humidity of Vietnam. A walking trail meandered across it. In the center of it all was a visitor's area with tented shelters and, of course, souvenirs.

Just as Phong swung the bus around to leave, a wire had fallen across the road, which was more of a trail, and hung there, suspended from a pole at one side and a tree on the other. Not knowing what kind of line it was, Phong stopped the bus. After a short deliberation, Ken Bartholomew volunteered to risk his life to see us safely out of the compound, and lunged from the bus to attack the offending cable. He readily found a broken limb of a small tree that he used to lift the wire above the bus and Phong drove beneath it.

Once again, a Vietnam vet rises to the occasion to ensure the safety of his fellow man. Of course, that's not what ensued when he returned to the bus. Only our light-hearted jesting and, naturally, a little humiliation. We were a fun-loving bunch.

At noon we were back on Highway QL1 following the coastline to the south. Spirits were high and that might have been because of a bottle of Scotch that was being passed around. Ed's Johnnie Walker Black was making its trek up and down the aisles and some of the fellows were taking advantage of it.

Tom Baca was burning up the airwaves with pictures from his

iPad. Pat Matheny, who was sitting behind me, talked with me about his column he wrote for the community newspaper back home in Shinnston. Don Hooper was explaining one of his many pearls of wisdom to Tom Horan. Jack Swickard was talking to Ken Bartholomew, who was answering with, "What?" The rest were enjoying the scenery or whatever they were thinking about.

At about 1:15, we passed by Tuy Hoa. The highway still ran along its sandy base, the sea visible beyond the beaches and dunes. I didn't recognize anything for the simple reason that I had never seen anything outside the Tuy Hoa Air Base during the war. About all I remember is the sand, clusters of olive drab tents, the smell of diesel and jet fuel, and the wind that blew in off the water. That and the searing heat that sucked all of the moisture from my body and deposited it in my drenched Nomex. From my new vantage point, it looked so different, like a tourist Mecca replete with hotels and condominiums.

About an hour north of Nha Trang the bus began laboring up mountains, weaving around them with the roads that hung on their slopes, cutting through the trees and shrubbery that reflected in the wet pavement. Murky silhouettes of other distant mountains barely broke through the rain that hid the valleys in between. The limited passing ability of our bus surrendered to the heavy truck traffic and our progress slowed even more.

The highway veered inland slightly behind small mountains that obscured the sea from view occasionally. I heard the bus lug down as the road rose more steeply. I watched Phong negotiate the curves and hills and wondered where he had learned to drive with such dexterity. He was not a large man, but seemed to handle the bus like a cowboy roping a steer.

We encountered a lot of road construction on this leg of the trip. Temporary roads were little more than gravel paths, largely neglected during the construction process. Phong slowed the bus to a crawl so it could scrabble its way back to solid pavement while we all bounced and swayed in our seats. Forget the steer. It was more like riding a bull.

The farther south we traveled the mountains lost some stature, with less jagged profiles that seemed smoother to the eye. Hillsides were heavily covered with trees, unlike the smaller vegetation in the north.

The toll booth was a surprise. I couldn't believe we would be charged to plod over roads that weren't really roads. We could just as well have gone cross-country with the same comfort. Well, just like most countries, it's government…you know.

We found relief at the next pit stop, our bladders having been tossed about like basketballs against our innards. Of course, some of the guys couldn't hurry as much as they would have liked, but we all emptied the beer and water that had swelled within us during the last few hours. On the way back to the bus, Don pointed to a blue semi-tractor trailer parked near the edge of the graveled lot. We hadn't seen many large trucks on the roads, not open ones, anyway. The trailer was a three-tier model packed with pigs. Pork was a popular food there so it shouldn't have been such a surprise. I hadn't thought about how food-stuffs got to market, assuming that everything might have been procured locally. There was the evidence that not all of it was. I certainly hadn't expected to see a truck full of pigs.

I doubt that Pat was expecting it, either. I don't think I he had much attachment to pigs. Especially after flying with them during his tour in the mid-60s. This is his explanation of his experience:

We were flying resupply missions for ARVN troops that we had inserted earlier somewhere in III Corps. LT Ken Chien was flying left seat and AC; Mr. Sam McGlone, was in the right.

We had loaded some C-rations and ammo, when here comes two ARVNs carrying a live pig. Its feet were tied together with a pole run through them and a rag tied around its snout for a muzzle. They threw it on the ship and went back to their truck and carried two more pigs over and threw them on. I had a feeling that this ain't going to be good. The two ARVNs climbed on board and sat against the firewall between my gunner and me. Now with the supplies and three pigs lying on the floor, there wasn't much room to maneuver in the old "B" model.

Mr. McGlone had the controls and when he picked the helicopter up to a hover, one pig started moving around. An ARVN put his foot on it and it settled down. About the time we got above 2000 feet, the pigs weren't buying this ride and started thrashing around. One pig got its hooves loose and got the rag off its snout. Both ARVNs jumped on it but weren't having any success in corralling it. Somehow, the pig got its front hooves up on the back of the console between the pilots. Its head was beside Mr. McGlone's left elbow; his hand was on the collective.

Very calmly, Mr. McGlone looked down at the pig's head, then looked over to LT Chien and stated, "Chien, shoot that son of a b____."

I could see LT Chien moving around in his seat in front of me, apparently trying to get his pistol out. At this point, I figured I'd better do something before gunplay broke out inside the helicopter.

I yelled on the intercom, "DON'T SHOOT, DON'T SHOOT!" There I am crawling over two other pigs and two ARVNs trying to drag that pig from the console. My main concern was its hooves busting the ADF radio (no rock and roll music).

After a couple of minutes, we finally subdued it. I was about to the point to see if pigs really could fly. The slobbers from the pig wasn't so bad; it was the pig manure all over the floor. I can't remember if my gunner helped or not, he was probably laughing too hard. He did help me clean the ship up later.

I don't think LT Chien would have shot … then again… That was the last time I carried pigs.

About a month later, there were two other helicopters with mine, and we were re-supplying ARVNs again. I spotted two ARVNs carrying a pig toward my chopper. I communicated to them very adamantly that the only way that pig was going on my ship was if I shot it first. They decided to put the pig on the ship behind me. The pilots on that bird weren't very happy, and they let us know about it when we got airborne. Mr. McGlone sympathized with them on the radio, while we were all cracking up laughing.

Finally, at 3:15, we saw an indication that a blue sky still existed beyond the clouds. The landscape brightened, the trees became a radiant green against the rich brown hues of the mountains, and the gloom disappeared. The wind, though, seemed to rise with the sunlight. Conversation picked up its pace and ribald humor was thrown around the bus for a good half hour until we reached Nha Trang, where we stopped at an outdoor coffee pavilion. We were directed to a table on the lower level, the floor covered in large pavers with a knee wall surrounding the dining area. Large thatch-roofed umbrellas planted in the floor shed the earlier mist that had dampened the floor between them.

We were served complimentary iced green tea. Several of us had the fancy for ice cream and we looked over the extensive offerings on the menus. I had difficulty selecting anything from so many. Then I spotted the word coconut. That was it. Coconut ice cream.

I mulled the cold confection around in my mouth for a few seconds. That's as long as it took for me to realize that ice cream in Indochina was not the same as American ice cream. I suppose that was a common mistake many travelers make when visiting a foreign country. It had a peculiar twang to it that I couldn't identify, maybe water buffalo milk. I ate it, but I wasn't going to order it again.

Not all of us ordered ice cream. Pat had selected Vietnamese coffee. Not just coffee, but "Vietnamese" coffee, so the menu read. The waiter brought a glass mug to his table and a metal affair with a saucer-like base and a hinged lid. It looked like one of those small pots that keeps water hot for tea. They were accompanied by a container of ground coffee, a carafe of hot water and a bowl of small ice cubes and a spoon. While he sat there, perplexed at the contraption that looked like a silver travel mug, Truc came up to indoctrinate him in the fine art of brewing Vietnamese coffee.

"You brew your own," he said. "You make as strong as you like."

Pat's quizzical eyes drew Truc closer and he demonstrated the process.

"Coffee go here," he said, placing the metal contraption on top of the glass mug and scooping coffee into the metal cup, about five spoons full of the stuff as if he were going to brew an entire pot. "That enough?" he asked.

Pat merely looked at him, his eyes confused.

"Then hot water."

Pat watched as Truc poured hot water over the coffee grounds and closed the lid. In just a moment, we could see brewed coffee dribbling through tiny holes in the bottom of the metal cup. Several of us watched in fascination as the dark brown, almost black liquid, collected in the bottom of the mug, dribbling like molasses, but thinner.

I thought to myself, that stuff is going to light up him up like a hyperactive mouse on speed. It took several minutes for the brewing to complete, all the time Pat's eyes were glued to the dripping liquid with a mixture of anticipation and trepidation. He finally set the dripping can aside and dropped an ice cube into the coffee. His reaction to the first sip was a twitch of the eyebrows. Then his face took on a Charlie Brown grimace. I wasn't sure if he liked it or not. He confided in me later that the taste was somewhere between melted asphalt and a bad batch of moonshine.

The Muong Thanh Nha Trang Centre Hotel was not far down the street. The bus pulled into the entry drive and we filed into the lobby to check in.

Thom and I took the elevator to the tenth floor. The doors opened onto a hallway as dark as a mineshaft at midnight. No lights. After our eyes acclimated to the darkness, we found our way to room 1011, the number on the door barely visible in the dribble of light coming from a small window at the end of the hallway.

The room was nice enough. At least as good as what we'd had so far. Thom slipped the key card into the slot by the door and the lights came on. The first thing Thom did was to attempt to connect his laptop to the Internet. He'd had trouble with this in Qui Nhon. The problem seemed to follow him. He still couldn't connect. His work on certain projects had to continue through the trip since no one else could take care of them, or so he said. I tried to connect with my phone, and even though the connection was successful, the response was slow. Not just slow, but excruciatingly slow. I had better luck using my phone's data stream.

When I opened the curtains and looked out the window, the re-alization of Vietnam's beauty started to hit home. Water the color of a blue jay's breast, a fleet of fishing boats dotting the surface, silhouettes of sapphire blue mountainous islands on the horizon, with broken gray-ish blue stratus clouds floating in the hazy sky. I had never experienced anything like that when I was stationed there. Only once did I take note of any beauty the country might have had, and that was my initial per-ception of the country during my maiden flight to my unit at Lane Army Airfield. All of the sights on this trip were an allure that had never oc-curred to me. I wondered how I had missed it before. I had been right in front of me. I guess it was because I just never knew or cared to look for it.

The sun fell away early and I looked out of the tenth floor win-dow through the fading light over what part of Nha Trang I could see. The hotel was about a block from the coast and the sea was losing its blue luster. The jumble of buildings that huddled beneath the hotel's summit were crowded into a dense hodgepodge of concrete structures, all of varying heights, and divided by narrows bands of tree-lined streets. Palm trees waved in the strong breeze.

As darkness settled further over the city, I looked out of the window again. I had anticipated a show of glimmering lights below, sparkling along the streets and houses. What I saw was widespread blackness broken only by the tiny points of a few streetlights glistening through the empty void of night. I wondered where all of the people were. The howl from the window told me that the wind was probably still raging. I would find out soon enough when we left for dinner at 6:30.

Truc was sponsoring the dinner; his treat. The eighth of December was the anniversary of the date he joined the North Vietnamese Army in 1974. He showed us pictures of his army days. He was quite a dashing young fellow. One of his many proud moments was when he served as an interpreter for General Giap during a meeting with a German contingent. During the war, the NVA and VC soldiers did not have the means of communicating with the folks back home.

"We no have mail, like you Americans," Truc explained. "Family wait for end of war to know if you were still alive."

Truc showed us a picture he'd had taken of himself after the war.

"I send photo to mother. I stand with arms and legs out, and fingers out. That way she see I am still whole."

He told us we would be eating at a barbeque restaurant and right away, some of the boys began salivating at the thought of real down to earth food. To think that you could get barbequed beef or pork in Vietnam. What a treat it was going to be. I, too, was looking forward to it, but a nagging suspicion hung onto my mind.

People had claimed every table but one at the restaurant. That one had been reserved by Truc. We gathered around it in anticipation of a familiar feast. Waiters filled our glasses and placed pots of hot coals into the three holes along the center of our table and covered them with grates. I sat across from Don, and Pat was on my right, Ken next to him. I could almost feel Pat's excitement of getting what he considered real food for a change.

After the wine had been poured, the parade of food began: raw chicken, which came on a plate. We were to select our morsel of meat and grill it to our liking over the coals. An interesting and fun concept. Then came the shrimp. That's when Pat started to have doubts about the rest of the meal. Someone said, "I thought we were going to get barbeque. What's this shit?"

The next plate contained something I could not identify, small nubbins that looked like discolored chicken, but an almost tubular shape. I thought I heard Pat moan. Don picked up the chopsticks and put a few of the pieces over the coals. We both looked at the things roasting above the glowing embers and wondered how we were to know when they were done. It wasn't long before he made a move to extract one from the fire and I took one off as well. After giving it a moment to cool, I picked up the chopsticks, firmly clasped the thing between them, and took a bite.

I was surprised to find that I had difficulty getting my teeth through it. I finally managed to rip off a piece and began to chew vigorously. It was very much like chomping down on a foul-flavored gummy bear. I was able to get the bite down my throat, then I set the rest of the mess aside to ignore. Someone told us it was squid. I'd never eaten squid. I won't want to again. I later discovered that there is a trick to cooking squid and, obviously, we failed miserably. I still don't want any more of it. It wasn't even on my bucket list, but I was tempted to put it there just so I could have the pleasure of scratching it off.

While all of this was going on, toasts were peppered in between courses and the wine bottle tipped non-stop. Salad came next. I call it salad because I don't know what else to call assorted strange-looking greens. The waiters came by with plates of another kind of meat in chunks, much like chicken nuggets before they are breaded. Once I popped one of the grilled morsels in my mouth, I enjoyed the rich flavor, different, but familiar. It was crocodile. Then another plate of steamed vegetables and kabobs of meat chunks that Pat seemed to take a liking to because someone mentioned that it was probably chicken, although I still detected a stern reservation in his demeanor. Ken had coaxed him into trying it. When I sampled it, I couldn't compare it with anything, but it did have a pleasing flavor. Then tuna. I knew tuna. I knew what it tasted like, but grilled tuna is much better than just tuna.

I looked back at the table and there sat yet another place with something rolled up in banana leaves. "Sea snake," someone yelled across the table. Another moan from Pat. Don and I looked at each other, then at the plate of green rolls. Sea snake? Well, I had eaten rattlesnake without incident and I figured what the hell. Don put several of the rolls over the coals and we watched them cook, the banana-leaf wraps becoming glossy and browning slightly.

"How long do we cook these?" Don asked.

I looked at him, surprised that he would ask me such a thing. I didn't know any more about it that he did. I shrugged and said, "I guess till they're done."

He smiled and almost laughed. We watched a bit longer then he looked at me again.

"I think they're ready," he said.

We each took one. I unwrapped mine to find a small roll of light colored meat. I hesitated grasping it with my chopsticks, but it eventually found its way to my mouth. I took a bite and considered what I was chewing. It was almost flavorless, but it did have a kind of revolting taste, grainy, like nothing I'd ever sampled. It was almost as bad as the liver that I detested. Another one for the bucket list. No more sea snake.

Much to Pat's delight, we made it to the beef and pork, both tasty. They were followed by clams. And this is where I felt akin to Pat. No, I didn't think I could do that. Like Pat, I don't eat anything that isn't dead and I don't eat anything that crawled when it was alive. That includes oysters, escargot, and now, clams. It didn't matter to me that they weren't alive. No.

So that was a Vietnamese barbeque. Although not what any of us had expected, they *did* have the rudiments of the barbeque there. It's just that they weren't quite the same as how we Americans would do it. We finished of the night with a final toast.

When we left the restaurant, there was a flurry of talk about the meal.

Ken came up to Pat and got his attention.

"You know that chicken you ate?"

Pat turned to look at him with those confused eyes of his.

"It was ostrich," Ken told him, laughing.

When we returned to the hotel. I called my wife again, then Thom and I settled in to read until we were sleepy. The next day we would travel to Phan Thiet, passing through Cam Ranh, a place I had been several times during my tour of duty. Like Tuy Hoa, I looked forward to seeing it again, although I had a feeling I wouldn't see much I would recognize.

CHAPTER 11

PHAN THIET, FIRST NIGHT

Wednesday, 9 December, 2015

It was nearly 6:00 and I was starving. Morning light seeped around the edges of the draperies and I looked over at Thom, still asleep. Breakfast started at 6:30 and I was down at the restaurant by 6:15. I was late. It appeared as though the entire population of the hotel had beaten me there and they were all jammed together like an army chow line.

I grabbed a plate and scanned the buffet of Vietnamese dishes, soups, breads, eggs, and drinks. What surprised me was the chicken curry and lasagna. For breakfast, I thought? What the hell. I took some chicken curry and by the time I headed for my table, food was dripping from the edge of the too-small plate.

As many varieties that sat on the buffet, and I'm not saying that I didn't like the Vietnamese food, but I would have given anything about then for a big, southwestern omelet with hash browns, sausage, and whole wheat toast. I might have been able to get something like that back at the egg station, but my plate was full by the time I got near it. And even though I relished the Vietnamese coffee, I longed for a big cup of Joe; big enough that I would know I was drinking coffee. The small cups used in the restaurants were a nuisance. You barely took two sips and had to refill the darned thing. If I was going to drink coffee, I was going to do it right.

Just as Tom Baca and Jack came in, I left them my table and went back to the room. Through the window, the rising sun reflecting off the water nearly blinded me. The sea looked as if a white sheet had been pulled up to the shoreline. Scattered clouds covered an already crystalline blue sky, and beneath, the sheen of white waves, barely visible, nudged the beach.

I looked across the town and several of the taller hotels, 12 stories or such, popped up along the coast. Mountains, softened by the diaphanous haze, rose from the horizon. I thought it was odd that little

119

traffic filled the roads. I snapped a photo with my phone and posted it to Facebook. That way my friends and relatives could keep track of my whereabouts.

At 9:00 we departed Nha Trang. We stopped at a small store where Truc purchased two bags of "VC lunches." On the way through the city on Highway QL1 along the coast, at that time of the day the beach was nearly deserted except for a solitary surfer, the first we had seen.

The lack of traffic control devices allowed us to zip along the streets without delay. Before we left the city, though, Truc promised us a stop at a coffee store so we could purchase some authentic Vietnamese coffee. Phong pulled to the curb in front of the Me Trang Coffee Store and the coffee connoisseurs tramped inside anticipating the rich, robust beans and powders that they would be taking home to pour into their coffee makers. The woman at the counter was all too pleased to help. Most of the fellows bought what was called "Weasel" coffee. The origin of the beans is that they are first consumed by a weasel, or civet, fermented by enzymes from the weasel's digestive tract, then excreted. Obviously, production of this kind of bean is very limited, as is reflected by the price, about $15.00 per 250 grams, or a half pound, even higher in other countries. The Weasel coffee has a peculiar mellow flavor that is cherished by serious coffee drinkers.

Although I enjoy good coffee, I opted for the Arabica coffee for about $5.00 per 250 grams. I figured I could always order "weasel" coffee later on-line if I felt a sudden pang of exaltation.

With our precious stores stuffed in the overhead racks, we made it back to the highway and skirted the mountains that bordered the South China Sea. The water, clear and calm, continually changed color from blue to green and back as the four-lane road climbed, then descended.

It was 10:00 before we approached Cam Ranh. A huge U. S. military base had been located at Cam Ranh Bay during the war. It had served as an airfield, supply depot, and processing center for troops entering and leaving the country. The several times I had been there I'd seen little more than a tent city, a sea of olive drab adjacent to a sea of blue. Sand stretched as far as I could see, and no matter where I had walked, it found its way into my boots, shoes, or whatever else I had worn. It was also hot. Except for a few occasions during the monsoon season, it was hot. Always hot. Especially on the sand that seemed to reflect and reradiate the suns deadly rays.

As I looked out the window of the bus cruising by mile after mile of sandy beach, it was hard to forget that first time I stepped off the plane at Tan Son Nhut Air Base in January of 1971 onto the fetid tarmac swarming with fumes from jet fuel and tar, cooked by the blazing sun into an anesthetic that would dull my mind to that of an emotionless automaton. The heat itself had been enough to numb my body into a spiritless mass of lethargic flesh; but the sun...oh, the sun. It bore down with the resolve of the Devil and leached the moisture from every pore in my body. That, I would never forget. The heat at Cam Ranh was not quite that severe, but my aging body didn't know much difference.

We passed by dunes that blocked the view of the sea from the road and patches of vegetation that dotted the beaches. Two large hotels were under construction on the beach. No work was currently being done on them, and the floor slabs hovered in the air, stacked like fallen dominoes, waiting for completion.

Then the commercial airport at the bay came into view where the military air base once spread out across the sand, but no one could recognize anything about it. Everything looked so different. No tents, no Quonsets, no revetments for aircraft, and no Hueys flying around. What was there 44 years ago had since rotted, been dismantled or moved. Even though what we saw was new to us, that didn't stop the déjà vu that forced me to remember, as best I could, what used to be.

As we left Cam Ranh behind, the mountains became more scattered, farther inland, away from the coast. The customary chatter on the bus seemed to have receded to dull mumbles, and the guys sat rooted in their seats like the road-weary travelers that they were. Many were occupied with whatever held their interest on their phones. In spite of the cool air inside our bus, even a short pit stop did little to invigorate anyone.

Road construction had obliterated much of the highway the farther south we traveled, leaving long stretches of nothing but gravel-covered holes and dips that gave the bus a kind of roller coaster effect. The workers we saw sluggishly moving the road toward some state of completion wore no protective gear, such as reflective vests or helmets. I had been so conditioned in America to the forest of traffic cones and maze of barriers at construction sites, that I was puzzled by the absence of all of that when I looked out the windows. There was little to indicate the idea of building a road other than the construction itself. No speed limits, no warnings, nothing. Of course, the speed limits were not that high anyway on pavement that was barely passable, being a mere 60 kph, or about 37 mph, not enough to get a car's engine broken in. I imagine American drivers would go nuts trying to keep their feet off the accelerators. That might not be an issue, however, because I did not see one policeman or the presence of law enforcement anywhere on the highways. But then, maybe I just wasn't looking.

At last, lunch. We all poured out of the bus in search of the facilities we had come so keenly to depend on. A bus full of 70-year old codgers doesn't pass up opportunities to unload, relieving the agonizing pressure in the aging bladders.

The restaurant was more or less the shell of a building with no interior finish work, only the inside surface of painted concrete block stem walls and metal paneling. We were told the restrooms were in the back, behind the restaurant.

The small building, located next to a chicken coop, was three tiny cubicles, each with a squat toilet. Now, if you're not familiar with the squat toilet, it is a china bowl type affair set at floor level. Unlike western toilets, you must place your feet on either side of the bowl and squat over it aiming with meticulous accuracy. There are usually instructions somewhere in the cubicle, but they take more time to read than it does to actually do your business and leave. Needless to say, being the macho male that I am, I merely aimed for the bowl and let her rip. I don't recall seeing any signs that said, "Employees much wash their hands before returning to work."

After we had disposed of all the water we had drunk on the way there, we ambled back toward the restaurant. That's when I noticed the fellow coming out of the chicken coop with two chickens held by their feet in each hand, wings flapping the air. He was moving toward the rear of the restaurant, an open porch affair. Just after he went inside, I heard a cacophony of squawking. No doubt, he was preparing someone's lunch. Fresh poultry, roost to plate. I felt fortunate that Truc had brought our VC lunches.

None of us were strangers to chickens, especially those who had grown up on farms or in rural areas. Then there was Pat Matheny.

Aside from pigs, he had also flown with the chickens in Vietnam and had gained valuable insight into the bird's capability of flight, as given in the following account:

We were solo flying direct combat support (we called them milk runs or pigs and rice missions) for the Phouc Vinh sector. My aircraft commander (AC) CW2 Sam McGlone, was in the right seat; don't remember who was in the left. We'd been flying since around 0600 (sunrise) and they had kept us pretty busy all morning. Around noon, we landed back at Phouc Vinh and were shutting down to eat. This was one of the few places in III Corps where we could get a hot meal, although we had to pay for it.

An American, unknown rank, came up to the ship and said that there was important disposition for us to pick up at III Corps soccer field back at Bien Hoa. We knew U.S. and ARVN top brass were having a big meeting at Phouc Vinh, although we weren't involved. With the urgency in the guy's voice, we figured it had to do with their meeting. Hell, maybe it was an important message from LBJ; we could be making an historic flight! Mr. McGlone wasn't very happy, but said, "Okay, let's go, fellows." We took off for Bien Hoa and landed on the numbered panel they told us to. An American with two ARVNS pulls up in a ¾-ton truck. The ARVNs got two crates of chickens out of the back and were carrying them to my ship.

I asked the American, "What's this?"

He said the ARVN general at Phouc Vinh wanted fresh chicken for supper.

I swung my lip mike out toward the American, keyed the mike and said, "Would you mind repeating that?"

When Mr. McGlone heard this, he came unglued. Now we might have picked up something else, but this is all that I recall. So, we take off for Phouc Vinh.

When we get up to altitude, Mr. McGlone asked me on the intercom if chickens could fly. I said, yeah, for a short distance. He said, "Let's see how they do from 3000 feet." I said, "Okay" and motioned for my Gunner, McBee, to give me a hand and we both unbuckled. I think there were four chickens in each crate. We get one crate open and I catch one by its legs and pulled it out. There were feathers everywhere. I finally got my hands wrapped around its wings to keep it from flapping. Mr. McGlone slowed down to 60 knots and I threw the first chicken out. It flapped its wings about four times and then gravity took over. We lost sight of it before it hit the trees. Mr. McGlone said, try it again; so I threw another chicken out, same result. Then I threw the other two out for good measure.

Now I've got an empty crate and have to get rid of the evidence, plus, I have a spinning tail-rotor behind me that doesn't like to be disturbed. Nervously, on my knees in the doorway, I threw the crate downward as hard as I dared and still about fell out. Now, my legs are shaking from the near disaster.

We land at Phouc Vinh, shut down, and were waiting to tie the main rotor down, when an American came over.

He looked inside the ship and, seeing only one crate, asked "Is that all there is?"

I looked him straight in the eye and said, "That's all they gave me," while feathers were still floating around inside the ship.

I always hoped that general choked on that chicken. When I went through aviation school, Uncle Sam figured it cost $500 an hour to operate a UH-1. That ARVN General got $750 worth.

We found a couple of tables surrounded by blue, plastic chairs, or what I would consider lawn furniture. Other diners were enjoying their lunches while food bits and chicken bones lay scattered about the concrete floor. Not high on ambience, it was out of the sun and a large floor fan provided a decent breeze to keep the air moving. Oddly enough, I couldn't detect any unpleasant odor except for a familiar smell: the heavy bouquet that only frying can impart to the air filled room, with a redolence of Quik-Trip cuisine.

Truc broke out the sandwiches and those who felt the need for a beer, which was most of us, grabbed a warm can of "333" from the box at the end of the table. Then I sank back into the harsh curves of the plastic chair and took in the rustic appeal of the place while munching on the bread, vegetables, and whatever kind of meat product was inside of the sandwich. The chicken bones on the floor lent an air of crude charm, the kind that evolves from a picnic in the woods.

It still surprised me that we could stop at a restaurant, use their facilities, bring our own food, and still be welcome. Well, we did purchase drinks. The country was just amazing.

Milling around outside after lunch, we bore the brunt of the sun's heat, a mere 88 degrees that felt like 100. We were glad to get back on the road in the comfort of air conditioning where we returned to our mumbling and Internet surfing, anticipating our next stop at Phan Thiet.

We passed several power plants along the way. Truc informed us that they were mostly geothermal plants, built by the Russians in the 60s and 70s. The Russians had made many improvements to Vietnam's infrastructure and invested heavily in the country. It appeared more so in the south than in the north.

The scenery had changed from the northern part of the country. Vegetation was more scarce on the mountainsides, their slopes bearing more rocks than trees. Even though parts of the highways were superior to those in the north, much of them were under construction and nearly impassible in places.

About two hours from Phan Thiet, I noticed a wind farm in the distance. I had seen their growing population in western Oklahoma, their giant blades swooping around in large circles, almost a novelty in the barren fields and pastures. But these were the first I had seen in Vietnam.

We soon departed Highway QL1 and ventured down a coastal road that was newly built and still under construction in places. I noticed resorts on the coast and not a lot of traffic. We passed building after building, all modern, tall, with crisp landscaping. The closer we got to Phan Thiet, the denser they became. Phan Thiet must have been a popular vacation spot.

We stopped at the Muong Thanh Mui Ne Hotel, a five-story resort tucked between two others. We would be in Phan Thiet for two days and Truc told us we would have the evening free to do as we pleased. The room Thom and I drew was large, simply furnished, but comfortable, an exterior door that opened onto a communal veranda that connected all of the rooms on that floor. We stepped outside to take in the inviting spectacle that lay before us. Behind the hotel sat a lush garden beneath a forest of palm trees and a walk that meandered its way toward a beachside swimming pool with a swim-up bar. Beyond, through the trees, I could see the bright blue South China Sea beckoning us like a painting on the wall.

It was mid-afternoon and Thom and I immediately donned our swim trunks and rushed to the beach. After a brief stop at the poolside bar to chat with Dennis, Duane, Jack, and Tom Baca, we got towels from the fellow at a small booth beside the bar and found a couple of lounge chairs unoccupied at the far end of the row. After dumping our gear, we hit the water.

I was never one for swimming in the ocean. The salt in the water was not my friend. But the moment I plunged through the white surf into the cyan swell of the sea, I lost any notion of time or place. The silky water cooled my skin and things I had worried about were no longer important. Things I wanted to forget, no longer seemed threatening. I swam out a short distance from shore, the water streaming through my fingers, my body surging over the surface. Even the slight stinging in my eyes did not dampen the exhilaration that had just erased all of the unsettled feeling that had consumed my mind during the last few days. So many memories, so many doubts, so many questions.

I stopped and stood on the bottom, the water about shoulder height and the cool sand pushing through my toes. I breathed in the fresh scent of the salty sea. Thom was beside me, the usual goofy smile on his face.

"This is fantastic," I volunteered. "A bit salty, though."

"The water is perfect," he said. "A lot calmer than the California coast."

"I could get used to this," I told him. I looked back at the thatched umbrellas on the shore, other guests lazing on the chaise lounges or in the sand. "Two days of this."

"And I plan to make the most of it," he said.

About that time, we saw a parasail in the distance. I pointed to it.

"There you go, Thom." I looked at him. "You ought to be up there."

"I wish I was." He was staring at the parachute with what I figured was envy. "You ever try it?"

"Hell no," I said. "I don't think much of parachutes. Much less being pulled around by a boat."

"I wonder where it is."

"What?" I asked.

"The boat."

We finally spotted it, a mere spec on the horizon.

126

"Did you ever swim in the ocean when you were here?" he asked.

"No," I said. "I never left Lane except when I had to. Some of the guys would traipse out the local villages or hitch rides to Qui Nhon, but I never had the inclination to do that. They usually wound up in the line at sick call afterward for a dose of penicillin."

"I never did, either," he said. "I never figured out what the big deal was."

"Well, the only time I went anywhere was on a mission or group excursions. I guess I was a loner."

"Yeah," he said. "I was too."

The sun warmed my shoulders and the small, cool waves lifted me gently at times, setting me back down onto the sandy bottom.

I found that Thom was a water person. Living in California on the banks of a river, he made frequent outings in his boat with his family.

We heard a roar and turned to see a fellow fire up a jet ski and shoot away from the shore. He turned a small circle, sending waves billowing onto the sand, then headed out to sea. After only a brief run, he sped back toward us standing on the runners, his nose in the air as if he had just won the Grand Prix. He rode it onto the bank and let it skid to a stop in the sand, then got off and swaggered up the hill toward the pool.

"I've ridden one of those things," Thom said.

I figured as much, since he owned a boat. He also told me he like water skiing and snow skiing. That's what surprised me.

"Ever try it?" he asked.

"I tried water skiing when I was 15 years old. Never was able to capture the idea. Jet ski? No. I just never saw the point of it all."

When I looked at him, I could see that smile again, the one that told me he was laughing at my lackadaisical attitude toward water sports.

We swam back to the shore, rinsed off the salt at the shower point, then headed for the bar. Some of the other fellows were still there, with reinforcements.

Thom ordered a mango smoothie. The two girls at the bar seemed to be a bit flustered by his request. After some discussion, they managed to gather the ingredients and the blender roared.

I asked one of the girls for a Scotch and water. I'd had my doubts about their efficacy at bartending, but a Scotch and water seemed to throw them into total confusion. I didn't think it was all due to the language barrier. I pointed to a bottle of Scotch on a shelf behind her. She looked at it as if she had never seen Johnnie Walker Black before. I pointed to it again and motioned pouring a bottle of water into a glass. Still nothing. Another woman appeared, who looked like a supervisory type, and I went through my pantomime again. The fourth try met with success and I walked away with a hearty glass of the magic elixir. I learned that effective communication in Vietnam takes patience.

We grabbed a table to the side of the boisterous group.

"So, what did you think of Vietnam?" he asked.

"I'm still not sure we did any good," I told him.

"You know, I feel the same way."

"I just never saw the point of it all," I said. "We kept guys alive so they could die later."

"Well, I like to think I saved some of them."

"Yeah, you guys were something else."

It was comforting to know that we both had doubts about the effect our presence was having at the time on the war, and those doubts had plagued us during our entire tours. I'd never talked to anyone about many the confessions we made to each other, and it weighed heavily on my pride and dignity that I was not alone in thinking the way I did. Few Vietnam vets discussed their feelings about the war due to the general ignorance of people about that time in our history. We wanted to avoid encounters with folks who might question the validity of our service to our country. We still do, at times.

I had done a lot of thinking on this trip, and the muse just wouldn't go away. Since several of the guys had been stationed at Bien Hoa, I figured they had a pretty large area of operation. Where the central highlands was, in the central part of the country between Cambodia and the South China Sea with tall mountain ranges to the west, Bien Hoa was farther south in a more varied geography. I wondered what it had been like to fly there, compared to the tornadic winds in the mountains. The weather was bad at time in II Corps, and I figured it might be just as bad down south.

Tom Baca, who had been stationed at Bien Hoa, had flown near there during the war on several missions. According to him:

There was a Special Forces Camp at Dong Xoai in Phước Long Province, South Vietnam, Shortly after, I was given aircraft commander status (6 weeks after arrival in Vietnam), I was told to pick up several field grade officers at the 5th Special Forces helipad and transport them to Dong Xoai. I had never been to Dong Xoai, but it was on the map so I figured we could find it. The biggest concern was the weather. It was terrible. Very low ceilings, low visibility and rain.

We went to the helipad to pick up our passengers. I landed and told the folks waiting that I was there to take them to Dong Xoai. It was noisy, wet and our passengers gave us a thumbs up, so we took off. As we headed north, the weather got worse. Maybe ¾ mile visibility, and the ceiling was about 200-300 feet. I tuned in several different non-directional beacons to keep an idea of where we were. When you are low-level and flying with only a tactical map in low visibility it was easy to get lost.

The distance to Dong Xoai from our take off location was about 50 miles. Back then it seemed like a long way. Today it doesn't. When you are travelling very slowly (40 knots) so you don't outrun your visibility, it turns into a long trip. The further north we flew the more the terrain went from relatively flat to hills covered in jungle. The tops of the hills were pretty much obscured in rain and fog. The tops of many trees could not be seen. I glanced back at the passengers and they were busy looking at maps and talking. I was not sure I could get them to Dong Xoai. We are now down to a 100' ceiling and one half mile visibility. This was not where you wanted to run out of fuel or land because of bad weather. The enemy was there.

After 1 hour and twenty minutes we stumbled into Dong Xoai. Damn good navigation on my part. Scary yet fulfilling that I had successfully completed my mission. I set the aircraft down, turned around to see my passengers with a puzzled look on their face. They wanted to know where we were. I told them Dong Xoai. They said they did not want to go to Dong Xoai, they expected to go to Lai Khe, which was due east from our departure point, not Northwest. I showed them my mission sheet. I told them prior to departure we were the aircraft to Dong Xoai. They said they didn't hear me.

Well nobody died on this mission. Although I thought about doing serious injury to the O-7 in the back. This flight was difficult, dangerous and absolutely a waste of time.

I have lots of other war stories with bullets, mechanical failures and tragedy. But for some reason this flight was always the one I thought of when thinking how stupid war can be to its participants.

The afternoon wore into evening and Thom and I bared many pictures of our lives to each other, the confidence assured that neither of us would be judgmental of the other. We understood each other and offered no advice, accepting each other for who we were.

There was no group dinner planned, so Thom and I spotted a place across from the hotel and wandered in. Thom had to stop in front to view the samples of seafood available that were on display. He was craving lobster and there, right in front of his eyes in a small tank, was a big fellow just waiting to be cooked. He was sold.

Thom joked with the little waitress about cooking the thing. I ordered some kind of pho, I don't recall exactly. Whatever it was, it was hellaciously good. I wish I knew the secret to Asian cooking that made it so tasty. The American versions of it just weren't the same. Thom swore that his lobster was better than my pho. Although I had serious doubts, I acquiesced to his sudden exuberance.

When we got to the hotel, we found that some of the less adventurous guys elected to eat in the hotel's restaurant. Pat was ecstatic. He'd had his first cheeseburger since leaving the U. S. I was happy for him, of course, but at the same time I felt sorry for his missed opportunity to sample authentic Vietnamese cuisine. Some folks just weren't meant for it, I suppose.

Thom tried to log into the Internet with his computer. He had limited success. I was writing notes for this book. Then he got up and pulled from his luggage a copy of "Boy's Life." I was stunned. I used to read that magazine when I was in boy scouts, some…well, a long time ago.

"Light reading?" I asked him.

"I love this magazine," he said. "Have you ever read it?"

I explained about the childhood I had outgrown.

"I think it's great," he said. "I love the jokes."

Then he proceeded to quiz me on the riddles he read from the back pages. They were still as corny as I remember, but I did recall how clever they had seemed at the time I had first read them as a boy.

It surprised me that he could be so enamored with a holdover from our youth, still enthralled by the stories and cheesy jokes that appealed to young boys. I had to admire him for not letting go of that simple pleasure; retaining a semblance of a young mind. I liked to think that I did too, but then I realized that no, I had left much of it behind after Vietnam. I wondered, then, if that's what had caused such a shift in my maturity and if I had taken Vietnam too seriously. But after a moment of reflection, I thought, how could anyone *not* take it seriously?

Tomorrow, Truc would take us to a local fishing village for a taste of true Vietnamese life. So far, what I'd seen of that life had been from the windows of a bus. I couldn't wait to step out among the locals and see how they lived in this region.

CHAPTER 12

PHAN THIET, SECOND NIGHT

Thursday, 10 December, 2015

By 8:30 in the morning, we were on our way to a fishing village at Mui Ne. The sun was already bearing down as if someone up there had ignited a blowtorch. I knew it wasn't as hot as I remembered it being in 1971, but age makes things feel more intense, even emotions. Something had kept my mind occupied with Vietnam over the last 44 years, but then that's what this trip was all about. It was working, whatever it was. Having established a connection with all of these vets on this trip, I felt more at ease with myself than I had in decades.

I watched through the window as the bus bullied its way through a narrow street skirting the shore, the smaller vehicles readily giving way. Phong parked alongside a short rock wall that separated the roadway from the beach area. I looked down toward the water, some 50 feet below, at the gathering of people and boats; it was as if all of the energy of Vietnam was concentrated right there on this quarter mile of beachfront, fishermen busy with their boats and nets, vendors sorting through the catch for what they would offer their customers that day, and curious onlookers milling around the sorting areas.

The instant I stepped off the bus, I met that energy head on when I was nearly blasted back through the door by the stringent stench that rose from the spoils scattered about the sand below us on the beach. I stifled the impulse to vomit and followed the guys down the long stretch of concrete steps that led to the center of the emanated miasma and the flurry of life.

The greenish-blue water of the bay was filled with a glut of boats and what looked like floating hot tubs. As I reached the bottom and ventured into the midst of the fierce activity, I examined some of the turquoise-colored craft. The circular vessels, about eight feet in diameter, looked like giant fiberglass spheres that had been cut in half. A thick, molded rim around the edge formed a gunwale with a socket that bore a

133

Vietnamese flag. The ones in the water bobbed about like fishing corks, the pilot of each small craft leaning over the edge pulling up a net.

Some of the tubs were equipped with a small engine and a tiny propeller driven by a shaft that protruded through a tube in the hull. I could see several of the fishermen hauling in nets with what looked like sea urchins and other small creatures. No matter what the catch, it was brought to the beach and dumped onto tarps or blankets and sorted into metal and plastic tubs. Tourists flocked around them in hopes of purchasing the fresh catch, or just watching out of curiosity. I'm sure many of the fishermen would be selling their catch to local restaurants and shops across the street.

With so much activity, it was difficult to take in everything that was happening. A young boy, about 9 or 10, zeroed in on us with a tray full of shells and jewelry, his feet clad in thongs, and wearing light blue shorts, dark blue tee shirt, and an orange cap. We all turned to look at him, his infectious smile hard to ignore. Dennis, Duane, Don, and Tom Horan warmed up to him, and the boy actually made a couple of sales. Dennis, in jest, referred to him as his son and photos were taken of the two, the boy smiling as if he had found his long lost brother.

I took time to just stand and look around. Fishermen in their baseball-style caps lugged their tubs ashore and pulled their nets out, depositing the day's catch. Women in their conical straw hats, squatted by the tarps. Sorting the catch, grabbing eels before they slithered off in the sandy beach, or dropping urchins and fish into assorted metal and plastic tubs. Prospective buyers stood anxiously by. Some women had begun transporting their fresh goods up the long rise of steps toward the shops that lined the street above.

Several shanties with tarps for roofs, stood at the back side of the beach in front of the slope that led up to the road. Litter covered the sand, paper, plastic, miscellaneous fish parts, and random trash. I had overcome the initial shock of the pungent fetor that had smacked me in the face when I stepped off the bus. Now it was merely the dull fumes of decay that sent my nasal passages into a kind of throbbing fit. Fortunately, Truc motioned us uphill back toward the road.

Back on top, I saw a woman squatting by a young pine tree just inside the short wall. A white bucket sat beside her, a cell phone to her ear. I had to wonder if everyone in that country had a cell phone. It sure seemed like it.

Truc led us along the street till we dived into a narrow passage, more like an alley, following a fellow with a plastic bag of fish swinging at his side. I was surprised to see some rather nice homes along our path. The constricted street was the only avenue in or out. I thought it strange that people would choose to live in such a secluded place with limited means of egress. I mean, how does one carry in all of the groceries, or move furniture in and out? There I was again, trying to superimpose my own standards of civilization on those of the Vietnamese. I had forgotten that I was not in America.

The fellow ducked into an opening in a fence to the right. We followed.

The first thing I saw was an army of large clay pots, about three feet tall and just as wide, the kind you might be tempted to plant a shrub in. Each had a colorful conical metal lid. At the base of each pot, a small clear tube emptied into a two-liter plastic soft drink bottle shored up against the pot with a brick.

It was explained that fish parts are layered with salt in the pots, with the addition of lime or lemon and maybe vinegar, and various vegetables for flavoring. The brew is left to ferment for about six months. The effluent drains from the bottom, leaving the clear nuoc mam sauce on top. The more it is filtered by draining, the better the sauce.

We had all known about nuoc mam, and we all had mixed feeling toward this fishy smelling sauce that the Vietnamese consume as if it were an elixir. The one exposure I'd had to during my Vietnam tour of duty was enough to bar me from ever smelling it again. I discovered that I had been a bit hasty in my assessment of it.

Tom Horan opened one of the pots and leaned over it. I guess the smell wasn't too bad because he didn't flinch or show any signs of distress. Inside the pot, blackish blobs sat in a pool of shit-colored stagnant fluid. It reminded me of some of bayous I'd seen around Lafayette, Louisiana, when I had lived there, only without the green overtones.

During our brief visit, I heard the constant clicking of camera shutters and dull murmurs about previous encounters with nuoc mam. I had let my mind briefly drift back to the Montayard village I had visited in 1971. I was unaware at the time that it was the fermentation process I had smelled and not the finished product. How naive I was.

We all left, a little more informed about Vietnamese culture and cuisine. We followed single file back through the alley to the main street where vendors squatted in front of shops with washtubs full of fresh seafood and fish. The diverse offerings, some of which I hadn't seen before, were somewhere between bizarre and disgusting. I saw a tub full of squid, which immediately brought to mind my unpleasant introduction at the barbeque restaurant. There were lobsters, of course, and sea snake, eel, crabs, a variety of fish, and except for the octopus, things I didn't recognize. I was never one to get excited about seafood, except for lobster and shrimp which I found to be just okay, and after seeing the sidewalk displays, it only hardened my case against it. Some of the shops along the sidewalk had glass cases in front displaying a variety of fish and seafood, fried or boiled or whatever they did to it. The ultimate in fast food.

Once back at the hotel, Thom and I arranged to have some of our dirty clothes picked up to be laundered, one of the many services offered there. It wasn't long until we heard a knock on the door. We handed over our duds, which the lady dutifully itemized without having to converse in Vietnamese, and we were left on our own. We took the opportunity to head back to the water.

There is something about cool salt water that seemed to pull all of the day's tensions from my body. Not that I had a lot of tension, but my mind had been struggling with all of the extraordinary episodes it had encountered, such as the happy, cordial people, the incredible food, and swarms of vehicles traveling the streets en masse.

The waves were more lively than yesterday, the sun just as bright and cheery, and the breeze just right. When Thom and I had had our fill of the sea, we showered and plunged into the swimming pool. That too, was refreshing. It seemed like most things I did there was refreshing. What a place.

After the pool, we sauntered over to the beachside chaises. All were taken but the last two on one end, but they had no cushions. While we stood there wondering what to do about it, a security guard (I guess that's what he was, since he was in uniform) pointed toward the two empty chairs and brought us cushions for them. Again, I was surprised that a uniformed employee would make such a gesture. In America, catering to the pleasure of guests certainly wouldn't be in a security guard's job description. The folks there were really accommodating.

Along the beachfront, people were stretched out on the lounge chairs like hound dogs basking in the sun, except that some these were wearing bikinis, a pleasant and stimulating sight. A few still hid their precious white skin under the shade of the large, thatch-covered umbrellas. The peace and quiet was complemented by the lull of the surf, slight waves gently rolling onto the sand. I spotted a few of the blue fishing tubs farther down off the beach. Thom and I dragged out our Kindles and spent a glorious rest of the morning reading. I took some time to scribble more notes in my journal.

We were on our own for lunch, so Thom and I ventured across the street to the same restaurant where we'd had dinner the night before. The small tanks in front had the usual display of lobsters along with some kind of fish, eels, and other things I wouldn't have put in my mouth. A waitress, short, petite, with a typical cute Vietnamese face bearing the eternal smile, greeted us, and of course Thom was all too ready to chat with her. I ordered chicken with ginger and onions, and Thom ordered a pizza of some kind that he scarfed down like a famished farmhand. About halfway through Thom's pizza, Don Hooper and Tom Horan joined us. Our foursome seemed to draw other customers. I think the waitresses were happy that we had come in.

Later that afternoon, we were drawn back to the beach and another dip in the sea. As I walked down the stone-paved path, my eyes were glued to the water. The Waves gently rolled under an undulating sheet of blue, not a bright or deep blue, but pale, almost pastel. We found a couple of lounge chairs and set up shop to read and write.

The time passed quietly while I wrote more notes for this book and read a Harry Bosch novel by Michael Connelly. I also took time to think about all of the stupid things I had done when I was young and... well, stupid. It was suddenly easy to take stock of my life and think that things should have turned out better. The term, better, is relative. I had to have something to compare my life to, but then I realized that I didn't. Not even in Vietnam during the war.

Aside from lingering thoughts about my mortality, at night, alone in the lumpy bed, I often wondered how I had managed to put myself into that situation. Of course, being young and lacking the wisdom that I like to think I have now, I had never found an answer. I was like a mouse in a maze with no exit. I just never realized it at the time.

Maybe it was that I had become frustrated with trying to figure out who I had become after all of the years since the Vietnam War, or it might have been the fact that I'd had enough writing and reading. We left our things on our lounge chairs, hurrying across the hot sand to the water, and waded our way out far enough to swim.

The water was cooling and fortifying, a potent antidote to the sun. The temperature was moderate, but the sun's rays still bore down. The intoxicating salty smell of the sea and the water lapping at my chest pulled worries from my mind and I found myself in a state of bliss I had seldom experienced. Well, not since I graduated from college, anyway, when I realized I no longer had to study, take tests, or worry about grades. I had few concerns at the resort, stroking my way through the waves and feeling like a kid again. That is what echoed through my mind: feeling like a kid again. That and the constant puzzle of why it is that as our bodies succumb to the years, our minds still think we are what we used to be. When I swam, I could only go a short distance, thwarted by my body's failing attempt to keep up with what my brain was thinking. There are always disappointments in life, and I've tried my best to endure them; but this one was a difficult challenge.

When we emerged from our plunge in the South China Sea, we headed toward the boisterous commotion beneath the thatched roof of the bar. Some of the fellows had taken up residence at a few of the tables and there was no shortage of cheer. After we showered, we joined the already sloshed group of exalted veterans.

Tom Baca and Sterling had command of one table while Jack and Pat had custody of another. Ed was hovering around the group like a bee looking for something to pollinate. Tom Horan sat at the bar in front of a tonic and lime and the rest had beers in front of them or in their hands. They all looked like they had been flying high for a while. I ordered a beer just so I would fit in. Thom stuck with his bottle of water.

It wasn't long before Ken, Dennis, Duane, and Don joined us. Pat lurked about with his iPad taking videos of us all. No one paid much attention to him; we were too busy imbibing in our "333" beers. Ken sat at the table with Jack and his chair was adjacent to mine. We talked about Vietnam, and I saw in his eyes the same harrowing cloud I had seen on the plane to Incheon. It was tempered by the deceiving smile that had taken root on his face.

"I'm still reading your book," he told me.

That reminded me of the anxiety I got whenever someone told me that. Most writers, I would guess, always wonder what readers think of their work, and I was one of those writers. I know the advice given by publishers, agents, and other writers, tell you to ignore comments about your work. You can't make everyone happy, and readers make inferences from your books and articles according to their own backgrounds and experiences. They're all different, so their take on your writing will be different. If the comments are negative, the author is dispirited. If they are favorable, the author gets the big head. But here were Vietnam vets, all having lived through the same things I had, and they were reading my book. I think if any of them had taken issue with it, I would have been dejected and defeated. So, I listened to what Ken had to say.

"The chapter where you made AC." He leaned over to me. "That was such a good story," he said, his voice low, eyes narrowed and brows down.

I nodded. "Everyone had a day like that at some time. That day was mine."

I remembered that day like it was yesterday. It was one of those rare occasions when a pilot melds with the helicopter in a way that they become one. I could do no wrong. That was my day.

A lot of the pilots grew into good aviators, mastering the Huey with finesse, and commanding their ship as an AC. I think each of us remembered the day we made aircraft commander. Something like that is hard to forget. Jack had remembered one of the first missions he'd had as a new AC:

One of my first combat assaults as an aircraft commander was one of the scariest missions I flew in Vietnam. A senior copilot was flying with me that day. Warrant Officer Lonnie Schmidt was a flight school classmate who joined the Thunderbirds with me. Our mission was to fly combat assaults into rice paddies southeast of Saigon. The formation of 10 Hueys then would break up and spend the rest of the day flying "pigs and rice" support missions. Four UH-1C gunships from our "Bandit" platoon would fly as our escorts during the assaults.

After loading 100 U.S. soldiers onto the lift ships, we headed toward the landing zone. As we began our final approach, the LZ came alive with gunfire. Tracers were flying at us from the ground and the gunships were firing rockets and machine guns toward the edges of the LZ. The rice paddy where we were to drop off the troops was flooded.

During short final, the assault helicopters held their course and glide slope. I was the third aircraft on the right side of a staggered trail formation, so mine was the fifth Huey back. I was about to stop at a hover just above the water. The GIs were sitting in the open doors on both sides of my helicopter, their feet on the skids, ready to jump into the paddy. They would leap any second, we would pull pitch, and the formation would be airborne, on its way to pick up the next load of soldiers.

I glanced back and saw the soldiers inching forward on their butts. They would jump any second now. I turned back forward in time to see the ground suddenly drop below us. We were rapidly climbing straight up. What had happened? I was on the flight controls, but I had not done anything to cause the Huey to climb.

The sudden upward acceleration caught the GIs by surprise and all of them remained on board. Within seconds we were 50-60 feet above the ground. It was now too high for the soldiers to jump without suffering serious injury or death.

I fought to stop the helicopter's climb, but the controls were not working. The vertical climb indicator was pegged straight up, yet, we were carrying a full load of soldiers in field gear. There was no way a UH-1D Huey with 1,100 pounds of shaft horsepower could be climbing at this rate. We passed 100 feet, then 150, 200, now 300. Our climb was not slowing.

"It has to be the fuel governor running wild," I thought. How else could we have received such a massive, instant power surge? I looked at the engine and main rotor tachometer, expecting to see the engine rpm off the chart. But it was registering normal, in perfect synch with the rotor rpm.

Now we were passing 600 feet. With my right hand, I swept the cockpit with the cyclic control. Nothing. I kept pushing down on the collective pitch with my other hand, but the Huey continued to shoot straight up, like a crazy elevator.

At 900 feet, I told Lonnie, "Check your controls. I think mine have been shot out."

Lonnie made the same wide sweeping circle as I had with the cyclic. "I don't have any control, either," he said over the intercom.

"Keep trying," I told him. Nothing. He passed the controls back to me. We now were at 1,100 feet. I knew the Huey would not continue to stay upright. At some point it would invert and we would dive, upside down, into the ground. We had no control over the helicopter's direction, attitude, airspeed, or altitude. It was out of control and continuing its rapid climb.

Around 1,200 feet, I made another sweep of the cockpit with the cyclic. I felt something in the controls, elusive at first. Then, very slightly, I could feel it bite. I must be getting back some control. Not much, but anything was welcome. Resistance from the cyclic started to return. In another 30 seconds, I had regained full command of the aircraft.

I turned the Huey and dove it back toward the landing zone. The other helicopters were about a mile from the LZ, flying back to the pickup point for another load of soldiers. Two of the gunships remained over the LZ, giving cover to the soldiers now on the ground. The other gunships were escorting the 9-ship formation.

My Huey came in fast and shallow, stopping at a hover near a small group of soldiers in the flooded paddy. After the GIs jumped from my aircraft, I took off to rejoin the other assault helicopters. I caught up with the formation just before it began its approach to the pickup point. Foolishly, I flew three more assaults into the LZ that morning with the Thunderbirds.

After the final lift, my aircraft spent the afternoon flying resupply missions. These were dubbed "pigs and rice" missions. When we supported the ARVN or U.S. Special Forces there usually was a pig or two and a load of rice on board the Huey.

I should have taken the Huey to aircraft maintenance to be inspected, but it was flying so well I continued with our missions.

Late that afternoon we returned to Bien Hoa. The day had been hot, so a cold beer would hit the spot. I ordered a San Miguel beer from Duc, the Vietnamese bartender. As I finished my first beer, Warrant Officer Tom Kagan walked up to the bar and bought a $5 book of chits. We didn't use cash at the bar, but paid for our drinks with chits. Beer was 10 cents a bottle; mixed drinks were 15 cents each. Tom tossed the book of chits on the bar, a standard practice when you screwed up on a mission. Everyone at the bar got to drink free while the chits lasted.

"What's that for?" I asked Tom, a former member of my lift platoon who had transferred recently to the gunship platoon.

"You don't know?" he asked. "I thought I shot you down." Tom explained that during a gun run, he fired a 2.75-inch rocket at the edge of the landing zone. However, one of the tail fins didn't open and the rocket veered toward the formation of transport Hueys hovering above the rice paddy. The rocket dropped into the mud under my aircraft, then exploded.

The force of the explosion had powered our wild ride more than 1,200 feet into the air. Fortunately for us, the mud absorbed the shrapnel and the fire from the explosion of the 10-pound warhead. I figured the rocket hit at exactly the right place to send us straight up. Had it exploded slightly behind us, slightly to the front, or on either side under our helicopter, we would have rolled up like a ball or been blown into the other Hueys in the LZ.

Later I learned that on final approach to the landing zone, Lonnie saw a machine gun firing from a bunker in front of us. He called the gunships and directed them to fire on the Viet Cong bunker. It was during this attack that Tom's rocket exploded under our Huey.

"You were in II Corps," Ken said to me. Then he took a healthy swig of his beer and looked my way, glassy-eyed. "What was the worst thing about Vietnam?"

I know I must have blinked my eyes, and I sat there bewildered for a moment. No one had ever asked me that question. I was glad they hadn't. I wouldn't have known how to answer it. But right then, I knew. It came to me as chapters of my book popped into my head.

"The body bags," I told him.

It had come back to me; that long line of body bags in the graves registration building at the Qui Nhon Air Base. Row after row of black bags, neatly aligned and waiting for transport back to the States. I had been investigating a death of an enlisted man at the time, a fool who had thought gasoline would make a good paint thinner while a sparking candle was burning nearby. My mind recalled the nausea that filled my stomach as I wondered then how they had died. It seemed as though we did more to kill ourselves than did Charlie. I tried not to think of all of the times I could have wound up in one of those bags.

That seemed to doom the conversation. He nodded his head and we both knew what it meant and how we felt about it. That's why most of us never said much about the war and were happy that few people had asked about it. It was the things we wanted to forget that made it difficult.

Flying in the mountains, with high winds and turbulence that often left cracks in the tail boom of my ship, I understood how easy it was to make a mistake. A fatal one. Not only for myself, but for the crew as well. We also had flat ground to cover and I never associated a great deal of risk with that kind of flying. But it wasn't about the terrain and weather. It was also about combat. I never knew the fighting was so heavy down south in III Corps.

Several of the guys had been stationed at Bien Hoa and flew around what was then, Saigon. The fellows who had been there had no shortage of tales. Jack had had another rousing experience there in 1967:

August 7, 1967, started quietly enough. That morning we were north of Saigon, flying a military courier from Bien Hoa Airbase to Tay Ninh City when my crew chief came on the intercom.

"Sir, there's a helicopter in trouble. It's going down!" SP4 Charles "Skip" Lyons told me.

I couldn't see the other helicopter because it was behind me, so I asked the crew chief to direct me to the aircraft. Using Lyons's directions, I put my Huey into a rapid descent from 2,000 feet.

Minutes later, as I made a sweeping right turn, I saw the other helicopter for the first time. It was about 100 feet ahead of me. I began overtaking the ship, which was a Huey like mine. I had closed to about 50 feet when the helicopter banked onto its side and dropped to the ground in a patch of grass about 10 feet tall. I saw one of the main rotor blades fly into the air and come back down. Then nothing. I had lost sight of the other helicopter. Not sure where the other Huey was, I landed so the nose of my Huey touched the wall of the grass.

I didn't dare risk hovering blindly through the grass without a firm sighting of the other aircraft. The long flat leaves were tall enough to get tangled in the tail rotor, which would have incapacitated our helicopter.

To my left was an open, dry rice paddy. In the distance, I could see a row of Viet Cong soldiers coming toward us, firing AK-47 assault rifles. Some were firing from hips level as they walked; others would stop, squeeze off several rounds, and then continue walking toward us. They were too far away to get off effective shots.

Lyons jumped from our ship, an M16 assault rifle in hand and wearing his flight helmet. Some 20 feet from our helicopter, his head jerked sharply to one side and he fell to the ground. I was certain an enemy round had struck him. But as I started to unbuckle my seat belt to drag him back aboard, Lyons stood up.

"I forgot to disconnect the damn intercom cord," he yelled.

He had run so fast that when he reached the end of the cord, the tightened line had pulled him off his feet.

As the Viet Cong came closer, their gunfire forced Lyons behind a rice paddy dike. We wouldn't be able to remain exposed much longer. In the meantime, Lyons had taken up a defensive position.

I thought about leaving the aircraft to look for survivors, though I doubted there was enough time. I also thought about making a high hover through the grass. As I weighed the options, a pair of hands parted the grass directly in front of me. My heart came to a momentary halt. It restarted when I saw the hands belonged to the other helicopter's aircraft commander who had led his crew to us.

I waved the four crewmen aboard our aircraft and then told Lyons to hop on. With all on board, I hovered our helicopter backwards, away from the grass. I then did a fast hover forward and eased the bird over a stand of trees along a nearby riverbank.

The trees now were between the Viet Cong and us. I gathered airspeed over the river, and then pulled the ship into a rapid cyclic climb.

After reaching 1,000 feet, we circled back over the downed helicopter. I wanted to be certain no one had been left behind. I had not yet had time to visit with the aircraft commander or his crewmembers.

None of the downed crewmen appeared to be wounded or injured. However, I decided to fly them to the 93rd Evacuation Hospital at Long Binh to be checked out. I later learned they all were okay.

On the way to the hospital, I asked the aircraft commander for his unit's radio frequency so I could call his commanding officer. When I told the CO I had picked up the crew, there were several seconds of silence. "Christ, I didn't know they were down," he told me.

It turned out the unit had made a combat assault into a landing zone where the enemy was massed in a live-fire exercise. Some of the helicopters had been shot down on approach, while others had been downed on departure. The bird we had followed to the ground was the only one that had gotten out of the LZ. However, it was badly shot up and didn't get far.

The next day I was told to take my crew to the main U.S. military base at Tay Ninh for an awards ceremony. After we landed, the crewmembers we had rescued rushed over to us and began shaking our hands and thanking us. They then escorted us to their battalion area.

A general pinned medals on us and other flight crews. That day I received a Distinguished Flying Cross and each of my crewmen got an Air Medal with "V" device for valor.

For days after the rescue, Lyons would ask me: "Did you see the look on the face of the courier when he thought I had been shot?"

Over the years, I've wondered if it was simply luck when Lyons saw the helicopter going down. I don't know how the Viet Cong soldiers could have missed us as they advanced firing their weapons. I also don't know if I would have been able to help the other crew had any of them been trapped in their Huey or been wounded. Fortunately, things fell into place for us very quickly, even though the rescue seemed to last a long time.

I know many other helicopter pilots who flew similar missions during the war. Some were awarded medals. Many others were never recognized.

The banter between Ken and I resumed and had reached toward folly, the beer taking its toll on our senses. I had been so absorbed in the frivolity that I was unaware that the group around us had become more animated and rowdy. Even Ed had abandoned his post by a column and was circulating among the tables with his gruff reflections on our trip. It had been several beers since I had set down at the table and even more so for the rest of them. Then Ken pulled out his phone and a small speaker.

"I think we need some party music," he said. "Sixties. I've got a bunch on my phone."

He looked at the bar in hopes of finding someplace to set the speaker. With a little help from the bartender, music blared forth over the tables. The metamorphosis was instantaneous. Our band of tottering, balding, and near decrepit old farts, our youth exhausted by life, had regressed into the abysmal behavior of the happy-go-lucky, immature drunkards that we all once were in Vietnam. The sing-alongs became louder and more robust, beers waving in the air. It was like a pack of old hound dogs howling at a squirrel they had treed.

My own metamorphosis was taking place as I sat there howling along with the Animals singing, "We've Gotta Get Out of This Place," one of the staple songs of the Vietnam era. Of course, our fitful rendition of the song was a tribute to what we had experienced. None of us wanted to leave that resort, or Phan Thiet. It was like a paradise, a place that could reshape even the most callous and bitter mind.

Ken and I continued to chat about our lives. The subject of college arose.

"I went through warrant officer school," he said. "I was in college for a while, but I wasn't paying attention to studying. My grades got so low I finally gave up and enlisted."

I laughed and said, "I knew what I wanted to be ever since junior high, and that's what I concentrated on. I had a tough course load with architectural engineering and ROTC on top to that."

Jack volunteered his own history. "I lost my deferment and enlisted. I didn't have a degree when I went over."

"Well," Ken said, "you brainy guys could do that. I like to party too much."

We looked at each other and I finally broke the stare-down.

"You know, it's amazing that after all of these years I can still find it possible to talk to slackers like you."

They both froze for an instant, then Ken's eyes widened and a grin plastered itself across his face just before he broke out laughing in the way a drunkard exaggerates a moment of levity. I imagine my face held a similar expression.

That afternoon, I had found men I could talk to. Men who had seen and done the same things I had. I think I could have told them anything and they would have understood. We were all men, but I looked at them as the boys they were back then.

At home, people tried to analyze what I said, because without the Vietnam War experience, they couldn't understand. I used to fault them for being crass and insensitive. I know now that it's just that they could not, and never would, understand it all. I'm still not sure that I do.

At some point during the melee, we decided to call it quits and return to our rooms. Most of us could still find our way there. Shortly after 4:00, the girl showed up with our laundry, clean and pressed. Only a few hours required. Together, Thom and I had about 30 pieces of laundry. It cost us a mere VND 660,000, or about $33.00. What a deal.

I stepped out onto the narrow balcony. Palm fronds whipped back and forth, about right for this time of day. It was hot, but it hadn't warmed to the searing heat I remembered. It rarely had for the past few days. The overcast sky that had hovered above us until Phan Thiet had kept the scorching heat at bay for the most part, but the rain and mist had made our travel disappointing at times. Not that I had been really disappointed, but I was hoping for better weather. There on the balcony, I relished the sun as it slowly slid toward the horizon behind me.

Truc, Ken, and Dennis planned to return to the fishing village for dinner at one of the small restaurants across from the beach. Thom and I strolled back across the street to our restaurant for dinner. The fried noodles and pork was especially appetizing that evening. The day had been as near perfection as I could have wanted. I didn't see how the trip could get much better. But it would.

Back in the room, Thom assailed me with corny jokes from his *Boy's Life* collection. I was astounded that he had more than one of the magazines. I tried to ridicule him about his curious interest in the magazine.

"You really like those things, don't you?"

"I think they're great," he said, proudly, head thrown back, the magazine thrust toward me. "The stories are interesting and the jokes are fun. You want one?"

"Ah, that's all right," I told him. "I've got my own reading material, thank you."

Before drifting off to sleep, I replayed the afternoon in my mind, and it dawned on me that this new circle of comradeship had been brought about by events in our lives that had taken place during a time of stress and danger, and in a place inhospitable to our physicalities. We all shared that bond, and I began to see in the others what I had seen in myself. We all harbored some memories that spawned anger and frustration, but that's all they were: memories. We couldn't change them, we couldn't forget them, we had to live with them. Some of the fellows had had it worse, some better. But we all knew what it was like, and I felt a tremendous burden lifted from my mind. I was no longer alone. That thought allowed sleep to come.

Our next destination was to be Ho Chi Minh City, or what we called Saigon when I was there before. We would spend three nights there before packing up to return home. I was not sure what to expect of the large city, since I had never been there. Those who had, inspired my anticipation of good times.

CHAPTER 13

HO CHI MINH CITY, FIRST NIGHT

Friday, 11 December, 2015

After the last breakfast in paradise, the bus pulled out at 8:30 in the morning bound for the excitement and fun we would have in Ho Chi Minh City. I think we were all hesitant to leave behind the peace and solitude that the resort offered and the closeness we had all felt there. For all of us, the Vietnam War had been such a significant influence on our lives, one that hardened our minds and bodies to the ravages of war. Its tentacles wove through our emotions, our beliefs, and our behavior to mold us into what we have become. We know it for what it is, and we see it in each other. To ask anyone else to understand it would be like asking him to describe what it feels like to die. How would he know?

I had relived some things I never wanted to, but at the same time I felt better about having done so. The book I had written about my experiences, as it turned out, had been only a teaser for the assimilation of all that had happened to me. The fact that it had happened to the others completed the circle in which I had been lost all of these years, knowing where I started, but never able to find it again. I felt as if I had arrived back where I belonged. With Ho Chi Minh City on the horizon, it was going to be one hell of a finale.

When we first arrived at the Muong Thanh Mui Ne Hotel, I thought we were in Phan Thiet. The hotel was actually located about ten miles north of Phan Thiet, although it was hard to tell. Like many American cities, the outlying towns tended to merge into one large metropolitan center, each town indistinguishable from the others. We passed dozens of resorts, all appearing to be upscale outfits geared to the international traveler, especially if they liked golf. I wasn't even aware that the Vietnamese knew what golf was.

We abandoned Highway QL1 for a road that paralleled the shoreline. Like the stretch of pavement from Qui Nhon, the sandy beach ran for miles nudging the pavement with its beige carpet and diverse assortment of small structures that could have been homes, shops, or anything. At nearly every access area to the water with any kind of beachfront at all stood a resort. What with everything being so inexpensive and the beauty that lay within the grasp of travelers of even modest means, I began to understand the glut of modern retreats.

Just before our reluctant departure from Phan Thiet, Truc stopped to pick up more VC lunches. Surely, we would see the end of these things, soon. I felt sorry for the VC; if's that's all they had to eat, they were far worse off than I had thought. C-rations were no treat, but after a while, these sandwiches begin to wear on the palate. We all took the opportunity to relieve ourselves at a nearby restroom to which a sign bearing the letters WC pointed.

"What's a WC?" asked Pat.

"The head," someone said.

"Water closet," from someone else.

"The pisser," from another.

"It's the toilet," I finally heard.

"Water closet." Pat's eyes narrowed a bit. "I always wondered what WC meant," he said. Then a satisfied look fell onto his face.

We filed into the aromatic lane filled with urinals and tried not to breathe while we did our business. Only one sink had the appearance of being useable without contracting something. I learned that if you need to "go" in Vietnam, public restrooms are not necessarily the best choice.

We ambled around a bit, curious about the local homes and shops on the street. We passed by one house set back from the sidewalk inside an iron gate. In the yard near the house sat an old jet fighter mounted on a stand at an odd angle to give the impression that it was airborne. It looked like an old Cessna A-37 Dragonfly used in the Vietnam War. An impressive piece of yard art. I wondered how the hell the owner got the thing in there. I figured it must have had some special significance for him. Or her.

Then back onto the bus to drift by more resorts. It wasn't until nearly 9:00 that we saw the last one and our route once more unfurled into rural Vietnam.

All of the small towns we rolled by looked the same. I guess after I'd seen so many of them, it was hard to notice any differences. Had I been familiar with the Vietnamese language, I might have been able to discern the distinctions of a particular town, kind of like noticing the signs on stores as I drove through small municipalities back home. I did, however, recognize a fire department. That was one of the few icons that was universal to the world.

Shortly after 10:00, we made a pit stop at a restaurant near the beach. Pat and someone else asked if the old Ke Ga Lighthouse was still there. I had no idea what they were talking about, but sure enough, out on the jetty stood a lighthouse. I figured that was it, since some of the fellows seemed excited about it.

Of course we all had to walk out to the concrete sea wall that separated the walk from the beach and take photos of the thing projecting up from the finger of rock jutting out into the water. I have to admit that it was picturesque. A number of the familiar blue tubs, like those at the fishing village near Phan Thiet, sat on the beach just outside the wall. What seemed like hundreds of small boats drifted just offshore, dancing on the rolling waves. With only hints of clouds in the sky, the water took on a teal hue, darkening as it stretched to meet the faded blue sky, a light haze adding drama to the landscape. Cameras rose to eye level and shutters clicked as if an army of hermit crabs had invaded the beach.

Then, naturally, group photos followed. I suppose this must have satisfied the curiosity of those guys who wanted to see the lighthouse, and we returned to the terrace by the restaurant for snacks and soft drinks. Oddly enough, and much to our dismay, no beer was available. While we sat at a long table, covered with a red and white checkered cloth, in the red plastic chairs on the red-paved terrace sharing our thoughts and other irrelevant matters, we notice a young lady at an adjacent table, tall, slim, with one of those faces that exhibits the lovely petite features common to Asians, but reflecting what might have been a French influence, also common in Vietnam. Her black hair, pulled back into a kind of pony-tail, revealed a nearly round face that lent her an unusual beauty. Her lips, a daring red, turned up at the ends in a provocative smile.

I believe it was either Dennis or Duane who spoke to her first. She proved to be friendly and curious about our lot. While smiling in that Vietnamese way that leaves you thinking she was truly happy, she told us she was on her honeymoon, which left no doubt that she actually *was* happy. She was from Hanoi and worked in a museum there. She started to remove the black and white checkered blouse that she wore and I wondered if she was going to do a strip tease. Much to my disappointment, she stopped at the tee shirt with a promotional print on the front beneath the letters, NYC. Yes, she had been to New York City.

Her husband, who soon joined her, was an attractive young man wearing a white pinstriped shirt with sunglasses hanging from the placket. That seemed to be a kind of uniform for professionals in Vietnam. His subtle swagger was typical of Vietnamese men. He was with the Hanoi police. We enjoyed talking with the couple, although it was she who did most of the talking. We wished them well.

Like just about everyone we met over there, the couple were charming, curious, and friendly. I just couldn't get my mind around the country and its people. It was so unlike America, where many folks tended to be distant and wary of strangers. I didn't know why that was so difficult for me to understand. But after nearly 70 years of growing up in the United States, spoiled and isolated from other cultures and ingrained in the luxury of the freedoms we enjoy, exposure to anything out of our element is a challenge. I was certainly being challenged there in Vietnam, probably more so than in 1971.

After the break, the bus ventured back toward Highway QL1 and its endless chain of towns, villages, and rice paddies that enriched the roadside with the exotic flavors of the country. The pavement widened into four lanes and a smoother ride, much to our delight. The scenery had subtly changed from flat, sandy stretches to mountain ranges in the not too far distance. The sparkling blue sky made a striking background for the now billowy white clouds loitering above the mountains, not in a promise of rain, but in a harmonious element of Vietnam's beauty, a majestic blend of greens and blues rising and falling across the horizon.

I remembered how the clouds emerged in Vietnam during the war, especially in the central highlands during the monsoons. The mornings would be clear, the sopping air heavy, then by late morning, small puffs appeared. Then in early afternoon, the puffs became solid white globs until mid-afternoon, when they grew to cover half the sky. Then late afternoon, all I could see would be a huge, billowing, gray, almost black ceiling just before they unleashed their fury in an unbridled eruption of rain. I could almost sit and watch the transformation take place. I figured the light clouds I saw from the bus would grow substantially later in the day. I felt certain that it would rain.

Watching the landscape stream by the window, I noticed electric power lines festooned between the tapered concrete poles flanking the highway. Not wood poles, like what I would have expected, but square concrete pillars. I guess they took their utilities seriously. At least the concrete ones wouldn't rot.

Although I had noticed the infrastructure evolving to maturity as we ventured further south, what I saw just north of Ho Chi Minh City was even more developed. The stores and other buildings seemed to be better maintained and bathed in brightly colored ornamentation. Their fondness for bright colors was evident in the wild splashes of red, blue, yellow, and green that embellished nearly everything.

In between the towns, rice paddies lay dormant, the young, green shoots reaching up through a blanket of water as still as glass. We passed several tracts of land with odd looking plants in ordered rows like an orchard, if that is the correct term. Concrete posts stood about three feet tall and six feet apart in a rows about every ten feet. I had never seen this kind of plant that sat atop each of the posts. The stalk grew up the square pillar and spread into what looked like fronds at the top like a giant starfish, it arms spilling down over the sides. Dragon fruit plants, or pitaya, I was told. It is a type of cactus with a bright red or yellow skin, about the size of a softball. Inside, the white flesh, almost crunchy, was dotted with tiny black seeds. I had eaten some of this at one of the breakfast buffets and found it rather bland. It is supposed to have a flavor akin to pears or watermelon, but I didn't care much for watermelon, either.

At noon we pulled into at a bus stop at Xa Xuan Hoa. The place provided restrooms, a small market, and a restaurant, none of which would have won the Good Housekeeping seal of approval. When I found my way to the men's restroom, not a difficult task if you just followed the smell, a cleaning lady was there, maybe cleaning, but I wasn't sure. At least she had a cart with all of the paraphernalia that I would associate with a janitorial service. I know that she saw me come in, but that didn't seem to make any difference to her. I figured if she didn't mind, I didn't either.

The restroom was large with a dozen urinals and as many sinks. In spite of the female company, I unzipped, and while taking care of business, I couldn't help but notice the number of inoperable and broken urinals and toilets. None of them were clean. Not even the floor. I thrust my hands toward one of the sinks before I realized what I was doing. I looked again at the scum and trails of whatever it was that seemed to growing up the side of the basin. It could have been alive, for all I knew. But the faucet handles didn't appear too contaminated, and with a bit of effort I managed to turn one of them on with the back of my hand. I just hoped the water was halfway clean.

We sat at one of the long tables and Truc passed out the VC lunches. Most of us got beers to wash down the sandwiches. When food hit our bellies, the frivolity hit the air. Eventually, the tide of conversation turned toward me. I'm not sure what had prompted this divergence, but I played along with it.

Now, I had received comments during the trip about my physical stature, since I am not a large man, small to medium build, and I'm certainly not muscle-bound, nor was anyone else there. However, I did have the making of a fledgling beer gut, but it was hardly noticeable unless a person caught sight of me in profile. At our age, some things are just beyond one's control. I could have starved myself, but I imagine the thing would still insist on hanging onto my stomach. Everyone at the table, except the bus driver, Phong, had pretty much filled out their middle sections which probably gave them some difficulty in seeing their toes. For some reason I had been singled out in jest for a bit of ribbing. Someone made a comment about the lot of distended stomachs and I heard another comment, "Yeah, Marc's so skinny, he must not eat much," or something to that effect. I caught a few other choice comments. I sat there taking it all in stride then finally had to speak up.

"Hey, guys," I said. "This isn't exactly fair. You know, in school we used to make fun of the *fat* kids."

It took just a moment of silence before that sank in and it pretty much broke the table up.

When things calmed down, I surveyed our surroundings and took note of the odd smell that seemed to linger. It was something like a wet dog with incontinent bladder and unbridled flatulence. And the rooster crowing somewhere nearby added to the rustic ambience. Notwithstanding the grime and mixed company in the restroom, I had to give the place high marks for the absence of chicken bones lying about the floor.

It wasn't long before we were back on the road, headed for Ho Chi Minh City; three more hours of obscure towns and villages. Some of them were larger than we had seen and possessed a more contemporary character, heavier traffic, more public spaces, wider sidewalks, and a greater variety of shops, some with display kiosks in front. The bright, colorful facades and signs indicated a state of good repair, in spite of their probable existence during the Vietnam War. I also noticed churches, which I hadn't seen since we had left Hanoi. I began looking more closely at the architecture of the towns, and there were a number of churches prominently visible from the main road.

According to Truc, religion was not a predominate characteristic of the Vietnamese. Of those who did subscribe to a religion, most were Buddhists, followed far behind by Catholics, then several other denominations.

Entering Bien Hoa, it appeared as though little rebuilding had taken place, the building wearing the same facades that I had seen in pictures from the 60s. The signs and colors might have changed, but the old building still stood behind crammed sidewalks.

I had seen many pictures of the area around Bien Hoa taken during the war, and back in the 60s, empty fields filled the twenty miles between Bien Hoa and Ho Chi Minh City. The cities had since grown into one and none of the guys had any clue as to what they were looking at. At lot had happened in 44 years.

Four of the fellows had been stationed at Bien Hoa Airbase during the war, some with the 118th AHC. They had stayed at the Officers Villa on Cong Ly Street. Pat and some others, wondered why on earth they would stay two miles from the flight line. I admit I had to wonder the same thing. When an emergency arose, I had to be in my flight gear and down to the flight line in two minutes. I had to run to do that, but I made it. It had surprised me that the crew chief and gunner were always able to beat me to the ship. I thought there might have been something fishy going on there, but I thought it best to leave it alone.

Phong stopped to let those fellows out who wanted to venture in search of the villa. I and Thom and some others traipsed along just for the hell of it. Phong then drove around, planning to pick us up later. We wandered through streets and alleys, the four guys who had been stationed there looking for anything that looked familiar. It wasn't hard to figure that nothing did. When the north took over Vietnam, street names changed, adding to the confusion. We finally came out on an avenue where the Hoa Binh Hotel stood. It was determined that it was the place once occupied by the Officers Villas, a kind of empty victory for the guys.

When leaving Bien Hoa, Truc took us by the Bien Hoa Airbase hoping to gain entrance for a brief tour. No dice. It was closed up tighter than a "fraidy hole" in a tornado; closed to visitors. It was a disappointment for Pat. He had wanted to get a photo of the "Birdcage," the Thunderbirds' flight line. Memories would have to be enough.

Duane Speirs, one of the four stationed there, carried his own memories of Bien Hoa, one of which was a near mid-air collision. As he put it:

We had just left the Bird Cage headed out to Xuan Loc. I was the peter pilot, Dale Moore was the AC. We had just formed up and passed under the Bien Hoa active at 300 feet. Dale had handed the controls over to me, when the lead helicopter and chalk 2 ahead of us meshed blades. We were in the trail formation, as normal for Dale, and I was concentrating on keeping our position in the flight. When Dale said something, I looked forward and watched as one aircraft came apart, blades going one way, the tail boom falling off and going another, the aircraft rolling over and going down, exploding on impact. The other ship went down, under some control, but not a lot. It hit the ground pretty hard. Dale took over and we landed not far from the burning hull. Not much we could do for them, so we moved over and helped out with the other damaged bird. It wasn't too long before the air force firefighting aircraft Pedro came and dropped fire suppressant on the burning helicopter. A little while later we took off, continued on to Xuan Loc and linked back up with what was left of the flight. We continued on with the mission as best we could. It was a long and sobering day.

I remembered that Ed Knighten had been introduced to Bien Hoa as an Operations Clerk. He had not been too happy with that job, hankering to get his hands on an M-60 as a door gunner in a Huey. He was fortunate enough to get the opportunity on several missions:

Upon arriving in Nam, I was to be stationed with the 120th in Saigon. That first day, they said they did not need me and to come back the next morning. At the EM club that night there was a lot of talk about Bien Hoa and some attack that was expected. I walked into personnel the next morning and was told I was going to Bien Hoa. On the way there I was handed an M14 and told to lock and load. I actually got to fire a clip at a mango grove where they said they received enemy fire.

At Bien Hoa I was assigned to the orderly room. One day the Operations Officer came in and ask the CO for a replacement for Griffin, who was leaving, and that he wanted someone a little older in operations. I was assigned as Griffin's replacement and spent the rest of my tour there. Many times they needed replacement door gunners for missions. I and my buddy Phil were often called on to fill in. The Stars and Stripes did an article on us, called "The Flying Clerks of the 118[th."]

I wound up flying with the Bandits most of the time. I had the honor of serving with now retired Brig. Gen. John C. " DOC" Bahnsen. We called him "Big Boots" but not to his face, since he wore tanker boots. I remember the day that then Captain Bahnsen made Major. He pulled up to operations with beer for all and said "I may not be the rankest Major here but I am the meanest."

I was very lucky to make it through without anything major happing to me other than a few scratches. There was one mission where we were going back to see what movement there was after three days of psy-war. A Buddhist Monk was walking down a road. We had a Vietnamese officer with us and he said to take him out. There were three firing passes make on him and the last we saw of him he was walking off into the trees unscathed. Makes a person stop and think.

Then there was the day we were out picking up troops from a hot LZ, flying cover for the slicks. While making a turn to come around, I thought I had leaned out too far and unplugged my helmet. I reached up to plug it back in and found out that I only had about four inches of cord left on my helmet. Lots of luck on my part.

Everyone who served in Vietnam has his own stories, some hair-raising, some humorous, and some that are both. It's when these experiences are shared that we begin to understand the significance of it all. The meaning will never be understood with any great degree of satisfaction; only the illusion of it.

The only indication that we had reached Ho Chi Minh City was crossing the Saigon River. That and the tall buildings visible in the distance. Otherwise, it was merely block after block of shops and traffic. Unlike Hanoi, the pace was livelier. I've never been to Times Square, but I imagine the activity there in Saigon would be pretty much like that; thousands of people and even more motor scooters. When I was in Hanoi, I never considered the possibility of traffic being more congested. The traffic in Ho Chi Minh City managed to cram more vehicles in a small space than should have been physically possible. I was in awe at the dexterity of the motor bike drivers riding knuckle to knuckle through the throng of traffic with no deviation of course or mishaps.

I was also amazed at what these clever people managed to fit onto the small, two-wheeled wonders. Lashed onto the back of the bike was anything from stacks of cardboard that rose higher than the operator's head, to lengths of lumber and pipe, possibly ten feet long, that were skillfully maneuvered through the swarm of vehicles. I also saw passengers in the back of a bike holding furniture, large boxes, crates, and a number of other things I could not have imagined could be carried on one of those things. The entire scene could have been a segment of "Ripley's Believe It Or Not."

It seemed as if it took as long to get from Bien Hoa to the hotel as it did just to get to Ho Chi Minh City from Phan Thiet. Threading our way through the sea of traffic in a bus required the dexterity of a driver like Phong. I don't understand how he did it without flattening a few scooters.

We disembarked at the Palace Hotel Saigon shortly after 5:00, when daylight was drawing the curtain over the city. Thom and I boarded the elevator for a trip to the 13th floor. My first impression of the room was a welcome surprise, seeing the generous pieces of furniture, but then I noticed the small beds. They were double beds, at least, which would accommodate the restless sleeper. However, they were positioned side by side, crammed together, I suppose, in an attempt to compensate for the lack of a see-through bathroom. The place certainly would take a bit of time to get used to.

Thom and I immediately went to the tiny balcony outside our room and took in the fantastic view of the city; tall buildings sprouted from the streets below and the Saigon River swirled around a corner just beyond the pillars of concrete that had risen within the last four decades. As dusk settled in, the tall buildings dazzled our eyes with colorful illumination. One tall structure had vertical strips of lights that, in sequence, traveled up and down the façade, changing colors as they went. Tiny blips of light glided along the streets 13 floors below and people were milling about in the giant mall between the avenues.

We would be there for three nights, and that evening we were on our own for dinner. We strolled the boulevard from end to end, taking in what used to be Saigon; the bright light, the symphony of happy voices, laughing children, and the purr of traffic, and the smell of newness, like walking into a large, recently built discount store, wafting onto the sidewalks. The boulevard bordered a mall located between two one-way streets, about half a block apart and four blocks long, lined by storefronts two to four stories in height, all lit up like Las Vegas, but in a more reserved and tasteful fashion. By the time is was dark, it seemed as if a million people has materialized out of nowhere, kind of like at night outside the wire of a compound during an attack. But these folks were friendlies, walking about the mall, kids, teenagers, and families, out for the night.

Water fountains spurted colored water jets into the air, pulsating from high to low, much to the children's delight. Actually, everyone enjoyed the spectacle, looking on, spellbound.

"Look at that," I told Thom, pointing toward spurt of colored water jumping into the air with kids dancing beneath them. "Look at them. I wonder if these people have never seen anything like that before."

Thom studied the scene a moment, then mumbled, "It doesn't look like it."

"They must be easily entertained."

"That they are."

"This place is great," I said. "I can't believe the people out here. Where the hell did they all come from?"

Thom just shook his head and we wandered back into the core of the Vietnamese life in the city.

What a pleasure it was to see families wandering among other families, girls giggling at whatever girls giggle at, and boys...well, just being boys, killing time. I thought some of them might be tourists, or folks from other parts of the country visiting the big city.

We saw several groups of street dancers, each performing to the music from a CD or MP3 player, or whatever they had. Some were break-dancers, others just dancing. One performer was instructing a girl on some of the steps. It was good entertainment and just like I would expect to see anywhere, the mall was not without various vendors selling glow sticks, toy airplanes, and other gadgets. The kids were loving them.

The four blocks of the mall sat between the Saigon River at one end and the Saigon Opera House (officially the Ho Chi Minh Municipal Theater) at the other. The avenues on either side glowed from thousands of motor bikes like burning lava creeping down the pavement, ceaseless and unstoppable. That's about as fast as they could go, considering the bikes were nearly wheel to wheel and handlebar to handlebar. Thom and I had forgotten our experience in crossing the busy streets in Hanoi, a life-challenging experience. We stood at a pedestrian crossing light for several minutes, never mind that it had turned green, then red, several times with no noticeable relief in the cascading traffic that glided past as if we weren't even there. We finally got enough nerve to venture into the street, playing chicken with cars and bikes and hoping the folks aiming for us would somehow stop before running us over. I looked into the annoyed faces and determined eyes as their hands instinctively grasped the handlebars and their feet stomped on brake levers. We did manage to make it across unscathed. Even the sidewalks weren't safe. If a driver found a wad of congested traffic in front of him he merely jumped up onto the sidewalk and went around. We really had to watch where we walked.

I had been astonished at the multitude of motorbikes in Hanoi. I believe every man, woman, and child must have owned one. It was the primary means of transportation. But in Ho Chi Minh City I honestly think the things were reproducing by themselves. There were places I couldn't even see the pavement for all of the two-wheeled machines in the way. And it wasn't just the abundance of those little things that amazed me; I found it amusing that the motor scooter served as the family car. Aside from the single rider, it was common to see at least two people on them, and sometimes three. What really shocked me was the scooter with Dad driving the thing with junior in front between his legs, and Mama riding in back holding baby. Go figure. And we think we have to have monster SUVs and trucks with huge tires and roaring V-8 engines just to go to the store. I have to wonder what has become of the American society.

Considering the number of vehicles on the streets and the people on scooters largely unprotected, except for the mandatory helmets, I was surprised that few accidents and injuries occurred. Of course, driving at a glacial speed tends to remove much of the danger from such congested traffic. We witnessed only one accident during our two-week stay, and that was a small BMW that had collided with a scooter. There were no injuries.

As Thom and I walked through the masses, I was cheerfully reminded of Christmas by the decorations displayed in store windows and marquees. Instead of the gaudy and overdone spectacles I had seen back home, the decorations along the mall were modest and tastefully done. Some were still in the process of being erected.

I continued to consider how different the Vietnamese were from Americans. Their reserved manner and polite demeanor make them affable and pleasant, appearing content with the world; unless they are astride a motor scooter. Children are monitored closely and I never saw them running amok or raising hell. To the Vietnamese, family was everything. Discipline was stern and decisive. If that mall had been in the United States, I would have been bumped, shoved, scowled at, cursed at and assaulted by the undisciplined brats of uncaring parents. Walking along the mall was like being inside a Norman Rockwell painting, a painting that captured the essence of Vietnam.

Hunger reminded us that it was time to find food. We passed by an obscure restaurant with a narrow frontage. We stopped to look at the menu posted outside the door. When Thom saw the lobster, that clinched our dinner destination. We were shown through a series of rooms into a back dining area. Supposedly an Italian restaurant, the waiter appeared to be Italian, as well, even with an accent. It took Thom no time at all to order his lobster. I selected the grilled salmon. I also ordered a Glenlivet, straight-up. The waiter brought two aperitifs to the table, some kind of lemon liqueur. It was a sweet-sour taste that stimulated the tongue. Thom did not indulge in alcohol, so I polished his off as well.

Talk during the meal fell into family histories. I have often tried to imagine what living in California would be like. I had spent a few days in Agoura Hills, near Los Angeles, and I found the whole experience stressful. Too much traffic, too many people, and too many of them concerned with acquiring possessions than living their lives.

I filled him in on my daughter and my wife's attempt to care for her aging mother. I think we understood each other fairly well. We were a good match for the trip.

Thom and I ventured into a craft shop and the girls who worked there were on us un a flash. It was like two mice walking into a room full of cats. If my eyes stayed on something longer than an instant, that was a girl's cue to move in for the hard sell. If I dared touch an item, that was pretty much it. It was nearly impossible to leave the store without the thing I had ogled. But these young ladies had no idea of my resolve. Thom, however, proved to be a soft touch. When we finally escaped from the store, he carried a silk scarf, a tie, and some knickknacks. It was his purchases that allowed me to abscond with dong still in my pocket. After a stop for gelato, we returned to the hotel and bedded down.

I had not stopped thinking about home and what my wife and daughter might be doing while I was cavorting with army buddies. I couldn't help but feel some guilt about my wife's vigil with her mother, but other than offering support for the house and equipment required for her mobility, there was little I could have done.

The next day we were scheduled to tour the tunnels at Cu Chi, an elaborate system of underground burrows that reached from Cu Chi nearly to Saigon during the war. I had never seen one of those famed tunnels, but I had heard about them. The thought of crawling through one left me with a tight stomach.

My mind wandered to what I had seen that night and I wondered if it was all staged for the benefit of the tourist. But I realized that that kind of charade on such a grand scale was ridiculous. My brain mulled it over until I managed to fall asleep.

CHAPTER 14

HO CHI MINH CITY SECOND NIGHT

Saturday, 12 December, 2015

Up before six and down to breakfast. That's what a good night's sleep can do for me. The bus was due to leave for Cu Chi at 8:00, and I wanted time to get the things together I would need for the trip.

The breakfast buffet was not as elaborate at other hotels, but it had all of the necessary things I needed; all of the foods I liked. The ambience was something like I remembered of army mess halls, but it was only breakfast, after all, not a romantic meal. I had no trouble scarfing down the food while refilling my miniature coffee cup a dozen times.

Phong pulled away from the hotel promptly at 8:00 and we engaged the resident scooters clogging the avenue, meshing with them like a finely tooled gear. On the way out of town, we passed by a BMW dealership and other international chain stores that I recognized. The world had quite a presence there. Near the city limits, I think, Phong pulled over in front of a small market with fresh meat of some kind hanging from hooks above various animal parts that were difficult to identify. No refrigeration, of course. I'm not sure the Vietnamese believed in it.

I took time on the bus to call my wife. It would be early in the evening at home. She was with her mother, getting things ready for the night. I assured her that I was fine, but that I missed her. Nearly two weeks in a foreign land, away from her, and the urge to go home became a bit stronger. I was unaware of the town's existence sliding by the windows. We said our good-byes, then I turned my head to see brightly colored shops floating by and people busy with their morning routines. I was back in Vietnam.

Tom Baca had already been to the Cu Chi tunnels and kept Sterling company, since he had elected to stay near a bathroom. Only ten of us left for Cu Chi. Tom was a bit under the weather and Sterling had contracted the Ho Chi Minh Two Step, a nasty affliction of the digestive tract akin to Montezuma's Revenge, but with more drama. Pat had also had experience with that illness. The following narrative explains the situation:

We were flying milk runs in the "B" model. AC Sam McGlone was in the right seat; don't recall who was in the left. In the afternoon, Operations notified us that we were to pick up an American general at a place we called the University, between Saigon and Bien Hoa, or it could have been Di An. We would be fly him to Vung Tau (for the weekend). The protocol was that any General flying was given a two-gunship escort (light fire team).

By the time we finished the mission we were already on, we were about a half hour late arriving to pick him up. The fire team that was to escort us radioed and said it'd be about 10 minutes before they would arrive.

As we came in to land, I noticed the general and his entourage were in two jeeps sitting right beside the helipad (they never learn). Well, Mr. McGlone couldn't pass this up. He brought the ship in very slowly and hovered around longer than necessary before setting her down. There were papers, hats, dust, and gravel flying everywhere.

I had the jump seats in, and the general and three or four others climbed on board. The general sat in the jump seat in front of me facing out; our knees could touch. We were at flight idle and the general motioned to me, asking why we weren't taking off. I yelled back at him that we were waiting for the gunship escort. I could tell by his demeanor that he was not in a chatty mood.

We sat there for approximately 10 minutes waiting. I unplugged my helmet twice and wandered around outside checking the tail boom so I didn't have to sit eye to eye with the general.

Finally, the gunships radioed that they were about 3 minutes out, for us to take off and they would pick us up as we came out. McBee and I closed the pilots' doors in front of us and we strapped in. Mr. McGlone started to pick up to a hover then set her back down. He started un-strapping and told my gunner to open his door, he said, "I've gotta go!"

Sam had an affliction everyone got while in Nam; it has many names. One is Ho Chi Minh's Revenge; back home we called it the "back door trots." He climbs out and jumps in one of the jeeps still there and takes off. The general is looking around and asks me what is going on. I tried to explain to him as delicately as I could what was happening.

In the meantime, the gunships had arrived and were circling overhead. Our other pilot explained the situation to the gunships. After about 5 minutes, the gunships radioed and said they were getting low on fuel, called for a fuel truck, and landed near us. Our pilot said, "Hell, we just as well fuel up, too," and shuts her down. The look on that general's face, when he shut the engine down, was a Kodak moment. He was not a happy camper.

Also, I had the privilege of, again, explaining to the general what was happening. By the time the fuel truck showed up, so did Mr. Mc-Glone. After topping off the three ships, we finally got him to Vung Tau, after approximately an hour sitting on the helipad.

I bet the next time that general needed a ride, he told his people not to get any helicopters with white birds painted on them.

The Cu Chi tunnels were located in...yes, Cu Chi, about 40 miles west of Ho Chi Minh City. One of several tunnel complexes in Vietnam, this one was part of the Vietnam War Memorial Park. The bus hadn't been out of the city very long before someone yelled, "Ken, put on your music."

He placed his portable speaker on the overhead luggage rack and we were soon rocking to the Animals' "We Gotta Get Out Of This Place" and "Hang on Sloopy" and "Wild Thing," and other favorites of that era. The two and a half hours seemed to pass quickly and we were pulling into the tunnel exhibit in no time.

I had always wondered what the famous tunnels were like. I had read books that referred to them, one way or another, and had read accounts of the tunnel rats that went down into them in search of the NVA or VC. It was a squeamish job that consumed many lives of the brave souls that wormed their way through the dark burrows not knowing what they would encounter.

Reading about things like that, things in the war I mean, a fit of apprehension usually engulfs me, much like reading one of those harrowing thrillers that keeps me on the edge of my seat. I don't know why, because most of those things never happened to me and couldn't happen now. But the idea of them still hounded me. When I think back to 1971, I lived every day thinking in the back of my mind it might be my last, but it didn't seem to have the effect that those thoughts have today. I knew

I had a job to do and I did it, just like everyone else over there. Now, I realize just how insane it all was.

When I first experienced this phenomenon, I was young and impressionable. I didn't know all of the bad things that could have happened, and I didn't know, with any measure, the probability of all the bad things actually taking place. But having lived for 69 years, I have seen and experienced more bad things than I could ever have imagined. Now, I know what can happen and how likely it might be. Most folks might say I'm a bit gun-shy, but it's only the wisdom that comes with age.

I just knew I would be going down into a tunnel. I'm not necessarily claustrophobic, but I do have my moments in confined spaces. Nine of us, in addition to Truc and Phong, would be taking the tour. Pat's legs were not up to the strenuous walking that would be required, so he stayed with the bus.

We entered a first-class tourist attraction carefully designed and orchestrated to inform visitors what the tunnels were all about and their impact on the war. Thatched roofs covered entrances to exhibits, and paths around the neatly maintained area were well marked. We passed through the entry pavilion where Truc purchased tickets, then proceeded to the complex. A guide dressed in green fatigues and sandals met us and led us through the wooded area with trees taller than any I had seen anywhere else in Vietnam, or at least they looked taller. Things look different from standing on the ground beneath them than they do from the window of a bus. The sky was obliterated by two levels of canopies, the larger, old growth trees rising high into the air and overhanging the tops of the smaller trees below. It would have been nearly impossible to view anything on the ground from above by looking through the foliage. That was the reason for the use of Agent Orange.

Our guide explained that the tunnels had been dug beginning in the late 40s during the French occupation. They spanned 250 kilometers from the Cambodian border to what was then Saigon, and contained up to eight levels, one above the other. The network had many entrances and contained living quarters, a hospital, a kitchen, a dining area, munitions storage, shops where unexploded ordinance was converted into other weapons, another shop where utensils were made, tires were made into sandals, a millenary room where clothing was made, and many ventilation shafts to the ground above. Other rooms were used for the making of rice wine and paper.

He showed us how the entrances were cleverly disguised. A small hole in the ground, barely large enough for a person to fit into, was dug in an area covered with leaves and brush. A board was cut slightly larger than the opening, and leaves, the same kind that surrounded the opening, were attached to the board. Once lowered into the opening, a person would stand in cutouts in the side of the hole while he carefully lowered the board over the opening. It was impossible to see it from our vantage point above. A large leaf from a nearby tree would be cut near the stem and the tip bent around and threaded through the slot, then left near the entrance. That's how the others knew that the entrance was nearby.

We saw along the way more entrances and mounds of soil with small holes in them to act as ventilation for the tunnels. They would be undistinguishable from the air. The guide explained some of the deadly traps that were used around the tunnels. One was a simple hole used as an entry to the tunnels, but four horizontal tubes were set into the sides around the interior of the hole. The tubes held sharpened bamboo stakes dipped in feces. After descending into the hole, a cover was pulled over it and the stakes were pulled into the opening. If a man fell through the cover, he would be impaled on the stakes. It would be nearly impossible to work free of them.

Another was the rolling trap. A wooden frame holding two horizontal revolving logs lined with stakes was set into the opening, much like an old wringer washing machine with spikes. Anyone falling through the concealed cover would find themselves lanced with several stakes, usually falling on through to the bottom of the pit. The scissors chair trap contained two wood frames with stakes that folded against each other as the victim fell into them. There were several other designs, just as deadly. A person would never see them until it was too late.

We heard gunfire nearby, and I think we were all wondering what we were getting into. Our guide led us further into the complex, stopping at each exhibit. The further we got along the trails, the louder the gunfire.

Other areas had dioramas depicting life in the tunnels; mannequins illustrating how they made tools, weapons, and clothing. We toured a kitchen complete with oven, stove top, and a water well. The fire was vented through a smaller horizontal tunnel that ran to the surface several meters away. If smoke was detected, any explosion would be at the point of the smoke, not the kitchen.

We were getting close to the source of the shooting, whatever it was, when we were led through a short run of one of the tunnels. Single file, we bent over and almost crab-walked through the hot, musty, confined shaft. The smell of fresh earth and the dank air gave me that closed-in feeling. It took me back to my backyard in Hobart, Oklahoma, where I would while away summer afternoons digging holes in the dirt for battles between my little green army men.

A woman from another tour group was in front of our guide. For some reason, she stalled halfway through, causing everyone else behind her to stop. Well, I hadn't planned on that and that little voice in my head that talks to me when I get in a cramped space started its moaning. It was my good fortune that our guide spoke to the woman rather harshly, instructing her to move on. I'm sure I wasn't down there as long as I thought I was, but I had a problem making my mind believe that. The fact that the tunnel was illuminated made it less of a fearsome adventure than it could have been, but the NVA and VC had no illumination. I don't know how they could have lived like that.

American troops made many raids on tunnels, but they could only scratch the surface of the extensive complexes. Pat was involved in one of these raids. From his article in the Pine Bluff News of February 7, 2016:

I know a little about the tunnels with firsthand knowledge. In Jan 1966, we were involved in a large military operation (Operation Crimp) with American and Australian troops in and around the Iron Triangle. My ship was flying C & C (Command and Control) for the 145th Combat Aviation Battalion, which was coordinating all of the air assault operations in the area. After a few hours, we heard reports of huge caches of weapons and documents being found in some tunnel openings that they had stumbled upon, so we landed to check things out.

I remember seeing several different types of weapons and anti-aircraft guns (first time I ever saw 12.7 mm guns) spread out on the ground. One guy told me they found tunnels eight stories deep. I've never heard of tunnels constructed like that. Some other guys had a bunch of documents that they were going through.

One of the fellows was reading papers with lists of names of different aviation companies. I asked the guy to look for my name and he found it. I was listed as PFC (E-3) Matheny, Patrick L. That made the hair on the back of my neck stand up. I knew it wasn't recent. I had been promoted to SP4 (E-4) the month before, but it was close enough. We knew Charlie had put a bounty on flight crewmen; pilots were worth more. Now you know why I remember this little escapade. By the way, the first 'tunnel rats' were the Australians. I've done some crazy things in my life, but that ain't one of them.

Our next stop was a break area where we sat on long, rough benches beneath olive drab canvas festooned between poles. We sampled chai tea and one of the VC staples, tapioca. It is made from the cassava plant (or yucca, not the yucca most of us are familiar with), a course stalk above ground with multiple roots shaped like brown carrots. The roots had been cooked and cut into chunks of what they called tapioca, and placed into bowls on the long tables. The only experience I'd had with tapioca was pudding, and I was never too fond of that. So it was with uncertainty that I took a bite of the white substance. It wasn't all that bad. A bit bland, but I supposed one could get used to it. The versatile root can be mashed, boiled into soups, or fried, as well being made into the tapioca we find at the market.

After we exited the tunnels, we headed for a break area with a gift shop and refreshment bar. It also serviced a firing range. That explained the sound of gunfire. Several weapons used in the war were available for visitors to shoot. You could purchase rounds at the desk, however many you wanted depending on how much you wanted to spend, and shoot your preferred weapon on the range. Thirty .30 caliber rounds cost about $2.00. Ed, having served as a gunner on Hueys, bought several dollars' worth of 7.62 mm rounds and fired an M-60 machine gun, the same kind he used on the Huey. I'd never seen him smile so big as he did when he came out from the range.

Veterans displayed a range of reactions to the war, some burying their experiences in their minds, some sharpening their lust for firearms, others skirting clear of weapons altogether, and some were just plain broken. When I came back, I never wanted to see another gun.

Just as we were leaving, two Vietnamese girls, typically attractive as most Vietnamese girls are, stood side by side taking a selfie. Duane sneaked behind them, his gray beard looming over their heads. It took a while for the scene on their camera to register with the girls. At first the smiles on their faces dropped to alarm, then hands flew to their mouths as hysterical laughter rendered them helpless. I found it charming that the Vietnamese were so easily entertained.

This experience of the tunnels was one the best things on the trip. It was something few people would ever have an opportunity to see firsthand. Even though I had heard about the tunnel complexes in Vietnam, and there were several, actually seeing them and being in them answered many questions and satisfied my curiosity.

As I sat there on the bus while everyone else was rehashing the tunnel experience, I was rehashing it in my own mind. The war illustrated the cunning ingenuity of the North Vietnamese. It made me think of the unique and clever adaptations of our forebears during the Revolutionary War. Seeing the Cu Chi tunnels solidified my respect for the Vietnamese and their determination.

Talk about the tunnels filled the bus when we pulled out of the park and headed for Nui Ba Dinh Mountain near Tay Binh. We passed through Trang Bang and Go Dau Ha to the 3200-foot-high extinct volcano, a landmark for the III Corps area of operations. Being the only mountain around for miles, kind of like a gopher mound in a desert, pilots used it as a reference point, and many helicopters had landed on its apex to resupply the small contingent of troops stationed there.

The small towns we ventured through looked the same as all the others we had passed before. The roads, however, had taken a turn for the worse, being little more than ancient strips of crumbled concrete or gravel. In spite of the rough roads and repetitive scenery, the camaraderie was high, chatter echoing from the windows.

We pulled into at a rest stop in Trang Bang to view the mountain and take group photos. The fellows who had been stationed in the area were absorbed in reminiscence, while the rest of us looked at a mountain that, to us, was just another mountain. Well, it did have a smattering of magnificence, but only that. It was a pleasant break, the partly cloudy sky softening the sun's impact on evaporating the moisture from recent rains.

That afternoon back in Ho Chi Minh City, Thom and I resumed our exploration of the stores around the hotel. We weren't exactly out to buy anything, although I thought Thom might have succumbed to the slightest temptation had we actually gone into a shop. We ambled down side streets where we found a different venue of merchandise, not so touristy and more practical. We passed by several clothing stores in which Thom seemed to take interest. He confided his weakness for on-line bargain clothing that didn't fit when he got it. He told me he was reforming and vowed that from now on he would invest in only quality clothing that fit right and made him look good.

Massage parlors and nail salons were everywhere. That was big business there. Passing by one of these places, we noticed a sign pointing upstairs. Another shop sat right below it. We stopped there and a girl met us at the door.

"How much for a massage?" Thom asked her.

"Sixty minute, 400," she said in the typical broken English, meaning VND 400,000, or about $20.

"Four-hundred-thousand?" he asked.

"Yes," the girl nodded, waving him inside. "You come in and we do you."

"I get the massage here or upstairs?" he said, just to confirm the location.

"We do here," she said, still smiling and motioning him in. In fact, the smile never left her face. "You come in," she said waving her arms toward the door.

He looked at me. "This is really a great deal," he said.

He turned to the girl and told her he would be back later. I had no doubt that he would.

That night, Thom and I ventured into the throng of people in the mall. We were surprised to find that the avenues on either side had been blocked off to traffic and it was a pedestrian's paradise. All of the cars and scooters were corralled behind barricades at the intersections.

More Christmas decorations had been brought to life with strings of tiny lights adorning the trees and additional displays in the storefronts. The entire area seemed to be alive with a harmonious interaction of its population. The only time I'd seen anything like it was at large holiday celebrations at home. Ho Chi Minh City seemed to be highly influenced by western culture, there being many upscale department stores with designer fashions and jewelry, skyscrapers, and hotels populated the central business district. There were also a ton of classy restaurants. Thom and I wandered into one.

The fellow at the door acted as if he was expecting us and opened the massive glass leaf for us to enter. We were shown to a table near the rear wall where we had an excellent view of the entire restaurant. Contemporary décor, sleek with a lot of glass and gold metallic coverings; a lot of glitz and glimmer. A waiter arrived with water and menus. He asked if we wanted drinks. Thom didn't drink and I ordered a Taj Mahal beer.

"Good menu," I said, looking around at the half-empty room. The locals tended to dine later in the evening.

"Do they have lobster?" Thom asked, looking from side to side on the extensive menu.

"You're still after that?"

"Hey, I want a really good lobster."

"I see they have lamb," I said. "I love that stuff."

"I like lamb," he said. "I just never think to order it."

"Ooh, they have Tandoori Lamb."

"I don't see lobster," he said, a bit dejected.

I finally selected the Lamb Vandaloo. I was a sucker for lamb and Indian cuisine. I also favored good fish, poultry and pork. Unlike most of the folks back in Oklahoma, beef is one of the last things I would order. I guess that's one of the reasons I'd never felt at home there, especially in Sallisaw. Well, that and the lack of a decent coffee shop or really good restaurant. Maybe I expected too much from a town with a population of 8,000 deep in red neck country.

I don't recall what Thom ordered. The wait was short and the waiter appeared with our meals. I dumped a glob of rice on my plate and dug into the lamb. The first taste was excruciatingly good. Thom was not disappointed with whatever he had. About halfway through our meal, Dennis and Duane came in and took the table next to us.

Dennis grinned and his glasses glinted form the overhead lights, his ever-smiling eyes behind them.

"This looked like a good place," he said, pulling out a chair and sitting. "We wanted something better than VC lunches."

The waiter came by with water and menus, and while Dennis and Duane looked through the entrees, I told them, "The Lamb Vandaloo is outstanding."

Duane mumbled something about Vietnamese food.

"Marc recommends the Lamb Vandaloo," Dennis said, looking over at my plate. "I think that's what I'll have."

They both wound up with the Lamb Vandaloo.

I was surprised to find such luxurious accommodations there in Ho Chi Minh City. The lifestyles there were certainly more affluent than up north.

Thom had mentioned earlier that he wanted to go up to the top floor of the tall odd-shaped building visible from our hotel window. It looked like a shiny gray banana standing in the air with a plate stuck in its side. We found out later it was the Bitexo Financial Tower. We made our way toward it and followed the crowd through the doors.

The interior was alive with people, even this late at night, and the expanse of glass and lights was nothing short of spectacular. Christmas decorations hung in the several-story-tall foyer, and shoppers were everywhere. We passed by designer name shops and found an elevator. Building officials, women in blue uniforms, asked us where we wanted to go. Thom told them the top floor, sixty some stories up. They said, no, that was closed for the night. One of the women said there was a club on the 50th floor, so that's where we went.

The club was packed, but a waiter found a table for two right in front of the small band. I ordered a Stella Artois and Thom ordered some kind of tropical thing with no alcohol. It was loud. I guess that wasn't unusual for a club, but this was loud. Being right in front of the band, I had no trouble hearing them. I could have done that without my hearing aids.

Three musicians sat on stools in the spotlights, behind trails of waitstaff lugging platters of drinks in front of them to the crowded tables. The players were all young. The one on the bass guitar wore a tee shirt and jeans. The rhythm guitar player wore a white long sleeve shirt and jeans. The singer, well this guy was decked out in a black and white plaid suit that would have made a used car salesman envious.

The music was good with a variety of genres, even Christmas music at times. I'm a music lover, so I was having no complaints. We listened for about a half hour then decided to call it quits. By that time it was after 9:00 and we made another trek around the mall, walking off our dinner, then headed back to the hotel.

With notebooks and Kindles at hand, we settled in for the night. With one last look out of our thirteenth floor window, I watched flocks of people still wandering around the mall as if the evening had just started. I wondered if they ever went home to bed. Bemusement still reigned over my mind as I considered the contrast between life there, in Ho Chi Minh City, and life back in the States. It was just so hard to believe that what I had seen of the Vietnamese people was all real.

The folks there seemed so laid back, no worries, no stress, or none that were apparent. It reminded me of the time I had lived in Lafayette, Louisiana, among the Cajuns. They were a delightful bunch and approached life in much the same way as the Vietnamese. Nowhere else in America had I experienced that.

We were supposed to have a walking tour of the local area in the morning. We would get to see other parts of the city first-hand, most likely absent of the commercial setting of the mall. I thought back to this morning with the streets already busy when we stepped out of the hotel to the bus, people already clogging parts of the sidewalk and the streets filled with traffic. Some of these people must never sleep.

CHAPTER 15

HO CHI MINH CITY, THIRD NIGHT

Sunday, 13 December, 2015

At 8:30 in the morning, Truc rounded up the VC platoon to start our walking tour of the city, all of us in our VC uniforms; red shirts and hats. Pat elected to remain at the hotel due to his uncooperative feet. We set off down the street passing by department stores selling upscale merchandise, such as Cartier, YSL, Louis Vuitton, and the like, the kind of stores I tend to shy away from, thinking they might have a cover charge. Smaller stops populated the side streets with a variety of wares, clothing appearing to be the most popular.

The striking difference between Ho Chi Minh City and Hanoi left me wondering how it happened that the south had westernized itself much more than the north. In Ho Chi Minh City, there was more bustle, more people, the dress less casual and more businesslike, more traffic, but less awkward odors. It smelled more like a large city with its exhaust fumes blended with formaldehyde, leather, and cigarette smoke and hot concrete; not the old, musty and sour smell of Hanoi, which seemed to be caught in a time warp that Ho Chi Minh City managed to escape.

We heard a band nearby, a pleasant break from the purr of the traffic. After a while, that resonating sound, like an army of muffled lawn mowers, got a bit annoying. I had always been a sucker for bands. We turned a corner and across the street, in front of a large building that looked like it might have been a museum, some 20 musicians were performing on the broad expanse of steps in front of the marquee. A crowd of maybe 200 had stopped to listen, most of them on motor bikes they had parked around the building's front. It was an unexpected pleasure to hear a concert. I had spent many of my school years playing a trumpet in the band and had a love of music, especially a live concert.

We passed by more stores, many of them with Christmas decorations plastered across their facades. The theme might have been Christmas, but the delivery was ultra-contemporary, all glimmer and sparkle, brightly colored. None of the nostalgic displays I was used to seeing in the stores back home. I guess it served the same purpose, although I was unsure exactly what Christmas meant to the Vietnamese. And as I thought more about it, I wasn't even sure if I knew what Christmas meant to Americans, anymore. It seemed to be about how much useless and unappreciated stuff we could give our kids, never mind what the true meaning of Christmas was.

As we approached a corner, a middle-aged man and woman were standing at ease, watching us, obviously tourists. Most of the people I had seen in Vietnam were Vietnamese, but I did spot a few folks from other countries.

When we got within a hundred feet or so, we all realized that the woman holding a camera was wearing a tee shirt just like ours above white slacks, red with a yellow star. I imagine that's why they were staring at us. It was why we were staring at her.

She asked us who we were and several guys burst forth with, "We're Vietnam vets," and "We're touring Vietnam," and "We came back…" I'm sure she caught most of it.

"Where did you get the shirts?" she asked, nearly laughing.

I believe it was Tom Baca who said, "These are our uniforms."

"Uniforms?"

Tom explained our situation.

"Where did you get yours?" Duane (I think) asked.

"Oh," she said, a bit embarrassed. "We bought it at a gift shop."

Her husband, who was not exactly amused by the gathering, watched suspiciously from the side.

"You have hats, too," she said, pointing at our heads. "Can I get a picture with you?"

That's all it took for our cameras to come out, and we lined up. She handed her camera to her husband and joined our group. Duane placed his hat on her head. She laughed at him and, in a coy gesture, tapped it into place with her fingers. Her husband took several photos, then some of the guys passed their cameras to him for more. I don't know how many times our images were transmuted into digital arrays, but I imagine the poor man was getting tired of it.

"Where are you from?" asked Dennis.

"Luxemburg," she said, which surprised me. I had never met anyone from there.

"Are you from America?" she asked.

We all responded with a verbal yes or a nod and her smile seemed to grow wider.

She returned the hat and we said our farewells. Imagine that. Luxemburg. It dawned on me that Vietnam was truly an international attraction.

We continued on our walk toward Independence Palace, formerly the South Vietnamese Presidential Palace. The streets were wide, clean, and many of the sidewalks had been recently covered in concrete pavers. Whoever made those things was probably making a killing. A few street vendors sat at the edges selling toys, pictures, and other touristy items. On the way near the heart of the city, we passed by Notre-Dame Cathedral, a twin-spired three-story neo-Romanesque structure. It stood alone in the center of a large intersection, across the road from the post office. Spires sat atop bell towers at either side and a transept spanned the rear of the cathedral. I saw that Thom had taken special notice of it.

We also walked past familiar places, such as The Coffee Bean coffee shop, Gloria Jeans coffee shop, Carl's Jr., Dunkin Donuts, Popeye's Chicken, and of course, McDonalds, not to mention Starbucks. I was surprised to see so many American corporations represented. But then, I recalled the articles I had read about Vietnamese capitalism that seemed to draw foreign investment like a magnet.

We strolled along a sidewalk across from a large park, thick with trees and shrubbery, and a carefully tended lawn. Motor bikes clogged the walkway at restaurants that had their doors opened to the pedestrian traffic, and trees lined the curbside. I enjoyed walking through this beautiful place instead of planting my butt in one of those seats in the bus. After the mildew and rain, the fresh smells of the big city were refreshing.

Independence Palace came into view as we rounded the next corner. A large, imposing three-story structure, a 1960s architectural marvel, presented a crisp, white façade against the verdant gardens and trees of the palace's grounds. Unlike the Presidential Palace in Hanoi, with its time-worn beauty of traditional architecture and old-growth trees, this place was a hallmark of modernism, almost stark but with something pleasing to the eye seeping from the edges. We commandeered an electric shuttle to carry us over the long street to the building.

The interior of the palace painted a picture of opulence, something not characteristic of the Vietnamese people. Even the rich carvings and ornate motifs of the Citadels presented an unpresuming presence, the gifts of ancient craftsmen who surely loved their work. Ho Chi Minh certainly understood the importance of maintaining a connection to the common people, something the South Vietnamese leaders had failed to grasp. Compared to the humbler facilities of the NVA, the contrast was garishly offensive. As I stood in the vast hallways, teeming with sculptures and grand artwork, and surveyed the generous rooms stocked with stylish, contemporary furniture, the contempt I had felt for the North Vietnamese suddenly turned and an aversion for the South Vietnamese regime crawled through my sensitivities leaving me with a repugnant view toward the government I had spent a year of my life fighting for. I began to see how it came about that the south had lost the war. The leaders, if they really were leaders, had been preoccupied with their own personal empires and paid little heed to their country and their people.

I'm normally not emotional. Even at funerals, if I can force myself to attend, I feel little grief for the departed. They don't know they're dead. I guess it's everyone else that doesn't realize that. But as I stood there in the midst of all of that grandeur, I truly felt compassion for all of the people who had lost their lives for such a wanton war and for the families who suffered because of it. I had a deeper understanding of the cost of the Vietnam War.

Thom and I found our way to the bunkers in the basement. Again, it seemed as if the ARVN commanders had everything in the way of communications and mapping gear; the NVA possessed a mere shadow of the resources I saw there in that bunker. It showed that all of the money and grand facilities in the world would not necessarily guarantee success.

By the time we neared the end of our tour, crowds were gathering in the hallways, tourists coming to see the grand palace. We made one last run through a hallway and found the white Mercedes-Benz that the president used for his personal vehicle. That and the gift shop that drew Thom in like a bug into a vacuum cleaner. It was an interesting store with a variety of goods I hadn't seen before, but like many of the other gift shops, it was a tourist stop for souvenirs.

Truc was assembling the platoon, finding us one or two at a time. We mounted the electric cart and it took us to a thatch-roofed break area behind the palace where we relaxed with soft drinks. We enjoyed our break and listened to an attractive young woman playing a kind of xylophone affair made of maybe 50 short lengths of bamboo arranged in 3 vertical rows, something like the bones of fish held on end. It was one of the most beautiful sounds I've heard; similar to a harp but more like a soft, mellow xylophone.

I looked around the grounds at the forest of trees, some gnarled with long, intermingling branches overhanging the grass, that might have been over a hundred years old. The majestic giants stood proudly, reaching their strong limbs skyward as if guarding the palace.

We gathered to return to the front entrance and Truc spotted a photographer, and he hurried over to him, his hand outstretched, fingers waving. After a brief negotiation, he had arranged to have a group photo taken with a copy provided for each of us. Of course, since this was an impromptu opportunity, we each shelled out $6 for a photo.

We had all lined up in rows with the palace in the background, and the photographer stationed himself in front, positioning everyone where he wanted. Another fellow with a camera stood beside the photographer, ready to take advantage of this rare opportunity to capture a group of Americans. While we calmly waited for the shutter to snap, someone said, "Hey, looks like we've got company."

I turned to my left and looked to the rear, and sure enough, one of the locals had joined in at the end of the back row smiling as if he had just won some kind of award. There we were in our VC uniforms with a local civilian in formation. It took a few minutes for everyone to realize what was going on. Then it hit Truc.

He broke ranks, and waving his hands in the air as if to signal a cease-fire, he stomped over the stranger and motioned for him to get out of our group. Several choice words in Vietnamese slammed the poor guy in the face, then Truc turned his assault to the other fellow with the camera, a friend, no doubt. He hurriedly snapped a picture before his friend left the group. They both sidled away, still looking back for another opportunity, smiling at their cunning.

I was amused by the effect of a camera in that country. It seemed to ignite the passion for photos of not just anyone, but of themselves. Even on the mall, Thom and I had roamed the night before, boys and girls would pose themselves with any motif nearby in front of the stores for photos. Selfies were also popular.

Those of the group returning to the hotel wandered back to the bus. The rest of us were free to explore the downtown area. Thom and I wanted to visit the market that some of the fellows raved about. After hearing of all the authentic goods that could be purchased, I was enthralled by the mystery of the Vietnamese market. We joined Don, Dennis, and Duane and we strolled off in the general direction of where we thought the market might be.

Thom had obtained a map of the city at the hotel desk, one of the last ones, and he was appointed as the official navigator. It didn't take long for us to realize that Thom had not done well in the army's map-reading course, and we had no idea where we were. We finally determined the direction of North and we immediately adjusted our course. Truc had given us basic directions, scant at best, but we recognized some of the street names. In traipsing through the city, we dodged trees and motorbikes clogging the sidewalks and passed by shop after shop selling souvenirs, restaurant after restaurant (I wondered just how much these people could actually eat), and sidewalk vendors selling fresh meat, vegetables and fruit.

Then we saw it across the street, stretching from one end of the block to the other. Swarms of people mingled on the sidewalks moving in and out of the building. We played chicken with the traffic to cross the intersection and gazed at the spectacle that stood before us. It was like a colossal sidewalk sale at a county fair. Shops and booths jammed side-by-side selling flowers, clothing, foodstuffs, everything I could imagine and some I couldn't. And we hadn't even gone inside, yet.

Being the impulsive shopper that he is, Thom was hooked and he darted into a clothing shop, still looking for the perfect outfit that he couldn't seem to get on-line. I humored him while he browsed, and I took in a belt shop, although I didn't really need a belt. I was surprised at the quality of the merchandise. I saw a few brand names I recognized, but most of it was locally made, I imagine, because I had seen nothing like them.

Thom finally emerged from a leather shop with a broad smile on his face, but then there always seemed to be a kind of smile there. He held up a new wallet, which explained a wider smile than usual. We garnered our courage and dived inside the market.

Only one step into the labyrinth of aisles and I was stopped dead by a pall of fish, raw meat, and cooking fumes that was so dense I could almost taste it and feel it as if it were a tangible, airborne cloud floating beneath the roof. The stench could have put some people into a coma before they reached the opposite side of the building.

I was accosted by what I thought was every species of fish or anything else that came from the sea. My eyes followed row after row of stands selling infinite varieties of strange, raw meats that came from... well, I'm not sure where it all came from, and I didn't really want to know. I believe that subconsciously I had suspected the source of much of it, but such notions had proven to be faulty in this country.

After the initial shock ebbed, we started down the main aisle at the center of the building, people swarming like bees in a hive. It was as if I were a child again left to wander through one of those mega-toy stores, my mind aflutter with wonderment and disbelief. Booth after booth of fruits, vegetables, beverages, flowers, shoes (very popular, by the way), clothing, belts, hats, jewelry, leather goods, artwork, crafts, tools, and things I didn't even know what were. If you couldn't find it there, you didn't need it. The folks there seemed to be in a kind of euphoric mist that made them smile whether they wanted to or not, min-gling among fellow shoppers as if they were neighbors or close friends. It was a far cry from the mayhem of American discount stores where growls, scowls, and rowdy kids fill the aisles.

The brightly lit booths and displays were inviting, and since I loved to wander about old stores with creaky, wooden floors and layers of dust on the shelves, I had to restrain myself from getting sucked into the glut of strange and exotic merchandise. I saw Don and Duane hurry toward something down the aisle, and I had to step up my pace to keep up with Thom's anxious enthusiasm.

It was all too much. I moved through quickly, because I knew by then that if I paused longer than a split second in front of something, the vendor would be on me like a fly on a cow patty. My swift drive through the aisles, though, didn't stop them from trying. I kept shaking my head and waving them off until Thom and I finally found an exit.

After gathering our senses, Thom said, "I'd like to go back and see the cathedral."

"Okay by me," I told him. "Where is it?"

He pulled out his map again, and after a few minutes found the church boldly marked. It didn't look like it was too far away, but then I took stock of where the market was located on the map and adjusting for scale, it could have been about a mile across town.

"Hey, we can walk that, can't we?" he asked, optimistically.

"Sure, no problem," I said, in spite of the angry temperature driven by the sun overhead. "Which way?"

I checked the compass on my phone, knowing that we would have to head in a westerly direction to reach the cathedral.

He looked at the map, not with any degree of certainty then said, "This way."

I looked to the north, the direction he was pointing.

"I'm thinking we probably need to veer off to the left at some point," I suggested.

"Well, we'll get there."

I wished like hell I'd had a copy of that map.

Off we went into the depths of Ho Chi Minh City, knowing where we wanted to go, but not knowing exactly how to get there. It was half a shirt of sweat later that we found ourselves at an intersection, one of those with five streets meeting. Just behind us on the corner was cycloped, a single-seat job, and the driver, a small man hardly large enough to sit on the seat, spotted us. I think there is some universal sign of distress that cyclo drivers used and we must given off the signal somehow from our innocent actions.

"You need ride?" he shouted in his clipped English.

Thom, never a stranger, took the opportunity to ask directions to the cathedral.

The driver, still smiling, pointed to the west (yup, wished I'd had the map) and said, "Five dollar."

Thom's grin widened as he looked at the small vehicle. "Five dollars?" he echoed, to make sure of the offer, and he held up his hand, all five fingers exploding from his fist.

The little man nodded, as the Vietnamese do, not just a nod, but an exaggerated articulation of the head and neck in a sweeping up and down movement.

Then he turned to the front of his cyclo and pointed to the seat, then at Thom. "Get in," he ordered.

We both looked at the affair, the back half of a bicycle behind a seat between two wheels. Just a single seat.

Thom pointed at me, "Where does he sit?" he asked, his eyes also questioning the man.

The fellow nodded again, and said, "Get in...get in."

The little man pushed the footrest down and putting the rear wheel into the air so Thom could mount the thing. Once Thom was tentatively settled, the little man spread his legs apart, motioning for Thom to do the same. I didn't like where this was going.

Thom followed the instructions and the fellow said to me, "Get in," with a sweep of his hand.

I stood there for a moment wondering if this was really happening. Thom looked at me, pleading with his eyes. I took a breath and climbed aboard, resting myself on Thom's lap and bracing my feet against the footrest in front. Then another man approached to pull the driver's seat out of the air and hold the rear of the cyclo down so our driver could mount up on the back of the contraption.

After a very slow start, we felt each lunge of the driver's legs as we loped off into the stream of traffic on our way to the cathedral, blocks away. I'm can't vouch for Thom's comfort, but I was miserable trying to keep much of my weight off of his thighs, and my legs felt the stress, as well as the sharp pressure from his thigh bones on my butt. We drifted along the edges of the streets while cars and motorbikes whizzed by us a mere breath away. I could see us winding up in some hospital there, victims of our own stupidity totally at the mercy of the Vietnamese medical expertise, whatever that was.

Lunge after lunge, our cyclo plodded along, and I thought the poor fellow was giving out, the forceful exertions of his legs waning at times. But soon after, a burst of energy recaptured our leisurely speed and propelled us along the street toward our destination, mingling with other traffic that errantly swerved to the side to pass or avoid a collision. Oddly enough, no one tried to bully his way in front of us or force us off the road. Such patience I would never see back home. We finally arrived at the cathedral and I carefully disembarked from the cyclo, since there was no one to hold down the back if the driver dismounted.

Thom held out VND 10,000, the $5 that was agreed upon, to the little man and he smiled and pulled out a rate card according to which we owed him VND 150,000.

"You said five dollars," Thom protested.

"Yes," the fellow replied, pointing to the card. "Five dollars."

"That's not five dollars," Thom argued, a smile on his face, obviously enjoying the dickering.

"Yes," the little man said. "Five dollars."

I still had a lot of dong left and fished VND 150,000 out of my pocket and thrust into fellow's hand. It was worth it to get off Thom's lap and stand on my own feet. The fellow smiled, got on his seat and pedaled away a happy man. It could have been an honest mistake, I figured, but I also thought the ruse was also intentional. What a con artist.

It was just before noon and my body had already burned through my breakfast. The rear of the cathedral sat before us in the middle of the intersection waiting for our approach. We saw a young woman in a wedding gown in the shade along one side of the cathedral, the train trailing across the sidewalk, her arms resting on her groom's shoulders, a romantic posture. The groom, outfitted in a tux, was looking into her eyes and I could pretty well figure out what he was thinking. Nearby stood the photographer at work making the bride immortal in digital imagery. A few feet down the sidewalk, we saw another couple in wedding garb, unable to take their eyes off each other. Then another couple with their entire party. There must have been six couples alongside the building posing for pictures.

"Don said there might be as many as 20 weddings here today," Thom said.

"Twenty?" I said.

"December is the traditional wedding season in Vietnam, just before the new year."

We passed by the wedding parties, each of brides in striking gowns, and the grooms fitted out with formal wear and strutting like peacocks. Some of them smiled and nodded to us. We nodded back and waved.

When we reached the front of the building, a sign on the door said the cathedral was closed until 3:00.

Thom's eyes drooped a bit, the smile giving up its hold on his face.

"It's closed," he said.

"What a bummer," I offered as consolation. "After all we went through and the damned thing is closed."

"Well," he said, "I'll just come back at three."

It was such a simple solution for him. Not for me. I wasn't coming back. I'm not sure what fascination the cathedral had for him, but I was starving.

We found our way back to the hotel by happenstance, in spite of our not knowing where we were going. Along the way, we passed an older lady sitting in front of a fence selling toys. Her face filled with age, the smile broke through the wrinkles, and Thom was instantly on alert. The paper snakes were clever and the little paper mice were cute, but that's all they were to me. It took a few minutes for Thom to come to his senses and we continued on to the hotel.

Once in the room we donned our swim trunks and headed to the pool on the roof. After a brief swim, and it *was* brief, I found that only one lap up and back, I thought I was going to die. That darned age thing really gets you.

We ordered lunch there and Tom Horan and Don joined us. The shade was perfect and the lounges comfortable. The company was better. We all were at ease, life was undemanding, and I melted into the camaraderie. I was not a talker, but there in the company of my peers, I held my own. I almost surprised myself that I could utter more than two words at a time.

We returned to the room where I dried off and cooled down. Thom got dressed to return to the cathedral. I eventually went downstairs and stopped at the hotel's casual café for a Sapporo beer, then ventured out on the streets. I had quite a bit of dong left in my pocket and I needed to get rid of it before I left the country. I hadn't purchased much except food, drinks, and the scarf for my daughter. My wife explicitly instructed me not to buy her anything (some of you guys reading this might die of envy, but she truly is a wonderful woman). Most of the stores along the mall catered to tourists with mass produced souvenirs, crafts, and clothing, none of which anyone I knew had a use for. Neither I nor my wife are into souvenirs and odds and ends to set around the house and collect dust. We have enough dust floating in from the gravel road in front our house to plant a garden in the living room.

I did find one shop with a nice variety of antiques and unusual items that drew my attention. I was tempted to purchase a table runner with an intricately woven pattern and attractive colors, but it wasn't long enough for our dining table. I thought about those small plastic tables in front of the shops. I considered folding fans, small sculptures, and such, but none of them would really look at home in our log house.

That night, Truc was providing a farewell dinner for us at a restaurant across from the hotel. The robust mood of the group made for a rowdy crowd. I was afraid we might get thrown out, but the staff seemed to take it all in stride. We started off with French fries, then won-tons, fried spring rolls (never a meal without them), and chicken and vegetables. This was followed by kabobs, bread and some kind of soup.

And it wouldn't be a VC Platoon meal without the wine and Truc's, "Yo...yo...yo!" Truc passed out copies of the group photo taken at the Independence Palace. Final toasts were made and even though spirits were high, there was a bit of somber restraint in the jovial group. Our adventure was nearing an end.

After dinner, Thom and I hit the mall one last time. We walked among the bands performing for large groups that encircled them, clapping and singing along in a festive kind of celebration. We stopped to watch the street dancing where young men and women performed solo or in groups. I think the Vietnamese were all hams, at heart, more than willing to perform for an audience. While Thom was enthralled by a small band with guitars, I headed into an ice cream shop. Actually, sandwiches and a variety of foods were offered, but the poster for ice cream bars caught my eye. I asked for a tiramisu bar. Once outside, I peeled open the paper wrapping and found a white, red and blue confection waiting for me to bite into it. At first, the coldness masked the flavor, but eventually, the taste of rich lemony cream that melted right there on my tongue and the unmistakable texture of sponge cake filled my mouth. It was glorious. I'd never had anything like it.

We'd had enough fun and returned to the hotel. Tomorrow we would be on our way home. We had a lot of packing to do. While I was folding clothes and stuffing them in my suitcase, it occurred to me that the last two weeks had been one hell of a ride. I had seen Vietnam north to south but I was only starting to understand the country and its people. I had expected to encounter hostility and indifference. What I found was a welcoming people with an earnest desire for friendship. Where I had expected uneasy memories to surface, I found answers to many of the questions that had gone unanswered for so many years. Where I had expected two weeks of exhaustive anxiety, I found a peaceful country where people are glad to welcome visitors and make them feel at home, sharing all of the beauty and pleasures Vietnam has to offer.

I wondered what the future would hold for them. I also wondered what the future would hold for America, given the lack of patriotism, the rift in political ideology caused by the radical factions. That and the sad state of our social interactions that seem to be disappearing in the face of technology and could easily be replaced with digital interactions that have no personal element. It scared the hell out of me.

But my time in Vietnam was coming to a close. I, for one, would be sad to see it end. Sure, I was looking forward to returning home to my family, but...this...Vietnam. It was so special, and for me, an educational experience. Actually, a life-changing event, so to speak. I had learned so much about Vietnam and its people, and I felt a bit of remorse at my unfair judgment I had made of them after the war. At least I felt fortunate to have had the opportunity to rectify that.

It would be an early morning to catch the flight to Shanghai. I had mixed feelings about that. I had never been to China. Had never wanted to go. And, unlike Vietnam, I'm fairly certain that if anyone had offered me the opportunity, I would have declined. There were too many reasons not to go. I had talked to friends who had been there and the implication was that it was not a friendly place for Americans. That was enough for me.

CHAPTER 16

THE RETURN HOME

Monday, 14 December, 2015

This was the day we split up. Don Hooper left first with a 5:30 flight, taking a cab to the airport. My flight left at 9:20. Thom was stuck on an 11:00 flight that night. There were 6 of us in my group. The plane, a Vietnam Airlines Airbus 330-200, 8 seats across (2-4-2 arrangement), seemed comfortable enough. I was stuck in the back of the plane away from the rest of the group in the midst of passengers looking as tired as I probably did. We were due into Shanghai at about 2:15. An hour and a half into the fight, Ken showed up at my seat.

"There's a lot of empty seat up front," he said. "If you want to move, it's only about half full."

I looked around my section at the passengers squeezed abreast like wieners in a package.

"I think it's a no-brainer," I said.

I got up and followed him forward. I found a window seat behind Ken and took up residence there. We talked about the trip for the remainder of the flight.

"What did you think of the trip?" he asked.

"I'm glad I came." I leaned forward so we could hear each other better. I was on his bad side.

"I really enjoyed the food," he said.

"Yeah, it was pretty good. Nothing like what I get at home. But you know, I'm ready for some good old American food."

My butt had grown weary from the seats of planes and buses, and the nagging pain in my right leg, most likely a nerve, had become more than just a nuisance. I found it hard to sit on my left cheek all the time. I would be seeing the chiropractor when I got back. I figured he had missed me during my three-year absence from his clinic.

We were approaching Shanghai, which I had given little thought to during the flight. When Tom Baca first told me we would be returning to America through Shanghai, a burst of excitement blew through me; an opportunity to see a new land, China. And the idea was that we might have a chance to ride the maglev train there, one of those gems of technology that enables a train to ride on a cushion of air while confined to the track by strong electromagnetic fields. The more I thought about it, the excitement waned. I remembered the stories Fred Chrenshaw had told us when I had worked at Coltec Automotive in Sallisaw in production control. He was part of an investigation team sent to China to explore the possibility of manufacturing automotive parts over there. His descriptions of the myriad fences around buildings that were used to keep the population in instead of other people out gave me the chills. That and the strict observance by uniformed guards, or whatever they were, to keep his party within a very tight corridor of visitation. China didn't sound at all like a place I would choose to visit.

The apprehension I'd had earlier about Shanghai had not deserted me and as I looked through the window at the airport as the plane descended to the runway and saw a tall fence with concertina wire all around the place. Recalling Fred's story, I didn't' know if the fence was to keep people out, or keep people in. As I walked through the ramp to the terminal, I think the hair on the back of my neck might have bristled. Once in the terminal, we had no idea where to go. Confusion took over.

The terminal was a beauty, obviously designed to impress. It impressed me. The soaring ceilings and vast spaces inside made me feel small and insignificant, as I guess it was supposed to. I guess the effect wasn't that much different from other airport terminals.

We discovered that Vietnam Airlines, for some reason, had not checked our bags through to our destinations. We would have to pick them up from baggage claim and check them again for the connecting flight at the ticket counter. What a crock.

Wandering through the cavernous building among an army of military types and police, our group made it to the immigration area. There we found three lines: Chinese immigration, foreigners, and special something or other. Well, we were foreigners, we weren't immigrating to China, and as far as we knew we weren't special. We were eyeing the foreigners' line when a stern looking woman in a police uniform directed us to the Chinese immigration line, the longest one, of course.

That's one of the things I noticed right off; all of the women I saw in uniform looked like they could chew through my arm or leg in seconds. The men looked like just...men. Stoic and stone-faced, but men. None of the pleasant and helpful folks I would expect to find in America.

If you're familiar with large airport terminals, you can imagine the long line weaving back and forth between straps of webbing on posts. I suppose that arrangement was universal to the world. I thought it strange that no one had been able to come up with a better system. When I reached the front of the line, I approached a cubicle with a serious woman in charge, obviously not given to smiling a lot, and who must have had an unfortunate encounter with a beautician. I did not get a chance to see her teeth. I placed my gate pass and passport on the desk.

"You have yellow card?" she asked, her voice stout as a bellowing ox and about as friendly.

"No," I said.

She handed me a yellow card and pointed to a desk at the side of the lanes.

I pulled my gear over to the desk and filled out the entrance form, then headed back to the cubicle. When the fellow there had finished getting checked through, I faced the woman again and handed her the card. In spite of the sneer on her face, she miraculously stamped me through.

Our group assembled on the far side of the immigration station and headed for the baggage claim area. By the time we got there, our bags were the only ones left. I was shocked that they were still on the carousel. Not knowing where to go from there, we inquired at a ground transportation desk as to the location of the ticket counters. The lady, who could almost have been attractive had it not been for the furrowed eyebrows and rigid jaw, pointed upstairs.

After escalators and elevators, we found ourselves facing another endless line of passengers waiting patiently in the winding lanes of the American Airlines ticket counter. Thirty minutes later, I was standing in front of a ticket agent. He routinely, without cracking a smile, handed me a ticket. I wondered by then if China had some law or rule against smiling. I tried to restrain myself from grinning, thinking they might take offense to it. This certainly was different from Vietnam. Even in the busy American airports, the employees joke with one another and seem to enjoy their jobs. When I studied the Chinese with their sour looks and submissive demeanor, I wondered just how unhappy they could possibly be.

I had placed my carry-on bag on the scale to check it through. It was processed and sent on its way riding the conveyor to where ever the things went. Then he put a tag on my large bag, but put it on another conveyor.

"You go to baggage inspection," he said curtly, jabbing his finger to his right. "Bag must be inspected."

I stood there for a moment, wondering why he had not sent other bags there for inspection. I tried to think of whatever in hell I might have put in the bag that would sound an alarm. Well, I figured something like this might happen. While I made my way next door to the baggage inspection room, I was rapidly replaying everything I had packed. I couldn't think of anything that would be suspicious except the dead camera batteries I was taking home to recycle.

My irritation was mollified when I saw that another fellow was already in the clutches of the inspector's eyes, two piercing black points with no humor or cordiality. In fact, his face was much like the faces of the other officials I had seen; like blank, unfeeling, automatons. The fellow in front of me was removing the contents of his large bag, a scowl on his face, obviously unhappy about the ordeal. He was told to open a large cardboard box, as well. I guess the inspector didn't see anything of interest, because he passed the man through. The poor man struggled to reclose the box then nearly threw it onto the conveyer before he left, throwing a nasty look at the guard.

It was my turn and the inspector yanked my suitcase off the conveyor and slammed it down in front of me. I automatically unlocked my bag before he could rip it apart and unfastened the covers over each side. The tactless fellow pawed through most of the items, but not as thoroughly as he did the bag of the man before me. Apparently, there was nothing of interest and he motioned for me to close my bag and put it back on the conveyor. I was done.

I hurried back to the ticket lobby and headed for the security area where I found the others. I was also thinking about my safety there. Were they profiling me as an American? Did I present some kind of threat? Or where they just paranoid?

"What happened to you?" asked Ken.

"I had to go through bag inspection."

"No shit?"

I shook my head. "I don't know…"

"None of *us* had to."

We fell into line.

Another long wait. Our passports were checked, then we were herded into the inspection area. My turn came up, and I put my boarding pass and passport on the shelf in front of the man seated there, his poker face revealing nothing of himself.

"You have yellow card?" he asked, his voice neutral, could have been either nice or not. I figured not.

Hell, I thought I'd just filled out a danged card.

"No," I said. "I filled one out at immigration."

"That was for entry," he said. "You need exit card." He pointed to the side.

Another desk. There I found yellow cards, two parts. The sour woman at the immigration probably should have given me both parts. I filled the thing out and returned to the cubicle. He stamped me through.

After nearly completely disrobing, I made it through the security inspection and headed for the gate. I was the last one out and again, Ken was waiting for me.

"I thought you might be lagging behind," he said.

"This isn't my day."

I followed him to the gate where Pat was waiting. He agreed to watch our bags while we went for something to drink.

We found a restaurant and selected a table away from everyone else. We each ordered Tsingato beers. The waitress, a young, smart looking Chinese woman with the first smile I'd seen there, brought the beers with two cold glasses and a small bowl of peanuts. I guess I was wrong about the law against smiling.

"So, you glad to be going home?" I asked him.

He nodded his head. "Yeah," he said. "It's time to go back."

"I really enjoyed this trip," I said, reaching for the peanuts.

"You know," he said, leaning in and narrowing his eyes, "I did too."

"I'm not coming back to China, though," I told him.

"What happened to you back there?"

"Well, hell, I don't know why they sent me to baggage inspection to inspect one my bags."

He chuckled. "Smuggling something?"

I laughed. "No, I think they're just being pricks. I guess I had the lucky number in their random search."

"What held you up in security?"

"Apparently, the first guard I saw at immigration was supposed to give me two cards, one for entry, and one for exit. She only gave me the entry card." A swig of beer." Then when I got to security, the guy asked for the exit card and I had to go fill one of those damn things out."

About that time, Jack and Ed joined us. Ken and Jack replayed a scene from Ho Chi Minh City.

"Remember that one girl in that one shop?" asked Jack.

Ken's playful smile spread across his face, his eyes laughing. "She told me she wanted a picture."

He showed me a photo of the two of them leaning against each other, that same smile on his face, a dreamy one on the girl's face.

It wasn't long before we returned to the gate for boarding. As we filed through the door and into the walkway, I'll be darned if guards didn't inspect us again. Holy hell! I wondered if I was ever getting out of China.

We eventually made it onto the American Airlines plane and things started to look better. We left a little bit late, and then I wondered if I would make my connection at the Dallas-Fort Worth Airport. I didn't worry too much, but the thought nagged at me the entire trip. I figured my connection would be in a different terminal and I'd have to race through the place to get to the gate on time, if I made it at all.

The flight was quiet, no one stirred much, and I didn't either. I tried to sleep, but that didn't happen. We were due in to DFW at about 7:00 that evening. I would wind up in Tulsa shortly after 9:00 that night, the day before. The International Date Line, again.

My luck changed heading back to America. Our flight arrived a bit late, but the flight to Tulsa was late getting off, too. I made the connection with time to spare.

That last hour was hell, even though it was the shortest leg of the trip. My leg was throbbing and there was no position that was comfortable. Boy, I sure wished that chiropractor was there.

Once on the ground at Tulsa, I sent a text to my daughter, Courtney, who was waiting in the cell phone lot. That's the small lot near the terminal set aside for folks awaiting arrivals. The parking was free and easily accessible to the arrivals doors.

I claimed my bags and burst out of the door to find my wife and daughter there at the curb. Bobbie helped me load my bags in the back of the car and off we went to Courtney's house in Coweta. And off went my mouth about the sights and experiences in Vietnam.

After a shower and a glass of Canadian whisky, tempered by more tales of Vietnam, I finally wound down enough to crawl into bed. But with the feelings I'd had revisiting Vietnam doing the back stroke across my mind, the tides of misery, delight, fear, and anticipation had not ebbed enough for sleep. I read for a while for distraction. I remember seeing the clock's hands approach midnight. That's the last thing I remember until morning.

I was up before 5:00, my body still on Vietnam time, which was around 6:00 in the evening. I awoke with the languor of the fascinating people of Vietnam still in my thoughts, like the punch line of an unusual joke that keeps you laughing well beyond the joke's end. The happy faces with smiles that bid you welcome and the high-pitched nasal voices resounded through my memory, like excited children in a playground, dominating the cache of impressions I had accumulated over the last two weeks. Nothing else seemed as important to me then.

I had difficulty identifying that lighthearted feeling on the trip. But now I realize it was almost intoxicating to be around the Vietnamese. Every person our group had met seemed delighted that we were Americans, as if we possessed some virtuous quality that played to their conceptions of another place to which they had never been. Reflecting back to my own country, I found it equally as difficult to imagine any of us being enthralled by visitors from foreign lands, instead, casting a skeptical eye at them.

It's sad to think that mainstream Americans choose to remain so isolated from other cultures, as if fearing an onslaught of discomfort. And there it is; everyone has a comfort zone. That's the place to which we retreat when threatened, or when we experience something new and unfamiliar, or something we don't understand. We all do it. I think it must be a part of who we are as humans.

As I began to sort through notes and photographs, I eventually reclaimed the life I had left for two weeks, but not without the vestige of what life *could* be like. The life I had lived for two weeks in Vietnam.

Once at home, I began sorting through my notes and writing this book. Being able to relive the Vietnamese experience was not an unpleasant chore. I had new friends with which to correspond, a new world to explore, and a new vision of hope. Sometimes we have to dig it up to find it. It lays buried beneath tons of neglect and selfishness. At least I had managed to unearth it.

CHAPTER 17

BACK HOME

When I left Vietnam in December of 1971, hot, sweaty, emotionally drained, and angry, I could not have imagined any desire to return to that sultry, forbidding pit of military and political mayhem. I was only too glad to climb the steps into the bouquet of formaldehyde and plastic, powered by jet engines that would shoot me back across the Pacific to my home and the life that I remembered from nearly a year before. The sudden sense of relief had drowned me in a slight euphoria.

I had been freed from the ugliness of war; however, it wasn't true freedom. I had continued to feel the sting of conflict and the uncertainty of survival. The war had laid a patina of disillusionment over me, a kind of haze that muddled my vision of democracy and freedom and all of that. It didn't dilute the sting, though; I still remember that feeling, just like the ones I remembered when I stood there with Thom in front of Nui Hon Cha Mountain. It's funny how that works, the mind pulling bits of my past from the abyss of images and events that lay hidden beneath reality; a kind of paramnesia where I wonder if it really happened at all.

I laugh now at the apprehension I felt on the plane to Dallas when I started this journey, and the doubts that dramatized my concerns about returning to a country that I was so anxious to leave behind. I always do that to myself. I guess we are conditioned by our experiences in life to be skeptical of what we don't understand. This can be a good thing at times, but it can also render a person's life banal and self-absorbing. As I have aged, I have begun to realize that I had missed out on so much of life just by playing it safe, keeping to familiar things and people, and avoiding connections to that dubious year of my life.

The return to Vietnam opened the door to the world I had shunned, and revived the thirst for excitement I had known as a young man, as meager as it was. The stop at Qui Nhon brought back a torrent of memories, some good, some bad, but they all played a part in making me who I am. Standing there on the road, looking again at Nui Hon Cha

Marc Cullison

Mountain 44 years after I had left it, I relived part of 1971. Much to my surprise, I wasn't incapacitated by fearsome flashbacks; I wasn't reduced to a diehard avenger; I wasn't filled with volatile feelings toward the Vietnamese. Instead, I found peaceful answers to the mistrust and antipathy I had harbored for those 44 long years; answers that relieved me of guilt and absolved me of my fear of inadequacy. Most importantly, it confirmed that the decision I had made in college to stay in ROTC and accept a commission as an officer was not a wrong one.

The Vietnam War had not been popular. How you felt about it was a very personal thing, known only to you and those close enough who would not judge you. But what you did about it depended on the company you kept. I am fortunate that I had placed myself in the company of friends that respected patriotism and had that same drive for duty that I had.

The journey also opened a vast circle of new friends, brothers of a kind, men like myself that experienced what I had experienced, endured what I had endured, and felt much as I felt. And other friends that once might have been enemies; an enigma that would have challenged my sanity so long ago. But now it all makes sense. This alone would have been worth the trip, but the two weeks I spent in Vietnam have given much more value to my life. All of the regrets that had shaped my attitudes and beliefs suddenly seemed so unimportant.

I also found it possible to stand back and look at America, now, more objectively. Where the Vietnamese seem industrious and congenial, I see Americans as self-absorbed and uninspired toward achievement, unless money is involved. Money seems to drive us; we judge ourselves by what we don't have that our neighbors do; we spend a fortune on self-gratification, especially at sporting events, rather than education; we think we are much better than we are; apparently, we think money buys happiness. But the Vietnamese don't have all of that money, and yet they seem a far happier lot than we are.

Of course, I saw only the surface of Vietnam. I suspect that had I delved into the depths of the country's humanity, I might very well have found much of the same oppression, corruption, poverty, and prejudices that I find in America. But if any of that was there, it was well hidden.

The trip has made me re-evaluate America. This book might seem to be a bit hard on The United States, but someone needs to be. We have

198

so much freedom, so much independence, and so much material wealth. But what do we do with it all? Many folks squander their freedom on berating others who disagree with them. Some waste it attempting to get something for nothing. Our independence has driven us to abandon the family unit in search of our own happiness and success. And still others have lost the ability to rationalize their feelings, instead reacting to things rather than attempting to understand them; or analyze situations objectively. They rely on others to make decisions for them. What has resulted is that we no longer know what happiness or success really is. We no longer have close ties to family, and obligations to our elders have been displaced by selfishness and indifference. And many of us rely on someone else to think for us, to tell us how we should behave, how we should live our lives; to tell us what is important and what is not.

As a nation of immigrants, which defines almost all of our ancestries, after over 200 years we have yet to outgrow the protectionist shield that denies compassion for those who would follow in our footsteps. After experiencing the generosity and kindness of the Vietnamese people to visitors from a country that was once a foe, I can only say that I am disappointed with the state of our own affairs. Our political system is in a shambles, given over to business and industry at the expense of the average American, dominated, it appears, by unscrupulous lobbyists and corrupt politicians. It used to be that we had the best and brightest of our lot to lead us. Now what do we have but, for the most part, self-serving pundits of rhetoric with little substance or patriotism?

I don't mean to belittle America. I love my country and I have served four years in its service, one of them putting my life on the line for it. But it could be so much better if we could only stop and see what we are doing to ourselves, especially to our families, children, and grand-children. Family has taken on a new meaning to me, even though much of my own family has passed on. I see where I could have made better use of my efforts.

I can see myself going back to Vietnam again, but with my wife and daughter. I know Courtney would fall in love with the place. Bobbie...well, it might have to grow on her for a while, but I think she would find the people there intriguing. I know, I do.

I once thought it ironic that enemies could become friends after 44 years. I now find it comforting that enemies can see through the hostility and politics of war to realize what humanity has been seeking for centuries: respect and consideration for your neighbor. That, after all, is part of what the Vietnamese are about. Friendship. It is one of the things I admire most about them: the capacity to be lifelong and dedicated friends.

In the brief two-week stay in Vietnam, I learned a great deal about those folks. Yes, they have a different culture, but it is not so very different from what we as Americans aspire to. It's just that they actually live it. We just hope for it. It seems like I learned so much about them, but in reality, I learned very little of what there is to learn. What I saw on the surface of each Vietnamese person was just that; the surface. Beneath the smile and amicable demeanor lies a deeper passion for fellowship that most of us will never know. That and patriotism. I'm sure there is another world in there; one that I would find welcoming.

As an American citizen, I am proud of my heritage, and having done my part to serve it and protect our freedoms that we cherish, I truly feel fortunate to be an American. I had always been taught that our country was the greatest in the world, a beacon of hope for the oppressed, an example for individual freedom and liberty. I consider myself to be a patriot. I also see that many Americans have forgotten what patriotism is all about. They shun the thought of serving to protect America and instead milk it for riches and personal gain.

This is one of the other things I admire about the Vietnamese. They are true patriots. They love their country and are willing to fight for it. They turned away the Japanese; they turned away the French; they turned away Americans. A country can't do that in the absence of patriotism.

The military machine changes a lot of folks. I think it changed me. I'm not sure what I would have been without it, but I'm certain I wouldn't be who I am today. The army's indoctrination, although sometimes subtle, was anxiously absorbed by us young college students. No matter what we had believed before the military sank its teeth into us, when we found ourselves in Vietnam, if people weren't in the U. S. military, or one of our allied units, they were the enemy. Period. Of course, when you're fighting a war, that's the way it must be. You certainly can't send troops to fight if they have any compassion for the enemy at all.

Another good thing came of this trip, other than the opportunity to replay my time there: the realization that I was not the only veteran who felt the way I did and that there is no need for guilt. We did our jobs, just like the enemy did their jobs. Each of us fought for our own reasons, just, or not. But anyone who holds the Vietnamese in contempt or harbors hostile feelings against them because of the Vietnam War has not found peace with himself, and that will needlessly torment him for the rest of his life.

I've been known to hold a grudge or two. Most of us have, at one time. But age seems to temper one's frustration and anger with a bit of compassion, if we allow it. If we don't, we age in misery and loneliness. I'm lucky to have found my way beyond that.

A Vietnam veteran's life is like an iceberg. What other people see and what they hear is merely that part of the veteran that is visible, the 10% floating on top of the insouciance of society. The other 90% lies beneath the surface, unknown to any except those who have fought in the Vietnam War; unknown even to many of the soldiers of subsequent wars. The majority of who and what the veteran is remains obscure and reticent, unwilling to surrender to the curiosity of others, fearing loss of what little dignity he has left. It is no wonder that these men and women who did their duty, just like the soldiers of World War II, the Korean War, and wars in the Middle East, had been largely disregarded by our country, so used to exhibiting pride in achievement. There was little pride to be had by a Vietnam vet other than the knowledge that he had served his country, even though the public rarely endorsed it.

As I wrote this book, I reached backward to retrieve the memories born in 1971, not to relive the darkness that had kept them buried, but to put them to rest. My life for the last 44 years has achieved a degree of normalcy, or as normal as anyone would see it. I have played out my role as husband, father, and veteran, and now, having been afforded the opportunity to return to Vietnam, the place where it all began, the memories resurfaced. It was during the two weeks traveling on the roads of that small country, seeing the beauty I had not seen before, that the color of those memories changed, a pale hue now dissolving that gray mist that had shrouded my life, like soap washing away a stain.

This journey has given me back my thoughts that no longer linger on the threshold of denial, leaving a nearly clean slate on which to lay them out and savor the experiences that once seemed so disparaging. I can honestly say that any Vietnam veteran who has doubted his or her worth should endeavor to go back; go back to the country where all of the grief began. Life puts you in places you never expected to be. We all had our own reasons for going to Vietnam. Going back seems to have validated mine.

I think everyone in our group gained something from this trip; new knowledge about Vietnam, enlightenment about the people, comfort from years of anxiety, or merely the motivation to seek help in putting their lives back together. As I said earlier, life puts you in places you didn't expect to be. I certainly didn't expect to be back in Vietnam.

Dinh Ngoc Truc made possible all of what this book is about. I didn't know the fellow before landing in Hanoi, but his jovial personality and integrity left us all with the assurance that he was indeed our friend. I regret that I didn't have the opportunity to meet him earlier. I would have cherished our new friendship even more. His efforts in orchestrating this tour is something I would never have expected of anyone, not even a close friend. It all seems so overwhelming, with the hotel reservations, transportation, meals, exhibits, official documents, the itinerary and schedule. It was a monumental effort that the "VC Platoon" will never forget.

Truc has since retired and is engaged in a veterans' tour business. I know he will be successful. He understands us as Americans, and that makes all the difference. I would do it again, once my financial status has returned to something acceptable. Tours like this aren't cheap, but Truc's tour gave us the most bang for the buck. I just can't see that happening with anyone who is not a veteran. Vietnam is a very affordable place to visit, and the food is …well, it's just too good.

So here's to Truc, full of cheer, fun, and adventure. I feel honored to have him and his family as friends.

MEET THE MEMBERS OF THE VC PLATOON

Dinh Ngoc Truc

Dinh Ngoc Truc started school in 1964 when he was 8 years old. He spent his first school year in Hanoi, but moved to the countryside with his parents because of U.S. bombing raids on the city, which forced most people out of Hanoi.

The family lived in a small house on the grounds of a small hospital in the village in Thuong Tin District, Ha Tay Province, where his father worked as an ophthalmologist. In grades 5 to 7, Truc moved to a primary school in Thanh Oai District without his parents. Truc's father had become seriously ill with heart problems, and his parents moved back to Hanoi, where Truc's mother looked after his father.

In 1968, when Truc was 12 years old, his father died. He returned to Hanoi for Grades 8 to 10 after the United States halted bombing of the city. The family lived in the Old Quarter near Hoan Kim Lake in a house that had belonged to his grandfather, until his grandparents moved to Saigon in 1954.

A U.S. bomb hit the house in 1967. No one was injured, but the roof was damaged. It was temporarily repaired so the family could continue living in the home. After the war, the damage was permanently repaired.

During high school, Truc and his friends listened to popular music on Voice of America and the BBC. Some of their favorites were "Red River Valley" and "Tequila" instrumentals. Other popular recording artists were The Platters. It was illegal to listen to VOA and the BBC because Vietnam and the United States were at war, so Truc and his friends listened to the broadcasts secretly in their homes. Truc and his friends also enjoyed playing football, fishing and swimming. There was no Internet there. It they had money, they would go to coffee houses.

He received an allowance from his mother. There were no jobs available to young people during the war, and there were no dances. Boys and girls saw each other socially, going to coffee houses and to the cinema.

Truc's first job after graduating from high school in May 1974 was as a construction worker, mixing mortar for new buildings in Hanoi. His mother lived on pension after her husband's death. At age 18, Truc was no longer covered by pension. While working, he continued living with his mother. Truc worked construction for three months, starting in October, and then joined the People's Army in December.

He received four weeks of basic military training outside of Hanoi. During training, he learned how to march, sing and get up early. After completing basic training, Truc and his fellow soldiers were driven south to the Republic of Vietnam border. There, during a ceremony, they removed markings from their People's Army uniform and put on a single red star. The trainees then underwent firearms training at a camp in South Vietnam. Truc was assigned to the 5-member crew of a .37 mm antiaircraft gun. His gun crew headed south on the Ho Chi Minh Trail to Vung Tau, at the mouth of the Saigon River, in a large Russian lorry. The truck towed a .37 mm antiaircraft gun.

The war ended in April 1975 after the People's Army — known to Americans as the North Vietnam Army — overran the South Vietnamese capital of Saigon.

On his first trip to Saigon after fighting stopped, Truc sought out a photographer and posed for a photo he would send his mother in Hanoi. He spread his feet widely, raised his arms their full length above his head and spread his fingers. The photograph showed all body parts intact. Truc had been unable to communicate with his mother throughout his time in South Vietnam.

Shortly after reunification, Truc visited Saigon to look for relatives living there. He went to Hai Ba Trung Street looking for his uncle, who worked as a doctor. He learned of his uncle's address while in route from Quang Tri to Da Nang on the Ho Chi Minh Trail when he met some South Vietnamese prisoners of war walking north. Truc had stopped for a meal break.

"I asked them, 'Where are you from?' One of them said, 'I am from Saigon.' So I asked him, 'Do you know Dr. Duong Dinh Tuan?' He said, 'Yes, I do. I know he has a clinic in front of Tan Dinh Market on Hai Ba Trung Street.'"

Truc was surprised that Saigon was so big. It was a coincidence that he had asked the one who knew his uncle. He was not sure he could go to Saigon. He was happy to know where his uncle was, but also worried he could not get to Saigon. He was a soldier and not a visitor.

Saigon residents were happy to take People's Army soldiers to look for relatives. As he was walking down the street, many people would approach and ask where he was going and offer to help. He climbed on the back of a motorcycle and wound up at the clinic.

"When I got there, I saw a sign with my uncle's name on it. I knocked on the door and the door opened. A soldier inside opened the door and asked me what I wanted. I asked him, do you know my uncle? He answered he did not know the owner."

The People's Army soldier, following orders, had been living in the house for a week.

Truc was upset because he did not know where his uncle was. This was the only address he knew for him and his other relatives in Saigon.

"I sat outside the house for about half an hour, then I went back and forth across the street. I stopped at my uncle's house and a lady came to me asked me who I was looking for. I told her, I'm looking for my uncle. The lady was a neighbor of my uncle and knew him very well. She told me my uncle and his family went abroad before the fall of Saigon. I asked her if she knew one of my mother's sisters who also lived in Saigon. She did, but she did not know her address."

"She asked me to give her my address, in case my aunt visited. I told her I did not know exactly where I would be, but I had been staying near Vung Tau. I told her the next time I came to Hai Ba Trung Street I would give her my address."

Truc returned to his company in Long Thanh District in Ba Ria Province near Vung Tau. He lived there in a beautiful durian garden. The owner of the garden lived in Saigon and sometimes he would visit the garden. He gave him his address and asked the owner to deliver it to his uncle's neighbor on Hai Ba Trung Street. One day, when he came back from daily military training, he received a written message from another member of his company.

The message said, "Truc, Please wait for your aunt. She will come and visit you at the garden at 9 a.m. in several days."

He was excited as he waited for her. At 8:30 a.m. on the day she was to arrive, he walked to the main road, about a five-minute walk, from his camp. At 9:00 a car arrived, driving slowly, then stopped at the garden. A lady about 65 years old opened the door and got out. She was looking around. He saw she looked exactly like his mom.

Truc had never met his aunt before, as she had moved to Saigon two years before he was born. The aunt, Bac Giao, was three years older than Truc's mother.

"I ran to her and shouted, 'Bac Giao! I am Truc here!' She turned and ran to me. When she reached me, she threw her arms around me in a hug. We both cried. Teardrops were running down both our cheeks for a long time. Neither of us could say anything. We just cried. Later, she looked at me again and said, 'You are exactly my nephew. You look like your oldest brother.

Truc's brother, Tuan, a biologist, was 20 years his senior.

Accompanying her were her son and daughter. It was the first time they had seen one another. Her son, Tuong Van, was the person who received the message Truc had given to the garden owner to deliver to his uncle's neighbor.

About 20 days later, Truc had a chance to visit Saigon. He went straight to his aunt's house. That day they were having a big family celebration. It was to celebrate the death day of his aunt's husband, who had died seven years before. He was able to meet all the members of her family. After lunch at the house, they took his to see his second aunt, the younger sister of his mother. After that, he was able to visit them every Sunday, if he had a chance.

After leaving the People's Army, Truc worked in railway construction and then attended university, where he studied English. He went to work for the Operations Centre of the International Press and Communications Company, under the auspices of the Vietnam Ministry of Culture and Information.

Thomas Baca

Retired Army Major Tom Baca, 70, a native of Albuquerque, New Mexico, is well known in the state's aviation circles. He enlisted in the US Army after high school at age 17. He served as an enlisted aircraft mechanic for two years, was appointed a Warrant Officer on completion of U.S. Army Flight School, and was given a direct commission during his second tour in Vietnam. He is a decorated Army helicopter and fixed wing pilot and had flown as a Air Transport Rated commercial pilot from 1983-2003. Baca was awarded the Soldiers Medal, Distinguished Flying Cross, Bronze Star and 38 Air Medals during two tours of duty in Vietnam. He has over 10,000 hours of flight time in all types of aircraft.

Baca is a graduate of the University of Southern Colorado. Tom served as the Aviation Director, New Mexico Department of Transportation from July, 2004, until his retirement in October, 2009. He was responsible for grants to the 59 federally funded airports in New Mexico. He has been married to Janet since 1969. They have two daughters, Sara and Stephanie, and 4 grandchildren.

I have returned to Vietnam four times since the end of the war. The first visit was in 1998. I visited what was called III Corps. The country was really starting to modernize. My second trip back was in 2008. In 10 years the country blossomed into a modern Asian venue. My reason for this trip was to be part of a documentary produced by National Geographic and the Smithsonian about helicopter warfare. My third trip back was part of a cruise and my wife got to see Vietnam. She fell in love with it.

I still had a desire to go back one more time. My friend Jack Swickard and I started talking about it and decided to go. By the time we left there were 12 of us on the tour.

Ken Bartholomew

I was born in San Diego, California in December of 1944 in the Naval Hospital. When I was about three my parents moved to Idaho. We lived there about three years until my parents split up and my mother moved my two brothers and me back to San Diego. We lived with my grandparents for about a year until my mom found a job and a place to live. My grandfather was a very significant figure for the rest of my childhood. By the time I was eight or nine, I became a master tricycle thief. My older brother and I would find tricycles and modify them; remove the seat and turn the frame upside down. This way we could ride them standing on the back. Reversing the frame gave them a lower center of gravity so going down the canyon trails at 20 or 30 mph, they were more stable. I didn't continue this life of crime; I became a Boy Scout and an Altar Boy, and I was totally afraid of girls. I loved my bicycle, camping, and almost any adventure I could find. We lived in the Kearney Mesa area of San Diego and Miramar Naval Air station, was not very far away. We went to an open house/air show when I was probably 15 or 16. I got to sit in the cockpit of a jet and instructed by a naval pilot on flight controls and instruments. I was hooked.

My life took a few turns in my senior year of high school. I ended up in Heyburn, Idaho, living with my father. When I graduated, I went to work with a neighbor who did contract hay hauling. After a summer and fall of hauling 2000 bales a day from field to stack, we moved to Boise. I enrolled in Boise Junior College, (now Boise State). I had a plan to get two years of college and apply for the NAVCAD Program with the navy. I just forgot that you have to get good grades to continue to get the academic deferment from the draft. But, along comes the Army Recruiter who says, "You don't need no two years of college. We will teach you to fly." That had Sucker written all over it. But this was December of 1965 and I knew that the Vietnam War would be over before I would graduate from flight school. I guess I'm not really that smart. The army got me again after my first tour in Vietnam. I was an instrument flight instructor at Hunter Army Airfield in Savannah, Georgia, when they offered me a direct commission to first lieutenant. My thought was only special people get this. Yeah, I was "special" all right. After my second tour in Vietnam, I was sent to Fort Dix as a basic training company commander. Then to Fort Benning for the Officer Advance Course. Daytona Beach and Embry Riddle for bachelor's degree (not so bad), then to Fort Carson, Colorado. The Reduction in force finally caught up with me at Aberdeen Proving Grounds, Maryland. I left active duty for a GS-11 position working on the Bradley Fighting Vehicle. I continued my military career in the Maryland National Guard and in the Reserves and am now a retired major. I also retired and closed my subcontracting business this past year.

Marc Cullison

I was born in Wichita, Kansas, in 1946. My father was a tool and die maker, my mother a typical stay-at-home mom. My brother, Keith, was three years older. Midway through the second grade, the family relocated to Hobart, Oklahoma, in the southwest corner of the state where red ants, goat heads, and "horny toads" ruled the dry, red dirt that seemed to infiltrate every crack in our house. My father had purchased a Western Auto Store and became a very astute businessman. I played coronet in the junior-high band, and that's when I first experienced flight. The band instructor, a pilot, gave some of his students rides in his single engine airplane. My fascination with airplanes never ceased.

I developed an interest in drafting and architecture and knew that that is what I wanted to do. After the eighth grade, we moved again to Blackwell, Oklahoma, in the north central part of the state. I continued with the band through high school. I loved marching. The Blackwell Marching Maroons won the state marching band championship all three years I was there.

I attended Oklahoma State University with a major in architectural engineering. And along with every other able-bodied male student, I took ROTC classes. During that first year, I pledged Pershing Rifles military fraternity. Numerous conflicts arose between my degree and the PRs, but somehow I managed to make it all work. The architectural engineering curriculum was a bitch of a five-year program and I had to take an extra summer school to make for the hours I missed due to advanced ROTC courses, which didn't count toward my degree requirements. While in advanced ROTC, I signed for flight training. During my last two years, I learned to fly fixed-wing aircraft, compliments of Uncle Sam. The only cost to me was an extra year's obligation on active duty. I thought it was a sweet deal. That's just how naïve I was.

I graduated with a bachelor's degree and a commission as a second lieutenant in August of 1969. From there I went to Fort Belvoir for Engineering Officers Basic training. Then I received orders for basic rotary wing school and found myself at Fort Wolters in Texas. Then on to advanced rotary wing school at Fort Rucker in Alabama. Upon completion and after a 30-day leave, I was on a plane to Vietnam in January of 1971.

I was stationed at Lane Army Airfield with the 129th Assault Helicopter Company. My life there is pretty well covered in my book, *The Other Vietnam War*, published in May of 2015 by Imzadi Publishing. I came out of it in one piece with an air medal and bronze star.

I was assigned to the Kaw Dam and Reservoir Project at Ponca City, Oklahoma when I left Vietnam. I worked there for two years and married my fabulous and amazing wife, Bobbie. I also made captain while I was there. Then it was time to go back to OSU for a master's degree. Bobbie graciously worked her tail off get me through. We moved to Oklahoma City, where my daughter, Courtney was born, then in Lafayette, Louisiana, and then Pearland, Texas. I worked for the metal building industry until the early 80s, earning my registration as a professional structural engineer, registered in twelve states. I left to return to Sallisaw, where we purchased five acres of land from Bobbie's parents and built our own log home. I worked as a quality control inspector, a quality engineer, in production control and eventually as the data processing supervisor for the plant.

When my computer programming days ended, I took a job teaching math and science at Connors State College in Warner, Oklahoma. After 13 years, I retired. Now I write and work on my house. The way I figure it, the day I hammer the last nail or drive the last screw, I'll probably keel over dead.

Sterling Essenmacher

I grew up in California. Aviation was in my family, and my older brother built and flew model airplanes. It rubbed off on me. I built stick and paper models but I set them on fire. I was a deputy sheriff in Ventura, California when a letter arrived from the local draft board inviting me to go on an all-expenses paid camping trip. I was drafted and off I went to Fort Polk Louisiana for eight weeks of basic training. Next came medic training at Fort Sam Houston, Texas, followed by an assignment to Fort Bragg, North Carolina.

I got tired of pulling KP and guard duty and applied for Warrant Officer Flight School in 1964. I got my orders for August 1965 and off I went to Fort Wolters, Texas and then to Fort Rucker, Alabama for UH1 transition and tactics. Upon graduating, my orders for Vietnam arrived.

Thomas Gilbert

The apprehension built as I made plans for my return to Vietnam after 47 years. My tour there lasted short of eight months but included 426 combat hours, 687 missions, 1014 patients carried, two Purple Hearts, and a Distinguished Flying Cross.

As a Medivac pilot (Dustoff 21) in 1968, there were many experiences I boxed up in my mind and rarely visited. This "trip" was an opportunity to deal with this form of PTSD, avoidance. Our returning group of 12 had a range of experiences that spanned a shared space in each of us. This opportunity for reflection helped me realize that what we were all good soldiers and that individual effort in combat is not the act of logic but an act of love, you follow your heart and love for fellow soldiers.

My military travels started in 1966 as I began playing the recruiter game: army, navy, air force, or the marines? I wanted to be a marine, but the army offered the best option, pre-qualification to learn how to fly a helicopter and the opportunity to be an officer/pilot. I went through basic training in 1967 at Fort Polk, Louisiana and graduated from flight school at Fort Rucker, Alabama in March of 1968. The day the members of our class, 67-25, received our orders for deployment I learned that I was assigned to the 498th Medical Evacuation Company. My instructor pilot looked me in the eye and said "Gilbert, you might as well kiss your ass good-bye." Being 20 years old and invincible, I never shared this with my wife or family. It did not take long after arrival to understand his comment. When Dustoff was needed, the "bad guys" were really close.

At graduation, my wife was 8 months pregnant, due shortly after my scheduled deployment date of April 19, 1968. My request for deployment delay was not approved, and we elected to have labor induced so that I could be present when my son Erik was born on April 14, 1968. Five days later, I was on my way to Vietnam.

I think often about the more than 58,000 U.S. soldiers killed in the war in Vietnam. Three stand out for me: James Granville, my crew chief; Major Pittard, air force rescue pilot, and Charles "Doc" Lumm, a medic and friend killed on a mission in another ship while I was on R&R. It's especially poignant as I write this on Memorial Day, May 30, 2016, 48 years later.

213

I think many Veterans struggle with the war and the many break-downs in civilian leadership that directed the war effort. Certainly after seeing my first KIA, I did not know the "why" that seemed clear in my understanding of World War II through history lessons and my favorite comic book, Sargent Rock. Recently I was reading an article by the author of the play, *Vietgone*, Qui Nguyen, whose dad, Quang Nguyen, was a helicopter pilot in the Vietnam Air Force during the war.

"My dad says to me it hurts him, (the war that is), still seen as a complete negative (by Americans)," his father told him. "I don't want people to think that the country I fought hard for, we lost absolutely, but I fought hard to try to keep as my home."

The war did not signify American aggression, it was a civil war. Like all wars, it had winners and losers."

Dennis Gulich

I was living in Vienna, Virginia, and going to college in West Virginia in 1968. Due to my normal habit of drinking and partying rather than studying, I was put on academic probation for the fall semester. And sure enough, in November I received my invitation from President Nixon to join the army.

When I got to the reception center at Fort Benning and took the battery of aptitude tests, there were posters on the wall of the most heroic men I had ever seen, called army aviators. So I requested a chance at that and passed the required tests for flight school, and thus began my flying career.

I went through the standard path for enlisted guys. Fort Polk, Louisiana. Then WOC school at Fort Wolters and Fort Rucker. I received my wings and Warrant Officer bars in January of 1970. I reported to the reception station at Long Binh, Vietnam, as described in Marc's book, *The Other Vietnam War*, on March 3, 1970. After 3 days, I was assigned to the 118th AHC at Bien Hoa.

I became a shiny new peter pilot and was assigned to the first flight platoon, the Red Flight, a slick platoon. I spent my whole tour there and went through the normal progression; peter pilot to first pilot to AC. Toward the end of my tour, the army was rifting pilots due to the winding down of US involvement. I was given the option of signing up indefinite or getting out of the army when I got home. I took the latter option, although I didn't dislike the army, and I had looked at my year in country with pride. I guess I just figured that I had pushed my luck enough.

After returning to the States, I wanted to become an airline pilot and I went to flight school to get my fixed wing ratings with my buddy and roommate from the 118th. I never got the airline job, but instead I got a very good corporate flying job and flew corporate for the next 35 years with 3 different companies.

I have lived in Denver, Colorado, since 1971 and have been married to my beautiful wife, Cher, for 44 years. We have 3 grown children and 4 grandchildren. And I am officially retired since October 2013.

Don Hooper

Donald Gleason Hooper (Don) was born October 19, 1954 in Providence, Rhode Island, to Doris Gleason Hooper and Albert Adams Hooper. He spent his early years in Providence where his father attended Brown University. His family consisted of Donald, his parents, and his siblings Beverly, Laurie, and Douglas. They moved to Richardson, Texas, a suburb of Dallas, when his father took a job at Texas Instruments. The family lived in Richardson for several years and then moved back East to Pittsford, New York when his father took another position.

Don graduated from high school in New York in 1972 and then went south to attend Florida Institute of Technology (now called Florida Tech). Don eventually started working full time at Harris Semiconductor and pursued a degree in Chemistry part-time. He enjoyed sailing, surfing, golfing, snorkeling, fishing, sky diving, riding his motorcycle, and spending time with his fraternity brothers while he juggled work and school. While attending his last class for his degree, he met his future wife, Lisa Zediker. She was pursuing her Master of Science in Environmental Science. They fell in love during Environmental Chemistry class and got married the following semester. They lived in Palm Bay, Florida, for several years after receiving their respective degrees. Lisa started work at Harris Semiconductor and Don left Harris and took a position with AG Associates. The family included Lisa's son Eric Z. Carlsen, and grew to include their daughters Ashley M. Hooper and Britney E. Hooper.

Don's position with AG Associates as a technical representative launched his world traveling adventures and sparked his wanderlust. Don traveled all of the world during the years he spent with AG Associates. Many weeks each year were spent in Korea, Indonesia, Malaysia, Hong Kong, and Taiwan. In 1989, Don had the opportunity to work at Intel Corporation. After a one-year temporary assignment to Beaverton, Oregon, the family settled in Albuquerque, New Mexico. In search of trees and some green, they settled in the North Valley. In his new position with Intel, Don was once again afforded the opportunity to travel; Israel, Ireland, Germany, France, and China were added to his "been-to" list.

Don had an amazing career at Intel Corporation; twenty-seven years and he still loved working there. His positions over the years included those as a manager and an individual contributor working in a variety of technical areas and on many diverse projects. He looked forward to working several more years before he considered retiring.

Don's stateside adventures included crewing with the Intel balloon during Balloon Fiesta and other ballooning events; flying his Mooney airplane from one end of the country to the other (including his annual pilgrimage to Oshkosh Fly-In); donating time to non-profits such as Roadrunner Food Bank, Habitat for Humanity, and New Mexico Hunter Jumper Association; and spending time doing woodworking, everything from making horse grooming totes to fine household furniture.

Don and Lisa created their travel destination "bucket list" and were checking countries off. They went to Egypt and India together in 2010 and 2014, respectively, and had plans to walk the Camino de Santiago in 2017 during Don's next sabbatical. Don traveled to Vietnam with friends in late 2015; he loved the country and the company.

Tragically, Don, aged 61, a loving husband and father, world adventurer, airplane pilot, hot air balloonist, carpenter, and animal lover, passed away on January 8th, 2016 as a result of vehicle-related accident. Don was known for his kindness, his wit, his adventurous spirit, and his sense of humor. Don lived life to the fullest and always had a positive outlook.

Tom Horan

Tom Horan became an army pilot in February 1969, but had wanted to fly from 1949, when as a 4-year-old at the Kirtland Air Force Base Kindergarten in Albuquerque, New Mexico, he would look up and see the air force P-51s, B-26s and the TWA DC-3s landing less than a half mile away at the Albuquerque airport.

He first flew on a TWA DC-3 from Albuquerque to Santa Fe, New Mexico, about a 20-minute flight as a 7-year-old, and then flew back to see his Aunt Mary in Rock Island, Illinois.

Like Tom Baca of Albuquerque, who organized the trip to Vietnam, Tom Horan always wanted to fly and used money he earned as a laborer on road construction on summer jobs in New Mexico to get his first 5 hours of flight instruction as an 18-year-old in the summer of 1964. Much to Tom's surprise, the University of San Francisco, where he went to college, had two years of mandatory Army ROTC. In the summer of 1965 he was offered and took an Army ROTC scholarship. With the help of then Captain Gerard Landry, an ROTC instructor who had just returned from Long Range Patrol Duty in Vietnam with the 101st Airborne, Tom got into the Army ROTC flight training program and received his private pilot's license in May of 1967.

Tom was commissioned in the Regular Army in June of 1967 and went immediately into the 2nd Armored Division at Fort Hood, Texas, and completed the Armor Officer Basic Course in September, 1967. He finished the first two and one half weeks of Ranger School at Ft Benning, Georgia, before being sent back to Fort Hood in a cast that stayed on his left leg for about 4 months.

"God bless that Pediatrician that said I had a stress fracture," Tom says, "or I would still be lost in the woods in Georgia."

He began flight school at Ft Wolters, Texas, in June of 1968, graduating from Ft Rucker, Alabama, in February, 1969. In April, he was assigned to the 3rd of the 17th Air Cavalry Squadron.

Tom is married to Mary Ann Campbell-Horan and they live in Albuquerque, where Tom has been a lawyer and lobbyist at the New Mexico state legislature. Mary Ann is a paralegal. Together they have seven children and five grandchildren.

Ed Knighten

Born in Longview Texas, Oct. 18, 1941, to Edgar and Pauline (Garoutte) Knighten. Moved to Oklahoma at the early age 5 and lived in Pawhuska, Oklahoma. Lived there thru the 7th grade when Mom and Dad started a bakery in Fairfax Oklahoma. I was up at 4 AM every morning cooking donuts and pies and making deliveries to the cafes in town. We were only there one year because the town was just too small to support us.

We moved to Broken Arrow, Oklahoma, where I started the 9th grade and graduated from Broken Arrow High School in 1959. I had various jobs there from shoeshine boy, to soda jerk, and finally working in a dry cleaner all the way thru college. I was lucky enough to get a scholarship to Northeastern State College in Tahlequah, Oklahoma. While in college, I had various jobs to help get me thru. I showed movies, worked in the cafeteria, but the best was custodian in the girls' dorm. I had a roommate who had fought in the Golden Gloves and he asked me to spar with him. I went on to have 16 bouts in college and the army. I finished with 14 wins and 2 losses. I dated a rodeo queen and got started riding Brahma bulls for a little extra spending money but never made much.

Pat Matheny

I was raised and continue to live in a little community called Pine Bluff located six miles from Shinnston, West Virginia. I joined the US Army in 1964 at age 17 and was discharged in 1967. I was trained as a Crew Chief (Mechanic) on the UH-1 Huey and served in Vietnam from April 4,1965, to April 1, 1966, with the 118th Aviation Company "Thunderbirds." The company was stationed on the Bien Hoa Airbase twenty miles north of Saigon. I was assigned to a 2nd Platoon (Choppers) 'slick' (Troop Carrier), call sign Blue Thunderbird 7, which I nicknamed SUZY-Q after my girl back home.

I spent 26 years as an underground coalmine supervisor with Consol Energy before retiring in 1997. Next month, SUZY-Q and I will be married 50 years.

Duane Speirs

I was born in Miller South Dakota. Then in the late 50's the family moved to Hill City, South Dakota, the middle of the Black Hills. Shortly after graduating from high school I enlisted in the army.

I knew I was not going to make it through college and, not wanting to get drafted, but wanting to choose what I wanted to do. Without talking to my parents, I visited the recruiting center in Rapid City. I so knew I did not want to go into the navy, as my brother did that; I did not like the air force, as there was an air force base in Rapid City; I was going to go into the marines, but as luck would have it the recruiter was out of town. Not wanting to wait, I talked to the army recruiter. I wanted to do something other than being a grunt. I looked through the book and came up with the Helicopter Warrant Officer Program. That seemed to be a pretty cool thing to try, so I signed up for Warrant Officer School. I went home and informed my parents, and a week later was on my way to Fort Polk, Louisiana, for Basic Training.

Jack Swickard

In 1954, we moved to England, where my father was stationed at South Ruislip outside of London. Our first home was in a large mansion in Stanmore, where my parents and our two younger brothers had a suite with a private bath.

I grew up in a military family. Though born in Big Spring, Texas, I had little contact with my birthplace, and moved to New Mexico within six months of my birth. My father, an Army Air Corps officer, was a navigation and bomb instructor at military airfields in Texas and New Mexico during World War II.

In mid-1943, we moved to Las Cruces, N.M., where we lived throughout much of the war. My father, Capt. Jack D. Swickard, was assigned to Clark Field on the Philippine Island of Luzon in 1949. Our family, including my twin brother, Jules, my younger brother, Jeff, and my mother, followed several months later aboard a military ship.

In the late 1940s and early 1950s, life was good for U.S. military officers in Southeast Asia. The U.S. dollar was strong in Far East countries, recently under the heel of the Japanese Empire. To help provide jobs for Filipinos living near Clark Field, officers' housing came with live-in housemaids and a yard boy. Rosie, our housemaid, had a bedroom and small bath off the kitchen. She seldom went home to visit her family, so she spent much of her free time with my twin brother and me. She would read to us from her Filipino comic books and describe the Japanese occupation of the Philippines. Rosie had spent the part of the Japanese occupation traveling with a band of guerrilla fighters in the jungles of Luzon. It was difficult for us to think of her other than as a kind and gentle woman who would do anything we asked.

Our house had a large, L-shaped porch enclosed by screening. It was where Jules and I played during typhoon warnings. When typhoons approached, we would stay on the porch until the rain came down so hard it forced us to go inside the house. The floor of the porch was covered with red wax that had to be buffed regularly. Rosie was in charge. She would cut a coconut in half and tie each half of the husk to her feet with the fibers pointing down. Rosie then would skate back and forth until the floor shined like a mirror. The yard boy spent his time outside with the banana trees, flowers, and my mother's vegetable garden. We didn't know him as well as we knew Rosie.

My father, who was making the transition from the Army Air Force to the newly created U.S. Air Force, flew as a navigator throughout Asia from Clark Field. The furnishings in our home reflected the purchases he made on those trips. We had rattan furniture in the living room and bedrooms, tables came from occupied Japan and India, vases and platters from Korea and China, and woodcarvings from Bali and the Philippines.

My first girlfriend was a Filipina who attended second grade with me at the Clark Field American Dependent Elementary School. She was the daughter of a cinnamon plantation owner. Each morning, she brought me a platter-size piece of cinnamon bark, which I would gnaw on in class. By lunchtime, I had eaten it all.

After living in the Philippines for two years, we returned to the United States, settling at Barksdale Air Force Base at Shreveport, La. Jules and I had our own room on the top floor. One other person, a retired British Army colonel in his mid-80s, lived on the floor. Jules and I got to know the colonel, who would invite us for tea and stories about his military service in India and World War I. It was the old colonel who introduced us to the exploits of Flying Officer Jerry Biggles of the Royal Flying Corps. The large house at Stanmore had some interesting residents, mostly retired senior army and Royal Air Force officers. Most sat ramrod straight, had thin mustaches, and brooked no insolence from young boys. During breakfast, one would eat his cornflakes with a fork.

After several months at Stanmore, we moved to a two-story home in North Wembley, a bit closer to downtown London. With the London Underground, or Tube, and double-decker buses, we could roam freely throughout the city and suburbs. A world of castles, museums, and theaters opened to us just as we became teen-agers.

After living in London four years, our family moved to the Midwest, where my father was assigned to the Air Force Reserve Officer Training Corps at Ohio State University in Columbus. We lived in Worthington, just north of Columbus, until Jules and I graduated from high school three years later. I studied at Ohio State University for a year, and then transferred to the Indiana University campus in Indianapolis. I worked various part-time jobs while attending the university, but none clicked until I took a position as clerk at The Indianapolis Times. I threw myself into the work, volunteering to write articles for the entertainment editor and the real estate section.

Within a year, I was writing obituaries for The Times. It was the first step in reporting. Six months later a position opened for a reporter on the police beat. I filled it with gusto, spending most of my waking hours chasing stories and writing articles on deadline. It was hard for me to believe I could have so much fun working.

Life changed in August 1966, when the Scripps Howard newspaper chain announced it was closing The Times. Though the newspaper had a circulation of 97,000, the parent company concluded it would be less costly to fold the newspaper than to invest in new equipment.

I moved to New Mexico and went to work for another Scripps Howard newspaper, The Albuquerque Tribune. By the time I began work in October 1966, I had lost my Indiana University student deferment and my draft board was nipping at my heels. I didn't want to be drafted, and my withdrawal from college meant I was not going to earn a military officer's commission through ROTC. One morning, while making my reporting rounds in downtown Albuquerque, I passed the army recruiting office. In the window was a sign promoting helicopter flight training. I went inside and inquired.

After a day of testing and a physical examination, I was sworn in as a recruit. The army was eager to enlist student helicopter pilots, so I knew I would be heading for flight school after I completed basic training. Standing beside me while I was sworn-in was Jim Mason, an Albuquerque civilian pilot. Jim would go through basic training and flight school with me, then would be assigned to a base not far from mine in South Vietnam. During the next 45 years, we would remain in touch, off and on.

Now I belonged to the U.S. Army, I didn't have to worry about meals or a place to stay. Jim and I were told to report to the recruiting station the following morning for breakfast and a bus ride to Fort Polk, Louisiana. In March 1966, I graduated from basic training and was granted a two-week leave before reporting to Fort Wolters for flight training.

After our leave was over, Jim and I boarded a Greyhound bus in Albuquerque. Rain started pouring as our bus rolled through the Texas Hill Country on its way to Mineral Wells, the community adjacent to

Fort Wolters. Jim and I had scheduled our arrival for Saturday night so we could relax before signing in at Fort Wolters on Sunday.

On our arrival at the Mineral Wells bus station, Jim and I sat on the bus, waiting for the heavy rain to abate. It didn't. The driver had a schedule to keep, so he got off the bus and pulled our duffel bags out of the luggage compartment. Jim and I took the cue and dashed off the bus. There was no place to shelter from the rain, so we carried our bags through downtown Mineral Wells, heading toward a neon sign that read: Crazy Water Hotel

We were drenched when we entered the hotel. I noticed the desk clerk gave us an odd look when we asked for a single room. Because we were only drawing $97.50 monthly pay, Jim and I decided to share the room. The next morning, we headed for breakfast. It was Sunday and we had until mid-afternoon to sign in at Fort Wolters. Leaving our room, a nurse walked past, pushing an older man in a wheelchair. In the dining room, it was clear Jim and I were the only diners below the age of 70. Later that day, when we checked out of the hotel, we learned we had spent the night in a nursing home. Apparently, the desk clerk had felt sorry for us when arrived wet, so he let us check in for the night.

We discovered there was not much to do in Mineral Wells on a Sunday, so Jim and I decided to sign in early at Fort Wolters. A taxi took us to the WOC company named in our orders. Jim Mason and I parked our duffel bags outside before entering the 1st WOC Company orderly room. WOC stood for "warrant officer candidate." To be designated army aviators, we first would have to be officers. The army had determined the warrant officer grade was perfect for aviators. Unlike commissioned officers, who were required to build experience in command and staff positions to meet career goals and be promoted, warrant officers could concentrate on flying.

For a time I thought I was a prime candidate to be washed out of training. My first flight instructor was a frustrated Texas National Guard pilot who wanted to go on active duty as an army aviator. He knew how to fly helicopters, but someone at the Department of the Army apparently had picked up on his sorry-ass attitude.

As I entered my second week of flight training, whenever I made a flying error, he would comment, "Do that again and I'll pink your ass." "Pink" referred to the pink slips of paper an instructor would give to a student pilot for a substandard flight. After two pink slips, student pilots had to fly with a standardization pilot who could wash you out of flight training or give you a reprieve. I flew with three standardization pilots, each of whom told me, "There's nothing wrong with your flying."

It dawned on me I had better ask for an instructor change or kiss flight school goodbye. My second instructor was very different. He was a 21-year-old, WO2 who had served in Vietnam with an assault helicopter company. He was a great guy and a terrific instructor pilot.

Before graduating from flight school, most of my class members received orders for aviation units in South Vietnam. With the orders were instructions to report to Travis Air Force Base in California, where we would take airliners to Vietnam. We were divided into three groups and ordered to depart on three consecutive days. I would leave on the first day. As we lined up to board our flight, classmates departing on the next two days made a special trip to Travis to cheer us on with, "See you in Vietnam," and, "We'll think of you tonight in San Francisco," and, "You're going to miss the party!"

I figured, what the hell; I'd leave earlier, but I'd get back earlier. Each of us had orders for a 12-month tour of duty. Our DEROS, or date of estimated return from overseas, would be based on when we departed.

Our first stop after leaving Travis was Honolulu, where the Braniff Airlines plane would refuel before continuing west. However, an hour after our flight departed Hawaii, the pilot announced, "We don't want to upset you, but we just lost our number four engine. We'll circle for 30 minutes, and then return to Honolulu for repairs."

Back at Honolulu International Airport, we were ushered into the passenger lounge and told to wait for a further announcement. After several hours, our bags were brought to the lounge and an airline representative explained the engine would have to be repaired before we could continue on our journey. In the meantime, Braniff would give each of us a book of coupons we could use to cover expenses.

"Report back here at 9 a.m. tomorrow and we'll give you a status report," the airline representative explained. "If you take a taxi, eat, or get a hotel room, pay with one of the coupons in the book we're giving you." It was like being handed free money while visiting one of the world's resort cities. I was tired, so I took a shuttle bus to Fort DeRussy, where I rented a room in the Bachelor Officers Quarters.

For the next 2 days, we would go to the airport, where we were told, "The engine's not fixed yet," and collect another day's worth of coupons. On the third day, the Braniff representative reported World Airlines had been contracted to bring a plane to Hawaii the next morning and take us on to South Vietnam.

The World Airlines flight landed at Bien Hoa Air Base, 20 miles northeast of Saigon. After deplaning, we gathered in an open shed, awaiting our duffel bags and watching GIs board our plane to fly home. We then got on blue air force buses, their open windows covered with wire screens, and were driven to Long Binh Post about three miles from the airbase. We halted at the 90th Replacement Battalion, a complex of dusty, wooden barracks, BOQs and offices.

On my way into the replacement battalion office, a classmate from a later flight from Travis asked, "Where have you guys been?" We heard that question a lot. The stopover gave us something we could rub in, particularly when we told them our time in Hawaii had counted as time in Vietnam.

The next day we lined up to show the orders we'd been given in flight school, assigning us to units throughout Vietnam. My orders assigned me to the 1st Air Cavalry Division at An Khe, to the north. The 1st Cav had been highly touted by some of our flight school instructors. I was looking forward to the 1st Cav, until the 90th Replacement Battalion clerk examining my orders said, "Sir, your slot was filled, so you are being diverted to the 118th Assault Helicopter Company in Bien Hoa."

Lonnie Schmidt, a classmate just ahead of me in line, also drew the 118th Assault Helicopter Company rather than the 1st Cav. We weren't sure if our life had improved, until we arrived at the 118th, which was known by its Thunderbirds call sign. An hour later, a Jeep pulled up to the 90th Replacement Battalion. The SP4 driver asked for the pilots assigned to the 118th. Lonnie and I boarded for the ride to Cong Ly Street in downtown Bien Hoa City.

We couldn't believe our eyes as the Jeep pulled into the courtyard of a large villa. The billeting officer showed me to a room where I would spend my first couple of nights before being assigned to one of the flight platoons. Each room had a flush toilet, a sink, and a shower. The villa was a nice place to live by any standard. It had two wings, which housed the 1st and 2nd flight platoons; a row of upstairs rooms that were home to the Bandit gunship platoon; a dining room with a palm tree growing through the roof; and a very nice bar, named the Thunderbird Lounge.

Lonnie and I were given temporary rooms in the villa until it was decided whether we would be assigned to the 1st Flight Platoon "Scorpions" or the 2nd Flight Platoon "Choppers." After changing into jungle fatigues, I wandered over to the Officers Mess and joined. Members' dues supported the mess. Because I was living in a villa and not in a tent or a bunker like many of my classmates, I was given a cost of living allowance to cover meals at the Officers Mess. The timing of our arrival was good because it was almost time for dinner.

The Thunderbirds employed a Chinese cook and three Vietnamese waitresses, who wore gray uniforms with white aprons. A mess steward made certain the kitchen refrigerators were full.

After flying pilot on slicks for two months, I was given a check ride to make certain I could be turned loose as an aircraft commander. My platoon leaders, Capt. Reed Kimzey, would be checking my flying skills and judgment. Reed didn't tell me it was a check ride, so I assumed we were flying regular missions that day. I didn't learn it was a check ride until Reed told me I had failed it. As Reed has told the story over the years, most of the day went fine. I flew reasonably well and didn't put the Huey or our crew in danger, until the final sortie of the day, when I shot an approach to a PSP (perforated steel planking) helipad on a soccer field at Di An north of Saigon. My approach went all the way to the ground, which was good. When the Huey's skids came to rest on the helipad, I lowered the collective and began settling the helicopter into a landing. That was not so good.

Reed saw something I had overlooked: The helicopter's skids were hanging off the back of the elevated helipad. Reed snatched the collective, raised the skids off the PSP, and moved the Huey forward so we were firmly planted on the pad. That's when he told me I had failed the check ride. The problem with my landing was the helicopter could have fallen or tilted backward off the helipad, causing the spinning tail rotor to strike the ground. This could have caused a balance shift and destroyed the Huey.

The next day, Reed and I flew again. This time I passed the check ride and became an aircraft commander. When word got around

I had worked as a newspaper reporter before joining the army I was given multiple additional duties involving writing. When I wasn't flying, I was busy as the company public information officer, awards and decoration officer, administration officer, piaster-control officer and civilian-personnel officer. My duties ranged from writing press releases about the 118th Assault Helicopter Company and its members, to writing up award recommendations for pilots and crewmembers, to traveling to Saigon every two weeks to pick up piasters to pay our South Vietnamese employees, to administering the hooch maids.

I looked forward to kicking back on the last week of my tour. The Thunderbirds had a rule that grounded all pilots during their last week in country. When that final week began I asked one of the other pilots to drive me to the airbase, where I turned in my .38-caliber revolver, my combat flight helmet and other organizational equipment. This took several hours.

On the way back to the villa in downtown Bien Hoa, I heard what sounded like fireworks. It was the beginning of the Tet holiday, so I wasn't surprised to hear the fireworks. Then I saw pieces of the street in front of us breaking up as AK-47 rounds shot up the roadway. My fellow pilot drove as fast as the Jeep would take us back to the compound in Cong Li Street where our villa was located.

Because I was grounded, I became the battalion staff duty officer. The other Thunderbird pilots, who could not leave the safety of the compound for the airbase, spent each night partying in the officers' club across the street.

Days later, after the Viet Cong and North Vietnamese Army troops were driven away from Bien Hoa, I boarded the first army bus to Long Binh for out-processing at the 90th Replacement Battalion. A tank preceded the bus, looking for stray enemy soldiers. Two days later I was back on a bus to Bien Hoa Airbase for my flight home. As the smoker, or airliner, taking me home taxied to the runway, I could see bodies of enemy sappers still on the perimeter fence.

Two days after arriving back in the United States I married to Renee Edwards, whom I had met in flight school. It was a cold February day in Sioux Falls, South Dakota. After a honeymoon in Europe, I was assigned to the 55th Aviation Battalion at Robert Gray Army Airfield adjacent to Fort Hood, Texas. Again, my newspaper background determined my duties. I started as public information officer and assistant adjutant and assistant S-1 personnel officer. Later, as a CW2, I was named battalion adjutant and S-1.

In December 1969, I left active duty and returned to Albuquerque, where I took up my old job as a reporter on The Tribune staff. Within three years I was promoted to city editor, with the responsibility for local news coverage.

A year later, I was asked to become editor of the Roswell Daily Record in southeastern New Mexico. After 15 years, the owner-publisher of the Farmington Daily Times in northwest New Mexico recruited me as editor. I later became general manager of The Daily Times.

In 1997, I returned to the Roswell Daily Record as general manager. I left the newspaper business in 2000 to launch The Triton Group, a public relations business. My clients included the New Mexico Institute of Mining and Technology, which headed a consortium of universities and businesses that operated the International Law Enforcement Academy for the U.S. State Department. I got to know hundreds of senior law-enforcement officers, prosecutors and judges from emerging democracies around the world, including Vietnam.

In 2008, Windfall Films of London filmed a documentary about a rescue mission I had flown in May 1967. I spent several weeks in Vietnam during filming. It was during filming I met Dinh Ngoc Truc, who was the Vietnam Ministry of Culture and Information liaison with the documentary crew. We became fast friends.

I have returned to Vietnam four times since my combat tour to visit friends in Vietnam's National Police, and Truc and his family in Hanoi. Additionally, Truc has visited Renee and me in New Mexico and has gotten to know my family.

After U.S. soldiers left Vietnam in 1973, Truc traveled south along the Ho Chi Minh Trail to Vung Tau in South Vietnam as a People's Army soldier. We would have called him a member of the NVA.

Almost 40 years later as we drove back to Hanoi from Ha Long Bay, Truc turned to me and said, "Aren't you glad we didn't kill each other during the war? We would never have become friends."

RETURN TO VIETNAM TOURS is owned and operated by Dinh Ngoc Truc, Tour Operator and Guide. For information about the tours, contact Truc by:

Telephone: +84 (0) 912 238 580
Address: 67 Tue Tinh Street
                Hanoi, Vietnam
Email: dinhngoctruc1956@gmail.com

Truc will assist with entry and exit visa forms, provide monetary exchange, pre-register hotel arrangements, and provide all in-country transportation. Suggestions are given for food, dress, and cell phone use.

Continue reading for an exclusive preview of

The Other Vietnam War
A Pilot's Life in Vietnam.

THE OTHER
VIETNAM WAR

A Helicopter Pilot's Life in Vietnam

MARC CULLISON

INTRODUCTION

In 1971, I was among the many who, for the promise of glory or the threat of fear, followed the call to arms. We were swallowed by the evil and goodness, the wretched ugliness and amazing beauty, the despicable sins and glorious honor of war. A war that wasn't urgent, a war against no real threat to America, a war undeclared by our government. A war with only three possible redeeming qualities: it was a war that would make pacifists drunk with arrogance, humiliate the hawks, and place a shroud of humility around the United States of America.

It was many things to many people, but to the soldier, it was a chance to come to terms with his own doubts, beliefs, and frailties as a human being. While in Viet Nam, he grew up, became broken, or died.

The male college student in the late sixies was screwed. If he had a clean nose, he could avoid the draft with a college deferment. But even a minor academic mishap could erase that and he would be on his way to see the world, courtesy of Uncle Sam. That's what they said in the commercials: "Join the army, see the world." Hell, I hadn't even been anywhere but Kansas, Oklahoma and Virginia. I had 47 other states to see in North America. I didn't give a rat's ass about the rest of the world. Not then, anyway. But as a student, I suspected Vietnam was inevitable.

Unless a guy had a shitload of luck, if he weren't in college, he was probably already on a plane headed for Vietnam. Another option was a medical deferment. If you were gung-ho, you had no interest in that. If you weren't gung-ho and had the money and knew the right doctor or congressman, you could buy one. Then there was always Canada.

Those of us who had enough drive to seek an education and the integrity to do what we thought was right ignored the ranting of our fellow students and peers who opposed the Vietnam War and pursued commissions as officers in the armed services. That was ROTC, the Reserve Officers Training Corps. All eligible freshmen and sophomores were required to undergo four semesters, or twelve credit hours, of ROTC training. Since it was a bona fide course, ROTC counted toward a student's grade point average. For those who loathed military training, this was a thorn in the saddle of education, at least to the students who were in college to actually get an education. To those who weren't, it was even more so, because they could easily jeopardize their draft deferment with

1

low grades in ROTC. To the few who were gung-ho, it was a cushion for their grades.

The draft was not a fair business, but without it, our nation's defense might have suffered. A strong military seems to deter aggression by other countries. So, I can't be too hard on the draft. It was a necessary bit of awkwardness that we had to go through. I don't begrudge our country taking young men to fight for it. I was glad to do it. That's not quite all there was to this scenario, though. It's what we were sent to fight for that's the problem.

Since advanced ROTC was optional, after the sophomore year, most of the fellows dropped out of it. Enrollment in advanced ROTC meant you belonged to the military machine. You were one of them. You studied two more years, got your degree, and along with it a commission as a second lieutenant. Then you served your time, usually two or three years on active duty before being released. Well, you were still subject to being called up for active duty again, but that didn't happen very often.

Those of us who didn't drop out knew what was coming down the pike and figured that instead of allowing the military to tell us that we were going to be grunts sloshing and slashing our way through the rice paddies and jungles of Vietnam, we would select our own means of risking our lives and satisfying our military obligation. Well, there was a slight chance that you might escape the draft lottery. All the dates of birth of all eligible men were put into a pool and the dates were drawn, supposedly, at random. If your birth date was the first drawn, you would be the first to be called up for service. The first 120 dates were almost assured of being drafted unless that person had a deferment. Because I already had an education deferment, I had no idea what my number was and I really didn't care. I'm sure I saw it on the notice I received from the Selective Service Board, but I paid no attention to it. At that time, it didn't matter. But if I graduated, I would lose my deferment and if my crappy luck held, it would be the only time in my life that I would be close to number one. I made sure that didn't happen.

I've always wondered, though, what my number would have been. And what kind of person I would be now if I were number one and didn't finish college? But all of that aside, I am who I am now because of what happened during that time in my life.

As I look back, the Army wasn't so bad. It could have been a lot worse. As you will discover after reading this book, I was not a career officer, and I damned sure wasn't out to be a hero or win any medals, even though the Army gave me some. I'm not the bravest sort, and I don't have a death wish. Never did. Sometimes a guy gets put in a situation that makes him do things he wouldn't ordinarily do. That's what Vietnam did to me

I didn't know it at the time I signed up for flight training, but statistics now show that a helicopter pilot in battle in Vietnam was twice as likely to be injured or killed as a soldier fighting on the ground. The statistics also show that one out of eighteen helicopter pilots in Vietnam never made it back. Somehow, I survived. I figure I was damned lucky.

We were essentially brainwashed by the military and the government to believe the Vietnam War was a worthwhile endeavor. Oh, there was the threat of Communism, all right. But I can only blame myself for caving in to the shallow arguments we heard in the ROTC classroom about how the South Vietnamese people were oppressed by the communist aggression from the north and how the government of South Vietnam pleaded for our assistance to drive the communists back. I'm sure they were and it did. But the government was corrupt to begin with and the people of South Vietnam suffered from their own government's leadership. I'm willing to wager that if given the choice, most of the South Vietnamese would have gladly accepted the Communist regime only to be rid of the burden of the corrupt South Vietnamese government.

We were hedged by visions of duty, honor, and country. Those that resisted did not necessarily do so because they were smarter. I imagine some of them just didn't want to get their shit blown away. Well, I guess in some respects, that was damned smart. I can't blame them for that. I never have. Others just thought it was wrong, but they chose to run away instead of facing the problem like men. At least I don't have to live with that embarrassment. I don't hold anything against those folks, either. They did what they thought they had to do, and that is what I have always tried to do.

My ambitions? Different now. Regrets? Sure, I have a lot of them. Would I do it again? I would do my homework first, but knowing what I know now, no way in hell would I do that again. Not for the reasons we were given. I don't regret having served in Vietnam. It showed me what I was, and made me what I am. I proved to myself that I was as good as anyone else. And it also taught me humility and opened the door for the courage

I never knew I had. I'm glad I went, but I wouldn't go again.

If you're expecting to read about white-knuckle exploits and heroics, or aggressive air battles, or blood and guts, you will probably be disappointed. That's not what this book is about. If you are easily offended by profanity and vulgarity, then this book is damned sure not for you. It's about an American serviceman's life in Vietnam. Many soldiers were profane and vulgar, but so was the Vietnam War.

So many books written by helicopter pilots in Vietnam elaborate on such themes. I'm not at odds with these books. I consider many of them to be well written accurate historical accounts of the war we fought, and I salute the brave souls who endured the hell of that country and lived to tell their stories. I also salute those who did not survive the experience. This book tells the story about the other war in Vietnam. The personal war I, along with each of the other soldiers, fought with myself trying to adjust to the caustic environment, trying to fit in with the other guys who were waging their own personal battles, and trying to figure out how to survive so I could return home in one piece. The day-to-day trials, the challenges, the predicaments, and the choices I made were the results of struggles with my conscience, my ego, and the oath I took as a commissioned officer in the United States Army. After forty years of wondering about it all, I finally was able to make sense of most of it. Some of it I still don't understand and probably never will. I'm fortunate to be able to tell this story. I'm lucky. I didn't realize this until just a few years ago. That's when I began remembering all the shit that happened. The gullibility, the courage, the stupidity, and the luck. They were all there, for all of us. How we negotiated them determined whether or not we made it home.

A lot of books have been written about Vietnam, many by soldiers, especially helicopter pilots. Most of them are good. They tell it like it was. But many of them dwell on the violence, killing, and battles. There was much more to that war. There was the self-doubt of the soldier that played hell with his courage. There was the drudgery and tedium of waiting, with plenty of time to think about if he would get it. When would it be? Where would it happen? Could he face the danger and act like a soldier? And then there was the ever-present question: what was he actually doing there? And why?

As a commissioned officer, I did more than just fly helicopters. The warrant officers flew. That was pretty much it. They didn't see much of the behind the scenes nonsense and politics of command. They were given missions and they accomplished them. Commissioned officers were different. We had the burden of suffering through all of the shit that was necessary to make the unit work. The administrative functions, the supervisory details, all of the crap that those above thought necessary for our presence in that war. No one ever tells that story. The one about conscience, morality, mortality, and faith, if there really is such a thing in war.

So, this is my story. Of course, the names of the people are different. If you hadn't served in Vietnam during the war, you probably might not believe much of the account, but that I leave to you to deal with. What is certain is that you can have no idea of the day-to-day dangers, tedium and dilemmas we faced. I WAS there, and I still have to think about the reasons for the things I did or did not do.

It's like believing your coach when he tells you that you're going to go out and win the big game. Well, maybe you will, and maybe you won't. Hell, he doesn't know one way or the other. I don't think most of our presidents knew one way or the other about the game in Vietnam. Each of them had to make decisions and that's what he did. It's just too bad that they screwed up. Life isn't always fair. You take what you can get and endure the rest. You can't control most of what happens to you. All you can do is adapt and learn from it and strengthen yourself to meet new challenges. Just like Vietnam. Once you are army property, you do what you're told to do. You might not agree with it, but that's your job and you do it. I didn't think about what I did when I did it. I just did it. Now I do think about it. I don't like a lot of it, but I did it, just the same. If I really did do something bad, I'll have to live with it. I just don't know what that is yet.

This story is not the whole truth because truth can't be told in a story. Only the experience can. I have to convey my experiences in Vietnam the way I lived them. That's why I'm telling the story in my own way.

Marc Cullison

JANUARY 1971

A NEW LIFE BEGINS

LEAVING HOME

Bitter cold swept in from the Kansas plains, blasting every house in Derby. It was like I walked outside naked. My lightweight khakis and flight jacket made me look good but were otherwise practically worthless. I got into the car, one of those behemoth Oldsmobile 98s that would suck gas from any fuel pump within fifty feet, and settled back into the posh seat, probably the last one I would sit in for the next year. My mother, her tiny four-foot-eight frame practically hidden behind the dashboard from other traffic, backed the car out of the driveway. The icy chill from the windows grabbed me by the balls, and I knew my life going to change. I just didn't know how.

My mother's silence on the way to the airport was as threatening as I imagined a bullet screaming toward my head would be. My father, a stoical relic of my youth, was at work. After all, his job as a tool and die maker fabricating parts to support good old capitalism was far more important than seeing his son off to Vietnam. So what if we might never see each other again? Good for him, I thought. I didn't need his indifference there in the car with us. The silence was trying enough. I just thank God, if he exists, that my brother wasn't there. I couldn't possibly imagine what kind of humiliation he would have put me through. The thought that I might never have to see him again left me with mixed feelings.

I had received orders in November, having successfully completed advanced rotary-wing aviator training. That was the most challenging thing I had done in my life. Learning to fly a helicopter, that is. And being good at it. Well, I thought I was pretty good. The certificate I received said I was in the top five percent of my class, 70-40. The white hats. My head was pretty big then, too, but my hat still fit.

I didn't listen to newscasts about the Vietnam War much. I didn't listen to news about anything. I was in a world of my own, isolated in my own thoughts. I really didn't think about Vietnam too seriously, but it was always in the back of my mind, waiting for me to realize I would have to face it soon enough. Hell, the army training shoved it down my throat twenty-four hours a day, and I sat through those talks with my head up my ass, thinking about something else. My folks and I never talked much about it, but I could tell it was eating at them. There was this distance between us, as if I were a stranger. We weren't the huggie, lovey family that some were. We were somewhat stoical about the whole thing. I was just trying not to think about it.

I never kept in contact with the fellows in my flight class. We all went our separate ways and I never heard from any of them again. I suppose if I had, it would have put a severe obstacle in my path to survival in Vietnam. I would always be thinking about how so-and-so got it and I would worry about how I would get it. I was not married at the time, either, so I didn't have the problem of leaving behind a wife and kid. I never worried about much of anything except making a fool of myself.

During that short drive my mind kept drifting to the thought that I might never see my family again, but only as short impulses that flitted through my head. It wasn't like I actually believed that I would never come back. My twenty-four-year-old brain didn't understand that notion. Not that I knew what was in store for me. The ROTC cadre, the officer's basic staff, and the flight instructors had been vague about that. We can only put things into the perspective of events we have already experienced, not those that are foreign to us. What I was about to do would be as foreign to me as my first day at school.

It was January 12, 1971. I was supposed to be in-country by January 14. Allowing for the International Dateline and the twelve-hour lead in South Vietnam, my tickets were for the twelfth. I was surprised that Uncle Sam paid for my flight to California.

The folks in the terminal stared at us, or maybe just my uniform. There were a few smiles and pointing fingers, but mostly blank stares. I couldn't tell if it was because they were impressed by my stature as a soldier who was sworn to defend the country against all aggressors, or if it was because I was a symbol of the controversial and unpopular war raging in Southeast Asia. It could have been either. It wasn't like I was coming home. But that wouldn't have made much difference. I was targeted by a lot of scowls, as well. Those I just ignored. That's all I could do.

My mother walked with me to the gate at the airport while everyone stared at us. No kiss, no hug. Just a few words of parting, not that I remember what they were. I waved as I went through the door and didn't look back. I have no idea how long she might have stayed there, but I'm sure she watched me cross the concrete ramp and board my flight to San Francisco. I knew what she was thinking, and she might have known what I was thinking, but I doubt it. I was gone. Out of there. My own man. Free. And heading toward glory. Or death. Then I remembered how fortunate I was not to have to say goodbye to a wife. And I felt so alone.

The flight was short enough that I didn't spend a lot of time thinking about where I was going. The smoke from my cigarette filled my lungs and erased what I was trying not to think about. I just wanted to get my ass to the plane at Travis Air Force Base on time. I damned sure didn't want to start out my army career on the wrong foot, even if it did mean I might get killed. Well, hell, that was going to be my job anyway. Maybe getting myself killed, I mean. The flight attendants seemed to take special care with me. I'm not sure why, but I hoped it was out of respect for my uniform. It made the flight more pleasant when I thought of it that way. The plane landed before I could become too distracted from it.

I took a bus from the airport at San Francisco to Travis Air Force Base. The bus stopped some distance away from the gate at the airfield, so I lugged my two-ton duffle bag and gear along the sidewalk toward the gate. I had no idea what I was doing and a young black man watching me apparently knew it, too. He offered to carry my bag for me to the gate, and I remember thinking how thoughtful of him. I was about to change my opinion of the folks in California because my arm and shoulder were getting sore from the dead weight of the bag. But just as we neared the gate, the fellow slammed my bag to the sidewalk and said, "That'll be five dollars."

I had just been had. It wasn't the first time. I was just too stupid to wonder why the fellow was lurking around an airport terminal with no apparent means of transportation and no one else around. I paid him the five dollars. It was worth it to save the wear and tear on my shoulder. I lugged my bags around the corner and inside the door.

I was processed through customs with over a hundred other souls who were as clueless as I was. We were herded onto a Boeing 707 and off we went to Anchorage, Alaska, bound for Vietnam.

We made a quick fueling stop at Anchorage, and most of us disembarked to the terminal to smoke. We all looked out the windows through the darkness at the lights shining on the snow and ice. I had never seen so much snow in my life. It was deeper than most cars. It could just as well have been the Arctic. I wouldn't have known the difference. Then, back onto the plane.

I pretty much remember what I was thinking when I looked out that little window by my shoulder and saw the lights of the United States of America retreating into the distance. I know I had this sort of excitement about seeing a new country, but at the same time I was dreading actually getting there. You know how it is when you're excited about leaving on a trip to a new destination, but you're not sure what's going to happen when you get there. Well, I damned sure didn't know what would happen. After hearing all of my military instructors harp on the dangers we would face, I thought to myself, would I be killed? Would I perform some superhuman feat of bravery? Or would I piss my pants and be a coward? I had never been in combat and I'm sure none of the other saps on that plane had, either. I imagine the army did its best to prepare me for the possibility of killing and being killed. I had never done any of that. It's not like something you can practice. So I wondered if I'd be a hero or dead. I had about twenty hours of flying over the Pacific to think about it.

ABOUT THE AUTHOR

Marc Cullison is a baby-boomer who grew up in an era when education was everything and duty to country was a responsibility. After receiving a bachelor's degree in architectural engineering at Oklahoma State University, he was commissioned as a second lieutenant in the United States Army Reserve Corps of Engineers through the ROTC program. During his four-year tour of duty, he served as helicopter pilot with the 129th Assault Helicopter Company in II Corps, Vietnam, in 1971. He returned from overseas to an assignment as a military assistant to the resident engineer at Kaw Dam and Reservoir near Ponca City, Oklahoma, where he met the woman he would marry there. After two years in Ponca City he was honorably discharged and returned to Oklahoma State where he received a master's degree in architectural engineering and honed his technical skills as a professional structural engineer. Then into quality control at a manufacturing plant which led him into computer programming. His most recent career was a math and science instructor at Connors State College in Warner and Muskogee, Oklahoma, from which he retired in 2014. He lives with his wife in a self-built log house near Sallisaw.

www.mcullison.com
email: marc@mcullison.com

Photograph courtesy of Kathy Taylor Photography

OTHER TITLES AVAILABLE FROM IMZADI PUBLISHING

I Found My Heart In Prague

The Hedgerows of June

The Rain Song

The Swamps of Jersey

The Other Vietnam War

Going To California

Gabriel's Wing

A Game Called Dead

COMING SOON!

The Weight of Living

The Blackstar Gambit

Dragon Bone

www.imzadipublishing.com

Made in the USA
San Bernardino, CA
17 March 2017